Immigration and Society

Immigration and Society

A HISTORICAL AND SOCIOLOGICAL APPROACH

First Edition

Augustine J. Kposowa

University of California – Riverside

Bassim Hamadeh, CEO and Publisher
Michelle Piehl, Senior Project Editor
Abbey Hastings, Associate Production Editor
Miguel Macias, Senior Graphic Designer
Stephanie Kohl, Licensing Associate
Don Kesner, Interior Designer
Natalie Piccotti, Senior Marketing Manager
Kassie Graves, Vice President of Editorial
Jamie Giganti, Director of Academic Publishing

Cover image source: https://commons.wikimedia.org/wiki/File:Awaiting_examination,_Ellis_Island_LCCN2014710705.tif.

Printed in the United States of America.

ISBN: 978-1-5165-0937-9 (pbk) / 978-1-5165-0938-6 (br)

Contents

Preface

The idea of writing this book grew out of my experience teaching undergraduate courses on immigration for more than 20 years. During that period it was increasingly difficult to prescribe a book for class because I could not find one that was comprehensive, and at the same time not laden with demographic technical jargon that bored students who lacked previous training in population. As I surveyed the literature, one theme was often encountered: Books that promised to be about immigration in their titles often ended up being testaments or stories about ethnicity and race, or how some ethnic group arrived in America and had fit into some melting pot or experienced some "American dream." I read stories about the English, the Germans, the Scandinavians, the Scots, the Irish, the Poles, the Italians, and so on. I found this focus on arrival of ethnic groups, especially from Europe, to be a major shortcoming. It's no surprise that among the many immigration books I read, rarely did I find any about the arrival of Africans, even though people from the African continent were in America as early as 1619, and before the arrival of the much more celebrated Pilgrims. I did not fault authors, but rather the outcome of an enduring national shame—the failure to confront slavery as an ever present and inescapable aspect of American history and legacy. After all, who would want to traumatize U.S. readers, especially students?

The other shortcoming observed was the tendency, especially in sociological coverage, to ignore original documents. Occasionally, there might be a reference to the Constitution or even the Declaration of Independence, but few books presented the documents themselves. The situation was worse for immigration-related documents, such as the very dangerous Alien and Sedition Acts of 1798, and the precedents that these set for future treatment of immigrants or those who government authorities single out as undesirables or threats to "national security."

This book overcomes these two shortcomings by first treating immigration as an ongoing process that began with the earliest acquisition and colonization of land now known as the United States, and from the organization of the government in 1789 to 2018. Hence, I avoid getting bogged down into how or when any ethnic or racial group came to the United States, and emphasize instead the social history of U.S. immigration in the tradition of historical sociology. Second, as much as possible historical documents are presented throughout the book, especially older documents that had undue consequences on immigrants. Ready access to original documents allows the reader to read and interpret them, and not rely solely on "expert" interpretations. Where some piece of legislation is too long, an abridged version is shown with emphasis on sections that changed immigration for better or worse. The reader is encouraged to read the entire document when presented, as policies developed that ultimately affect the immigration process and immigrants, current and future, derive from interpretations of law. What also emerges throughout the book is responses to questions such as: Who influences immigration legislation and policy? In whose interests are laws passed? Who benefits? Who is targeted and why?

Immigration has been a polarizing topic in much of U.S. history, and many issues are invariably controversial, and emotionally and politically charged. I have tried to present facts as they happened—the good, the bad, and the ugly. Thus, many readers will find things they like, and a lot they do not like. This is inevitable in human social life, in which debate and the free exchange of ideas from diverse perspectives make the learning environment richer and more pleasant.

Augustine J. Kposowa
Riverside, California
USA
22 May, 2018

1 | Introduction

... My father was a foreign student, born and raised in a small village in Kenya. He grew up herding goats, went to school in a tin-roof shack. ... Through hard work and perseverance my father got a scholarship to study in a magical place, America, that's shown as a beacon of freedom and opportunity to so many who had come before him. While studying here my father met my mother. She was born in a town on the other side of the world, in Kansas. ... My parents shared not only an improbable love; they shared an abiding faith in the possibilities of this nation. They would give me an African name, Barack, or "blessed," believing that in a tolerant America, your name is no barrier to success. ... I stand here knowing that my story is part of the larger American story, that I owe a debt to all of those who came before me, and that in no other country on Earth is my story even possible.

—Illinois Senate candidate Barack Obama, July 27, 2004

Source: Washington Post (http://www.washingtonpost.com/wp-dyn/articles/A19751-2004Jul27.html)

In 2004 Barack Obama, then an unknown senator from Illinois, gave the keynote address at the Democratic National Convention on July 27 that year at the Fleet Center in Boston. In the speech the senator spoke of there being no Black America, White America, Latino America, or Asian America, but only the United States of America. The speech captured the imagination of many Americans, and it was to propel Obama to the forefront in the race for the White House in 2008, and ultimately to the U.S. presidency in 2009. His story was unlike any other presidential candidate that the American nation had experienced before.

Barack Obama had been born to a native-born White American mother and a Black African immigrant in Hawaii only 43 years earlier, during a period in U.S. history when interracial marriages between White and Black couples

Barack Obama in New Hampshire
Source: Copyright © Fogster (CC BY-SA 3.0) at https://commons.wikimedia.org/wiki/File%3ABarack_Obama_in_New_Hampshire.jpg.

were frowned upon in most states, and even banned in others on the mainland, especially in the South. The story of Obama's parents—a native-born White woman and a foreign-born Black man—illustrate in a vivid way how immigration has affected American history, and how it may continue to do so in the future.

Immigration remains a fundamental process in both the growth and the changing composition of the population of the United States from the earliest Colonial times to the present. Perhaps without waves and waves of immigrants that made their way to the North American continent—first by sea, then by air, and later by land—America's economic, social, and political development from an agrarian society to an industrial or postindustrial one may not have been as rapid. Of course, given that there were already people on this land before European immigrants arrived, it will never be known in which direction North America would have moved without colonization. Despite the fact that, with the exception of Native Americans, everyone in the United States is either an immigrant or born here as a descendant of immigrants, the nation at various periods in its history has demonstrated some ambiguity or unease with regard to newcomers based particularly on who they were, where they came from, and how they looked. Indeed, the term "aliens" continues to be used in legislation and public policy parlance with reference to foreign-born, non-naturalized persons, as if they had dropped from Mars or some other distant planet in outer space.

The early settlers from England, to what would later become the United States of America, appear to have placed no limitations or controls on who arrived during the Colonial period—roughly from the establishment of Jamestown in 1607 to the Treaty of Paris in 1783, a very long stretch (176 years) of American history. In the Declaration of Independence, one of the specific charges brought against the "present King of Great Britain," and used as justification for severing ties with the English Crown, was that he (the king) was not approving new appropriations fast enough. The early settlers from Britain accepted new arrivals from Europe as a way to increase the White population, develop the land for sustenance, make fortunes, and protect themselves against the native inhabitants whose land was being taken away gradually via treaties, disease transmission, and, later, force.

There were no restrictions on entry in the Colonial period until well after the adoption of the Constitution, although even in Colonial times charters to establish colonies were often drawn in such a way that they sought to exclude Catholics through various mechanisms, such as double taxing Catholic lands or, in some instances, having them declare oaths of abjuration. As an example, the founding of Maryland as a colony for Catholics by the Calvert family in 1634 grew partly out of resentment toward Catholics not just in England, but also in the American colonies. For instance, despite passage of the 1649 Toleration Act by the Catholic legislature in an effort to appease growing Protestant unrest and complaints of anti-Protestant discrimination (among other allegations) in the colony, Protestants in 1695 seized Maryland, moving its capital from Catholic Saint Mary's to Protestant Annapolis, where it has remained to the present day (Daniels 2002). Although people emigrated from Europe to avoid prejudice and persecution, many still faced unequal treatment in the American colonies due to questionable legislative actions undertaken by Protestants.

Despite lack of restrictions or controls in Colonial days, subtle distinctions began to be made in a relatively short time about who had or did not have rights in the New World. For example, Africans who were being brought to provide free labor as early as 1619 were not considered immigrants, although their arrival took place a year *before* that of the much more celebrated Pilgrims who landed at Plymouth Rock in Massachusetts (Pinkney 2000). It is very likely that Africans were not considered immigrants due to the nature and circumstances of their arrival (Kposowa 1998), seen rather as units of labor, not as human migrants. In the eyes of White colonialists, their complexion and skin tone disqualified them as well. Failure to recognize African slaves as immigrants (at least immigrants through compulsion) was to have consequences later in American history. When family reunification gradually became a cornerstone of U.S. immigration policy, groups that had existed in the United States for much shorter periods could take advantage of the policy by bringing in family members, but descendants of Africans could not, even though their ancestors had been among the earliest settlers of the land. Accordingly, beneficiaries of U.S. immigration policy—at least from the Colonial period until 1965—remained predominantly White.

Recording of immigration to the United States did not begin until passage of the Act of 1819. Titled, "An act regulating passenger-ships and vessels," and popularly remembered as the *Steerage Act*, the Act of March 2, 1819 (3 Stat. 488), stipulated that as of January 1, 1820, the captain or master of a ship destined for the United States from abroad must deliver a manifest of all passengers taken on board. It was to be delivered to customs officials upon the vessel's arrival at a port of disembarkation located within collection districts. The manifest was to list passengers by name, age, sex, occupation, and country of origin. Due to concerns over unusually high mortality rates on board immigrant ships at the time, the manifest was also to record the number of passengers who had died during the voyage. It was noted, for example, that in the year before passage of the law, a ship had left Antwerp, Belgium, with 5,000 passengers, but 1,000 were unaccounted for upon arrival in New York harbor (Hutchinson 1981, p. 21). As passed, the Act is presented below, except Section 3, which was about ships departing the United States for abroad.

ACT OF MARCH 2, 1819

An Act regulating passenger ships and vessels

Be it enacted by the Senate and the House of Representatives of the United States of America in Congress assembled, That if the master or other person on board of any ship or vessel, owned in the whole or in part by a citizen or citizens of the United States, or the territories thereof, or by a subject or subjects, citizen or citizens, of any foreign country, shall, after the first day of January next, take on board of such ship or vessel, at any foreign port or place, or shall bring or convey into the United States, or the territories thereof, from any foreign port or place; or shall carry, convey, or transport, from the United States or the territories thereof, to any foreign port or place, a greater number of passengers than two for every five tons of such ship or vessel, according to custom-house measurement, every such master, or other person so offending, and the owner or owners of such ship or vessels, shall severally forfeit and pay to the United States, the sum of one hundred and fifty dollars, for each and every passenger so taken on board of such ship or vessel over and above the aforesaid number of two to three five tons of such ship or vessel; to be recovered by suit, in any circuit or district court of the United States, where the said vessel may arrive, or where the owner or owners aforesaid may reside: Provided, nevertheless, That nothing in this act shall be taken to apply to the complement of men usually and ordinarily employed in navigating such ship or vessel.

Sec. 2. And be it further enacted, That if the number of passengers so taken on board of any ship or vessel as aforesaid, or conveyed or brought into the United States, or transported therefrom as aforesaid, shall exceed the said proportion of two to every five tons of such ship or vessel by the number of twenty passengers, in the whole, every such ship or vessel shall be deemed and taken to be forfeited to the United States, and shall be prosecuted an distributed in the same manner in which the forfeitures and penalties are recovered and distributed under the provisions of the act entitled "An act to regulate the collection of duties on imports and tonnage."

Sec. 4. *And be it further enacted*, That the captain or master of any ship or vessel arriving in the United States, or any of the territories thereof, from any foreign place whatever, at the time that he delivers a manifest of the cargo, and, if there be no cargo, then at the time of making a report, to the collector of the district in which such ship or vessel shall arrive, a list or manifest of all the passengers taken on board of the said ship or vessel at any foreign port or place; in which list of manifest it shall be the duty of the said master to designate, particularly, the age, sex, and occupation, of said passengers, respectively, the country to which they severally belong, and that of which it is their intention to become inhabitants; and shall further set forth whether any, and what number, have died on the voyage; which report and manifest shall be sworn to by the said master, in the same manner as is directed by the existing laws of the United States, in relation to the manifest of the cargo, and that the refusal or neglect of the master aforesaid, to comply with the provisions of this section, shall incur the same penalties, disabilities, and forfeitures, as are at present provided for a refusal or neglect to report and deliver a manifest of the cargo aforesaid.

Sec. 5. *And be it further enacted*, That each and every collector of the customs, to whom such manifest or list of passengers as aforesaid shall be delivered, shall, quarter yearly, return copies thereof to the Secretary of State of the United States, by whom statements of the same shall be laid before Congress at each and every session.

Approved, March 2, 1819.

Source: U.S. Congress (1850) Chap. XLVI: 15th Congress. Sess. II, CH, 45, 46 1819 The Statutes at Large of the United States of America.

Early Manifesting of Passengers

The Act of 1819 (Steerage Act) as passed by Congress did not amount to federal control of immigration with regard to number of persons to be admitted. That was to come later with the emergence of anti-immigration sentiments. Rather, the Steerage Act should be understood as a limited data-collection effort on immigrants with the objective of addressing some of the outrages that were being committed on immigrant ships destined for America, along with making it more comfortable for Americans traveling to Europe, often on vacation. Copies of the completed manifests were to be given to the secretary of state, who was required to submit the gathered information in a summary report to Congress on a periodic basis. Although the law was later repealed and superseded by the Act of 1855, manifesting of passengers has survived to the present day, and it is one source of immigration data that will be covered in Chapter 2.

The manifest has been used in recent years for purposes for which it was never originally intended in the 19th century. In response to crises, for example, the attacks on New York City and Washington, DC, on September 11, 2001, far more detailed information about passengers is now collected. These include the name, age, birth date, sex, occupation of passengers, port of embarkation, and intended port of entry. Data are also gathered on passports, visas, and information submitted on visa applications at U.S. consulates abroad. The collected information is cross-checked for potential terrorists, terror suspects, or other "suspects" with other federal databases and the secret "No Fly List." Data collected by airlines on their passengers at ticket points of sale, including method of payment, are also detailed in the manifest reports. All of these and other classified data on passengers are known to immigration and customs officials long before an aircraft departs a foreign country for the United States, for the paper-and-pen manifest of the 19th century has for long been superseded by its electronic counterpart, the Advance Passenger Information System (APIS).

Lack of control over immigration is attested by the fact that data collection on immigration had a rough start. As observed by the U.S. Bureau of the Census (1975, p. 97), the number of immigrants who arrived in the United States prior to 1819 is unknown. Bromwell (1856, pp. 18–19) estimates that 250,000 passengers of foreign birth arrived in the United States from the end of the Revolutionary War in 1783 until 1819.

Controls on the number of people allowed to enter began becoming restrictive in 1891 when Congress adopted the first comprehensive immigration laws for the United States and established a Bureau of Immigration. Thereafter, entry would become even more restrictive as increasingly more groups were added to an ever-expanding list of "excludables." Who was allowed to come and who was not permitted tended to vary according to the racial, economic, and political climate of the day. As seen in subsequent chapters, source countries of immigrants would play a crucial role in the development of immigration policies for the nation.

Figure 1.1 presents immigration to the United States from 1901 to 2001. The rate (per 1,000-resident population) was highest in the 1901 to 1910 period

FIGURE 1.1: Immigrants Admitted: Number and Rate, 1901–2000

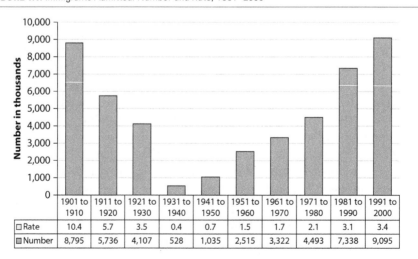

	1901 to 1910	1911 to 1920	1921 to 1930	1931 to 1940	1941 to 1950	1951 to 1960	1961 to 1970	1971 to 1980	1981 to 1990	1991 to 2000
Rate	10.4	5.7	3.5	0.4	0.7	1.5	1.7	2.1	3.1	3.4
Number	8,795	5,736	4,107	528	1,035	2,515	3,322	4,493	7,338	9,095

Source: U.S. Bureau of Citizenship and Immigration Services, *Statistical Year Book 2001.*

and the number of arrivals, along with their countries of origin, were to create an anti-immigration movement that culminated in passage of laws in 1921 and 1924 that permanently embedded race as a continuing feature of immigration policy. Nativist movements of those days and the havoc they created for innocent people are discussed in later chapters.

Global Imperialism and Immigration

Movement of people from one country to another, or even from one region to another within the same nation, is universal and appears to have existed throughout much of human history. In the Old Testament, there are several references to migration. One involves the Israelites migrating to Egypt (Gen. 46:8): "These are the names of the Israelites, Jacob and his descendants, who migrated to Egypt" (New American Bible, 1987). The return migration of their descendants under rather dramatic circumstances under the leadership of Moses and later Joshua is given extensive coverage in Exodus. Egypt appears to have been a particularly popular destination for migrants, for "Joseph rose and took the child and his mother by night and departed for Egypt" (Matt. 2:14 New American Bible, 1987).

In the premodern period of imperialism, migration was largely movement from north to south as European powers embarked upon empire building. The imperialist expansion took the form of seizing land in Africa, Asia, Latin and South America, and Oceania (Australia, New Zealand, and islands of the sea) for purposes of exploiting raw materials that were sent back to the mother country. Creating colonies often meant the colonial power had to send administrators, civil servants, police, and armed forces to subjugate the native population and prevent uprisings. Native resistance was never successful. British historian Snellgrove contends that Europeans were superior in discipline and organization so they always managed to master non-European races. From 1815 to 1914, 40 million Europeans went to foreign lands to seek fortunes, and by the start of the World War I in 1914, 700 million people living on other continents were either European immigrants or their descendants, and the United States had become a massive extension of Europe (Snellgrove, 1974). The scramble for colonies along with the concomitant subjugation of other peoples was not devoid of racial undertones. Cecil Rhodes, who lived from 1853 to 1902, was a great advocate of White colonial expansion and racism, and he wrote in a rather celebratory tone in his *Confession of Faith*:

> I contend that we are the finest race in the world and that the more of the world we inhabit the better it is for the human race. Just fancy those parts that are at present inhabited by the most despicable specimens of human beings what an alteration there would be if they were brought under Anglo-Saxon influence, look again at the extra employment a new country added to our dominions gives (Rhodes, 1877, p. 1).

It is hardly difficult to conclude that the beings Rhodes described as "despicable specimens" were unlikely to be White, and more likely to be colored persons. The reference to extra employment reminds one of the true aims of imperialist expansion: exploitation of foreign peoples and lands, and enrichment of the mother country and its Anglo-Saxon population—the finest race. Elsewhere, Rhodes (1877, p. 2) writes:

> Africa is still lying ready for us to take it. It is our duty to seize every opportunity of acquiring more territory and we should keep this one idea steadily before our eyes that more territory simply means more of the Anglo-Saxon race more of the best the most human, most honourable race the world possesses.

Some could argue that Rhodes was too young, merely 24 years old when he penned the four-page *Confession of Faith*, and perhaps did not understand the implications of what he was writing. The fact remains, however, that even until death he never reversed his racist views and was a proponent of north-to-south migration. A further question could well be, if he were that young, from where did he learn such racist beliefs?

Reversal of Fortunes

With the end of World War II it was becoming evident that European hegemony in the colonies could not be sustained permanently. Germany had lost its own colonial possessions in Africa during the war; the French kept its colonies, and despite persistence that they should be maintained, the status quo was not to last forever. In the United Kingdom, there were even clearer signs that Britannia would never rule the waves again. African and Indian troops had served with British forces in places as far away as Burma and had fought just as gallantly as their British counterparts—or, in some cases, were even better in repulsing Japanese Imperial Forces. The notion of White racial superiority and invincibility had been shattered in the war, and so a wave of nationalism developed, first in India, and later in West Africa, following the war. Decolonization began as previously ruled people began to seek independence. India was the first to gain independence in 1947, and 10 years later, Kwame Nkrumah also demanded independence for Ghana, becoming the first former British African colony to attain independence. Not long after that, Nigeria and Sierra Leone followed suit. The British Empire, which Prime Minister Winston Churchill had proclaimed during the Battle of Britain would last for a thousand years, was never to rise again. Addressing the House of Commons on June 18, 1940, in the midst of a humiliating defeat of France by Hitler's Germany, the prime minister ended his speech with the memorable sentence: "Let us therefore brace ourselves to our duties, and so bear ourselves that, if the British Empire and its Commonwealth last for a thousand years, men will still say, 'This was their finest hour.'" (Churchill, 1940). An empire builder himself, Churchill would live to see some parts of that empire break away.

Whereas migration flows in the prewar era had been largely from north to south, that is, from Europe to the colonies, a new phenomenon gradually emerged after World War II. European nations that had been ravaged and destroyed in the war began to reconstruct destroyed infrastructure, rebuild economies and institutions, boosted in part by the Marshall Plan initiated by the United States to help in postwar economic recovery. With the high casualties, especially of able-bodied young men, sustained by many European countries in the campaigns of World War II, and with declining fertility rates in some of the war-ravaged countries, there were labor shortages.

Postwar Economic Growth and Guest Workers in Europe

In the postwar era, some European countries welcomed immigration for various reasons including infrastructure rebuilding, economic survival, and labor shortages. In France, for example, the 1939–1945 war had resulted in the deaths of at least 557,000 (National World War II Museum, 2015). Although these casualties were lower than the number experienced in World War I, they were mainly of working-age men who could not be replaced immediately post-conflict. The situation was worsened by the decline in French fertility following the war. The overall result was shortage of labor at a time when the nation needed more workers. In response, the French government not only kept a rather liberal immigration policy that it had had prior to the war but expanded entry of individuals who were not necessarily intended to remain in France permanently. From the 1950s through the early 1980s, specific targets were set regarding how many to admit. It was not only immigrants that France wanted, but guest workers. France, similar to other nations that often invite guest workers in times of labor shortages—for example, as the United States did with its *Bracero* program from 1942 to 1964 (Kposowa, 1998, p. 21)—those allowed entry were not intended to stay permanently, but many did. The immigrant stream of guest workers came largely from the French former colonies of Algeria, Morocco, Tunisia, and West Africa. After the Arab oil embargo of 1973, in response for Western support of Israel in the Arab-Israel war, the French economy faltered, and as ordinary French citizens complained, immigrants (guest workers and their descendants) became easy scapegoats for rising unemployment and other economic woes. The government reacted by imposing limits on legal immigration, which had the unintended consequence of creating an illegal immigration problem in France for the first time in its history, when a substantial percentage of the previous temporary guest workers failed to depart (Adolino & Blake, 2011).

Worker shortages also occurred in Germany following the war, and as in France, the response to migration was to call for temporary guest workers instead of permanent settlers. The country had experienced an estimated 8.8 million deaths (both civilian and military) in the war (1939–1945) (National World War II Museum, 2015). Rapid economic growth in the 1950s, coupled with a declining fertility rate, created labor shortages and a demand for foreign workers. Initially, Germany turned to Aussiedlers (ethnic Germans, mainly in Eastern Europe and the former Soviet Union, with a right to return to their ancestral land), but this was not a realistic expectation, given the geopolitical context in Europe at the time—most notably in the massive Soviet Union, which maintained strict control of population emigration. The nation, therefore, resorted to importation of guest workers (Gastarbeiter) from countries such as Turkey, Yugoslavia, nations in Central and Eastern Europe. As a consequence of its guest-worker program, Germany gradually moved from being an emigration to an immigration country. By 2006, the foreign-born population in the country stood at 6.7 million or 8 percent of the total population (Adolino & Blake, 2011, p. 123).

The change from an emigration to an immigration nation has not been welcomed by all Germans. Indeed, it remains an area of contention, for as the economy went into recession in the early 1970s, increasing unemployment was blamed on the foreign-born, so the German government put an end to its guest-worker program in 1973 (Adolino & Blake, 2011).

Today, despite official denials, Germany has become a major immigrant destination, with the country receiving more immigrants, including asylum seekers, than any other European nation. As in many other countries in the European Union, Germany has not been without fierce debates regarding immigration—whether too many people are taken in, and how the rate is affecting the country's European character. The issue of illegal immigration has become contentious as immigration and nationality laws have been passed, toughening conditions for asylum approval, and making it more difficult for non-European Union nationals to immigrate. In short, immigration policies have become more restrictive, with a German public still in denial about its nation having changed from an emigration to an immigration country. As Adolino & Blake (2011, p. 128) assert, "The German population's response to a continuing inflow of foreigners continues to be conditioned by a widespread and deep-seated belief that Germany is not (and will never should be) a country of immigration." Despite observations by Adolino and Blake, Germany was relatively generous during the Mediterranean migration crisis (2014 to 2016) relative to other European nations and the United States in terms of the sheer number of people it welcomed, especially Syrian refugees. Furthermore, in the past 20 years, the country has made substantial progress regarding acceptance and integration. German citizenship was once extremely difficult to acquire largely due to numerous and rather burdensome requirements, and the complexity of application forms has been simplified. The country's new immigration law that went into effect in 2005 is consistent with European Union standards, and offers a legal framework based on a comprehensive approach and administration of immigration policy.

Apart from France and Germany, many other northern European countries set up guest-worker programs in the post-World War II period to help supply the workforce needed to maintain booming economies. A look at Table 1.1 provides a summary of how these previously emigration nations became immigration countries between 1950 and 1975, largely due to various guest-worker programs. France and Germany (the former Federal Republic of Germany) top the list.

Due in part to their colonial history, by 1950 the United Kingdom and France already had larger shares of foreign-born persons than the rest of the countries shown in the table. Britain (which included naturalized persons in its figures) had 1,573,000 foreign-born in 1950, rising to 4,153,000 by 1975.

TABLE 1.1: Minority Population in Main Western European Countries of Immigration, 1950–1975 (in thousands)

Country	1950	1960	1970	1975	Percent of Total Population, 1975
Belgium	354	444	716	835	8.5
France	2,128	2,663	3,339	4,196	7.9
Germany (FRG)	548	686	2,977	4,090	6.6
Netherlands	77	101	236	370	2.6
Sweden	124	191	411	410	5.0
Switzerland	279	585	983	1,012	16.0
UK	1,573	2,205	3,968	4,153	7.8

Notes: Figures for all countries, except the UK, are for foreign residents. They exclude naturalized persons and immigrants from the Dutch and French colonies. UK data are census figures for 1951, 1961, and 1971 and estimates for 1975. The 1951 and 1961 data are for overseas-born persons, and exclude children born to immigrants in the UK. The 1971 and 1975 figures include children born in the UK, with both parents born abroad

Source: Stephen Castles, Hein De Hass & Mark J. Miller, "Minority Population in the Main Western European Countries of Immigration, 1950-1975 (in thousands)," The Age of Migration. Copyright © 2014 by Guilford Press.

France began with a higher number than the UK in 1950 (2,128,000), which rose to 4,196,000 in 1975. The German figures are quite startling, for prior to 1950 the country was not a particularly welcoming place for immigrants, especially non-Europeans. The Federal Republic of Germany (then headquartered in Bonn) had 548,000 foreign-born, which by 1975 had increased to 4,090,000, representing a rise of 646% in the two and a half decades. This rather rapid change was not due to Germany liberalizing immigration policies to allow naturalization of foreigners; rather it was the guest-worker program needed to fulfill labor demands of its economic growth that brought so many people from less robust economies.

U.S. Foreign Policy and Immigration in the Global South

International migration, especially from south to north, or in some cases from east to west or south to north, has increased rather rapidly in the past 40 years, and political instability plays an important role. Although there were Koreans in the United States prior to 1950, significant and sustained Korean immigration did not begin until after the Korean War, which began in June 1950 and ended in July 1953 (with an armistice). An estimated 5 million people, soldiers and civilians on both sides are believed to have perished in the conflict (History. com staff, 2009). In 1950, the number of Korean immigrants was too small to be reported by the U.S. Census Bureau without breaching confidentiality regulations, but by 1960 there were 11,171 Koreans (U.S. Bureau of the Census, 1975), representing only 0.11% of the total foreign-born population in the United States. In 1970, the number of Korean immigrants had increased to 88,711 or 0.92% of the foreign-born.

Similarly, until the 1960s, before full-scale U.S. involvement in that country's civil war, Vietnam was not a major source of immigrants for the United States. From 1961 to 1970, the number of immigrants admitted from Vietnam was 4,600. Between 1971 and 1980, however, the number of Vietnamese immigrants rose to 179,700 (U.S. Department of Homeland Security, 2005), an increase of 3,806.5%. Most of this sharp rise was due to the collapse of the U.S.-sponsored government in South Vietnam in Saigon (Ho Chi Ming City), the hasty pullout of American forces, and the displacement of a population that had previously held hope that U.S. troops would defeat the North Vietnamese and Viet Cong forces; some were fleeing a South Vietnam that had served or otherwise supported U.S. presence in the country. Table 1.2 shows immigrants admitted from Cambodia, Laos, and Vietnam from the decade of U.S. military involvement in the region (1961–1970) to at least a decade following U.S. military presence.

The effect of the wars in Indo-China on immigration was also evident in refugee flows following those campaigns. Refugee act admissions for Korea were 3,116 from 1951 to 1960. In contrast, due perhaps to the rather dramatic circumstances under which the United States left Vietnam in 1973, and also the duration of the war there, massive refugee flows followed the American defeat. Between 1971 and 1980, refugee admissions under the Indo-China Refugee Act of 1977 were 150,266, rising to 324,453 in the 1981–1990 period. Similar consequences of American involvement in Southeast Asia on immigration played out in Laos and Cambodia, two nations brought into the conflict via circumstances that still remain a source of controversy in the United States, as with the entire Vietnam War itself. Refugee flows from Laos to the United States were 21,690 from 1971 to 1980, which covers the time of massive bombings and U.S. incursions. From 1981 to 1990, the number of refugees from that country admitted to the United States was 142,964, representing an increase of 559% in the two time points. As for Cambodia, refugee admissions from 1971 to 1980 amounted to 7,739, a figure that increased to 114,064 between 1981 and 1990 (U.S. Department of Homeland Security, 2005), an increase of 1,373.9%.

TABLE 1.2: Immigrants Admitted From Indo-China and Korea 1961 to 1990 and Percent Change at End of the Period

County	1961–1970	1971–1980	1981–1990	Δ1961–1990
Cambodia	1,200	8,400	116,579	9,614.9%
Laos	100	22,600	145,646	145,546%
Vietnam	4,600	179,700	401,392	8,625.9%
Korea*	35,800	272,000	338,801	846.4%

Source: U.S. Citizenship and Immigration Services (2001). Change (Δ) calculated by author.

Note: Korean War began in 1950 and ended in 1953, but it had created migration streams.

While wars in Indo-China created streams of migration that have likely continued to the present, other streams have also been created via conflicts in other parts of the world. American intervention in nations such as Guatemala, Honduras, El Salvador, Nicaragua, Panama, Cuba, and Chile, to name a few, contributed to subsequent migration flows from those countries as a result of civil wars, assassinations or foiled ones, and death squads that got established.

In the 1980s, the Reagan administration often claimed that some Latin American country had become or was turning into some communist "beachhead," a site on a beach defended by military force and has been taken from the enemy by landing forces, and could later be used as a place from which an attack could be launched against the United States or other "allies" in the Western Hemisphere. He used that rhetoric to support dictatorial and repressive regimes in the region against genuine efforts to overthrow some of those governments by nationalist liberation movements that were often described in Washington (in the mainstream media and government parlance) as communist or socialist.

In the case of Chile, the people of that country elected Salvador Allende as their president in 1970. As head of state, Allende engaged in reform measures aimed at improving the quality of life of average Chileans. For instance, he nationalized the cooper mines that had previously made huge profits for U.S. corporations, such as Kennecott Copper and Anaconda (Kloby, 2004)—profits that did not benefit Chileans but these multinationals and their U.S. stock holders. U.S. multinational corporations, including International Telephone and Telegraph and United Fruit Company (Bucheli, 2006), came to view Allende as a threat to their profits, despite clear evidence that his policies of economic reform were having significant positive benefits on ordinary Chileans.

Behind the scenes (or perhaps not so behind the scenes), these corporations began to exert pressure on the U.S. administration to remove Allende from office. In response, the United States imposed an economic blockade on Chile, cutting off credit lines, and letting the CIA loose on Allende and on the unoffending people of Chile. In September 1973, the popularly elected government of Allende was overthrown in a CIA-inspired coup d'état for the crime of trying to improve life conditions for his people—apparently interpreted in Washington as socialism—and as being a threat to U.S. multinational corporations—also interpreted in Washington as socialism. The coup, most likely organized in the White House with Secretary of State Henry Kissinger and President Richard Nixon fully in the know, saw the Presidential Palace in Santiago bombed, and Allende murdered. Whether he killed himself or was killed by bombs dropped on the palace is irrelevant as he had been popularly elected by citizens of Chile, not citizens or the government of the United States. The installed puppet regime of Augusto Pinochet ruled with such a heavy hand that unknown thousands of Chileans lost their lives or simply "disappeared." One consequence of repression was the flow of immigrants to other countries in fear of persecution, torture, and/or disappearances. Others fled as asylum seekers. Why did people flee? One only has to read the following description of torture under Pinochet by Parenti (1993, p. 146):

> The torture delivered upon Pinochet's victims included application of electric shock to different parts of the body, particularly the genitals; forcing victims to witness the torture of friends and relatives; raping women in the presence of other family members; burning sex organs with acid or scalding water; placing infected rats into the vagina; mutilating, puncturing, and cutting off various parts of the body, including genitalia, eyes, and tongue; injection of air into women's breasts and veins (causing slow, painful death); shoving bayonets and clubs into the vagina or anus, causing rupture and death.

Table 1.3 details the migration flows from Central and South America from the 1960s through 2000.

TABLE 1.3: United States Hostile Involvement and Migration Flows: the Americas, Selected Countries, 1961–2000

Country	1961–1970	1971–1980	1981–1990	1991–2000
Chile	11,500	17,600	23,449	16,892
Cuba	256,800	276,800	159,245	178,715
El Salvador	15,000	34,400	214,573	217,306
Guatemala	15,400	25,600	87,903	103,045
Honduras	15,500	17,200	49,524	66,716
Nicaragua	10,100	13,000	44,062	94,553

Source: U.S. Citizenship and Immigration Services, *Statistical Yearbook 2001.*

Western intervention was also present elsewhere in the world, including the Middle East. A series of events in Iran in the early 1950s impacted Iranian emigration, and had consequences for the world to the present day. Following the end of World War II, Britain was heavily involved in the internal politics of Iran. The Anglo-Iranian Oil Company (AIOC) had been established years earlier to drill for oil in the country. Britain had a 51% share in the company, but Iranians did not reap any benefits from oil proceeds. Instead, most profits from the oil went to the UK due to an unfair oil agreement that had been struck years earlier. In 1951, Mohammad Mossadegh was popularly and democratically elected prime minister of Iran, with a mandate to let Iran benefit from its natural resources, including oil. The United Kingdom government reacted by imposing sanctions on Iran and threatened the country with military invasion. In tandem, the United States along with major American oil companies orchestrated a global boycott of Iranian oil, an act that failed to destabilize the Iranian government as had been intended or dissuade Mossadegh or cause his ouster (Kloby 2004). It seemed then that action was needed to target the prime minister more directly. In this regard, the American CIA and British intelligence agencies conspired to overthrow the Iranian government. The coup, led by the grandson of former U.S. President Theodore Roosevelt, Kermit Roosevelt (The Mohammad Mossadegh Project, 2015; Kloby, 2004), toppled Premier Mohammad Mossadegh and installed Shah Mohammad Reza Pahlavi as dictator of Iran. The immediate aftermath of the coup was to create a bonanza in the region for U.S. oil corporations, with Gulf Oil, Standard Oil, Mobil, and Texaco obtaining a 40% share in Iranian oil based on a new agreement (Kloby, 2004).

The coup that toppled a popularly elected prime minister of Iran in 1953 sowed the seeds of resentment against the United States that has residually survived in the minds of some Iranians to the present day. The shah turned out to be repressive, autocratic, and accumulated one of the worst records for human rights abuses in a relatively short time. His secret police, the SAVAK, was notorious for suppressing dissent, filling Iranian jails with political prisoners, torturing people, and executing those the state found troublesome (Chomsky & Herman, 1979). Those who could flee the shah's persecution into exile did so in large numbers to foreign countries (Britain, the United States, and Australia included). In the late 1970s as the shah's oppression reached high levels, and as it became increasingly clear that the United States would rather stick with a repressive dictator than listen to the aspirations of ordinary Iranian citizens, voices for change rang. The animosity harbored by many Iranians for the United States boiled over into a revolution that saw the shah overthrown, a former Iranian in exile in France returned to declare an Islamic Republic, and ordinary Iranians and some students seized the U.S. Embassy, holding 52 Americans hostage for 444 days. It is events such as these that influence emigration, typically first by those targeted, running for their lives into exile, and then followed by waves of others when the revolution did not go as expected.

The Post-Soviet Era

The post-Soviet era has been characterized by a proliferation of civil wars, some of which have been especially predatory as in places such as Sierra Leone, Liberia, Somalia, Sudan, and South Sudan. Some of the conflicts produced genocide or politicides as in Rwanda and Burundi (Kposowa, 2006). As wars have increased in number and kill power, so have migration flows developed in the form of refugees seeking escape. International migration has increased greatly in the post-Soviet era for a combination of economic, political, and military reasons, and it would be a mistake to attribute all movers to non-conflict. Indeed, there is evidence that most refugees are concentrated in the Global South. Even if they wanted to move to foreign nations in the Global North (Europe, North America, Australia, or New Zealand), there are significant barriers to entry, including reluctance by those nations to accept sizable numbers of refugees. Despite this, the number of refugees in the modern era is in the millions of people. A look at Figure 1.2 shows that in 1990, worldwide refugees totaled more than 18 million.

FIGURE 1.2: Total Worldwide Refugee Migration, 1990–2013

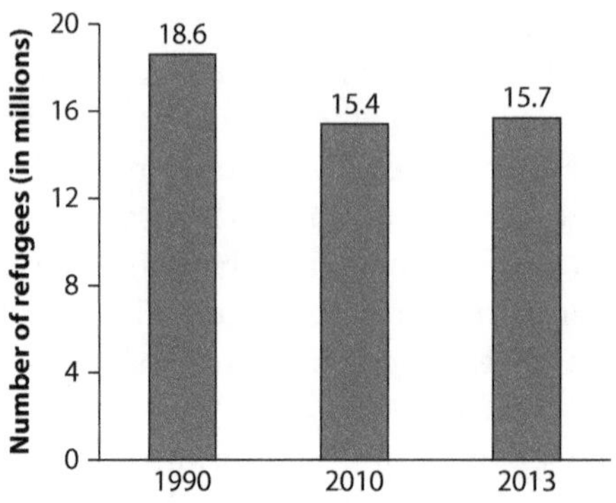

Source: United Nations Department of Economic and Social Affairs, Population Division, Population Facts No. 2013/2, September 2013.

A decade later, it had declined to 15.4 million people, but in 2013 it had barely changed.

A 2013 United Nations report shows that the world is literally on the move. It indicated that the number of international migrants worldwide had reached an all-time high of 232 million people. According to the report (United Nations 2013, p. 1), the number represented an increase from 154 million in 1990 and 175 million in 2000. From 1990 and 2000, the international migrant stock, which is the cumulative number of immigrants, grew by an average of 1.2% per year. In the 2000 to 2010 decade, the annual growth rate of international migration accelerated, reaching 2.3%. Since then the pace has slowed and declined to around 1.6% per year from 2010 to 2013.

Figure 1.3 shows the alarming rate of international migration depicted in the UN report. In 2013, "136 million international migrants lived in the global North, while 96 million resided in the global South. Since 1990, the share of international migrants living in the developed regions has increased. In 2013, the global North hosted 59 per cent of all international migrants; up from 53 per cent in 1990."

Invasions of Afghanistan and Iraq very likely created migration flows whose effect will take years to comprehend. Although a topic that still has the potential to divide the American nation, the Iraq invasion was a strategic blunder of monumental consequences; it created unknown numbers of displaced people within the country, intensified hidden religious divisions, and united groups that would probably dislike the United States for generations to come. The invasion also dramatically lowered U.S. prestige and claim to moral leadership abroad. We may comprehend the fact that there were demonstrations against the possibility of an invasion on every continent, yet the Bush administration ignored the entire world, deceived its domestic population, and went to war anyway. We may ask ourselves, "What did the whole world know that the Bush administration did not know?" Even after the U.S. exit from Iraq, a new group seized territory in a very dramatic fashion in 2014, and one consequence has been continuous

FIGURE 1.3: Average Annual Rate of Change of International Migrants, 2000–2013 (percentage)

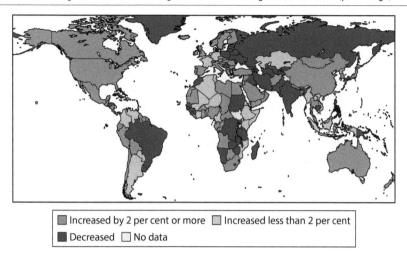

Increased by 2 per cent or more ▪ Increased less than 2 per cent
Decreased ☐ No data

Source: Population Division, United Nations, "Average Annual Rate of Change of International Migrants, 2000-2013," United Nations Department of Social and Economic Affairs, Population Division, Population Facts No 2013/2, 2013.

population displacement within Iraq itself, and the creation of refugee flows. For the United States, the mistake of 2003 continues to exert a toll on the U.S. economy with unknown billions spent on reconstruction, and recently on a new air war to defeat or degrade Islamic State fighters who had seized territory in both Iraq and Syria. The fighting waged by the Islamic State had the added effect of causing more population displacement as entire ethnic or religious groups were singled out for extermination. In 2017, the United States claimed to have pushed out Islamic State fighters from Mosul, Iraq's second-largest city; fighting was continued in Raqqa, Syria, the group's nominal capital city. Only time will tell what are the long-term consequences of these invasions. What is clear is that unknown thousands of innocent civilians in both Iraq and Syria have paid the ultimate price in loss of lives. A war of choice that could have been avoided in 2003 by never invading Iraq in the first place greatly destabilized the Middle East and contributed to a European refugee crisis unseen since the end of World War II.

Refugee flows also resulted from the so-called Arab Spring, with previously weak and repressive, but stable, governments, in Tunisia, Egypt, Libya, Yemen, and Syria either falling or putting up resistance, and in the process creating civil wars that have led to population movements. The cases of Libya, Yemen, and Syria have been especially poignant. Autocratic rulers often have a way of not having a clear line of succession, given the level of mistrust toward even former comrades. Thus, Colonel Mu'ammar al-Qadhafi was basically the only contender in town in Libya. His ouster by France and the United States created a political vacuum that had not been considered by French and American rulers prior to dropping bombs and cruise missiles. The chaos and lawlessness prevailing in the country, along with fear of death and economic uncertainties in the Libyan population, contributed to the migration crisis in the Mediterranean that had still not ended as of fall 2017.

Qadhafi had come up to power with a misleading image whereby he presented himself to sub-Saharan African countries as some pan-Africanist working for African unity—referring to himself as "brother leader." He opened banks and built mosques in nations such as Sierra Leone and the Gambia as a way to win support from Muslim populations in those countries. In Freetown, Sierra Leone, he bought the main hotel, the Bintumani. He would endorse Black Africans to come to Libya to obtain jobs in the oil sector, even as unemployment among Libyans was rising. Resentment grew between the light-skinned Arab population of Libya and the darker-skinned Africans migrating so easily into Libya. With his downfall, the Arab population turned on the darker-skinned immigrant population for revenge. Their protector had been killed by the French and the Americans. Thus, migrants (from sub-Saharan or Sahelian Africa) who would have otherwise found work in Libya no longer had any chance there; they also risked being killed.

An unscrupulous group of traffickers emerged to take advantage of the situation, charging thousands of dollars per "migrant" and promising to ferry migrants across the perilous straits of the Mediterranean to Europe. Although people had in the past tried to enter Europe by crossing the Mediterranean, Qadhafi's fall and resulting instability exacerbated the situation. The movement of migrants was fueled by wars in the Middle East itself, poverty and inequality in sub-Saharan and Sahelian nations, and the increasing weakness of nations wracked by corruption.

The Syrian civil war was another crisis that fueled refugee flows. It is a war whose solution defies reason. Western powers initially wanted the government of President Bashir Assad to leave office, and for a while it even seemed the United States might launch cruise missiles on the country for suspected use of chemical weapons on the civilian population. There was a rapid change of the situation when the Russians prevailed on Assad to give up its chemical weapons arsenal, and so the threat of an American attack was lifted. Yet, more Syrians have died from war-related events and trauma, not due to chemical weapons. Western powers have found themselves in a quandary: If Assad goes, who would take over Syria? Different warring parties, while opposed to the Assad regime in Damascus, are not united as to how to achieve aims, let alone govern in a post-Assad period. Fear of fighters whose loyalties are unknown or questionable and the ability of the Islamic State to seize a considerable amount of Syrian territory added to the complexity of what to do about Syria. For the time being, however, unknown thousands flee the country as refugees, and European nations and the Americans have been slow to accept large numbers of these refugees. The London-based Syrian Observatory for Human Rights monitors events in Syria for the international community and estimates the number of war deaths in the Syrian conflict at 210,060 in February 2015 (Syrian Observatory for Human Rights [SOHR], 2015). The number of displaced people was put at 12 million, and refugees at 4 million. Of this number, the UK agreed (at the time of this writing) to accept only 187 (SOHR, 2015). The Syrian civil war, and the number of refugees it has created, has added significantly to the migrant crisis in the

Mediterranean as people enter into unsafe boats commanded by unscrupulous traffickers whose only aim is war profiteering.

As migration moves to target Europe, citizens there, especially pushed by anti-immigration political parties (such as the National Front in France or the UK Independence Party), became scarred by an image of immigrant "invasion," resurrecting old racial divides that made it harder for governments to take decisive action in case they were perceived as weak on immigration controls. Debates in the European Parliament at Strasbourg and conferences of European Union heads of government tended to focus on capturing and returning migrants caught at sea, or even launching military strikes against traffickers and the physical boats before they left Libya (WikiLeaks, 2015). The conservative UK government, first under David Cameron and later Theresa May, appeared especially unwilling to accept any Mediterranean migrants, with the argument that doing so might encourage more people to take the perilous journey. As of spring 2017 Italy and Germany appeared to be bearing the brunt of the refugee crisis, of which there seemed to be no end in sight. In early 2017, the United States, under its new leader, Donald Trump, largely shut its doors to refugees, especially Syrians with claims of potential terrorists entering the country in spite of unusually long "vetting" that applicants must undergo.

Despite fears of some immigrant invasion from less developed countries, available data show that most refugees are in the Global South—in developing regions. Most will never even attempt to travel to Europe, America, Australia, Canada, or to any of the countries so fearful of taking in more immigrants from presumably less desirable nations. As shown in Figure 1.4, of the estimated 15.7 million refugees worldwide in 2013, only 2 million were in the Global North (which also includes Australia and New Zealand), while 13.7 million were in less developed countries of the South.

It has been shown in this chapter some factors that influenced immigration to the United States in the earlier days along with the variables, such as foreign policy decisions that have played key roles. For all the problems, the United

FIGURE 1.4: Refugee Location Worldwide, 2013

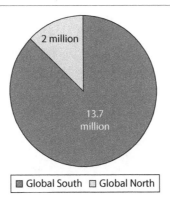

Source: United Nations Department of Economic and Social Affairs, Population Division, Population Facts No. 2013/2, September 2013.

States remains a relatively welcoming place for newcomers compared with other settler nations or those fighting to avoid becoming immigrant receiving countries. No other nation receives as many immigrants per year as America, and the openness shown has transformed the nation in more positive than negative ways. President Barack Obama stressed these positive economic benefits in his immigration address at American University in 2010.

> It is this constant flow of immigrants that help make America what it is. … To this day America reaps incredible economic rewards because we remain a magnet for the best and brightest for people around the world. In an increasingly interconnected world … . Being an American is not a matter of blood or birth, it is a matter of faith. "E pluribus unum." Out of many, one. That is what has drawn the persecuted and impoverished to our shores. That's what led the innovators and risk-takers from around the world to take a chance here in the land of opportunity. That's what has led people to endure untold hardships to reach this place called America.
>
> —President Obama's Immigration Address, July 1,
> 2010, at American University, Washington, DC

Source: http://www.state.gov/j/prm/migration/index.htm

FIGURE 1.5: Oath of Allegiance at Naturalization Ceremony, 2012

Source: Official White House Photo by Pete Souza, "Oath of Allegiance at Naturalization, 2012," http://www.state.gov/j/prm/migration/index.htm. Copyright in the Public Domain.

A more predictive and less chaotic way of admitting immigrants to citizenship has evolved over the last hundred years. In big cities such as Los Angeles, naturalization ceremonies are held in large convention centers. Others are more private in courthouses. Still, others are given special ceremonial importance, such as for would-be citizens currently in the armed services. For example, in the photograph in Figure 1.5, President Obama listens as then Secretary of the Department for Homeland Security Janet Napolitano administers the oath of allegiance during a military naturalization ceremony for active duty service members in the East Room of the White House, on July 4, 2012.

REFERENCES

Adolino, J. R., & Blake, C. H. (2011) *Comparing public policies: Issues and choices in industrial countries*. Washington, DC: CQ Press.

Bromwell, W. J. (1856). *History of immigration to the United States, exhibiting the number, sex, age, occupation, and country of birth of passengers arriving in the United States*. New York, NY: Redfield.

Bucheli, M. (2006). *Good dictator, bad dictator: United Fruit Company and economic nationalism in Central America in the twentieth century* (Working Paper 06–0115). College of Business, University of Illinois at Urban-Champaign. Available at https://business.illinois.edu/.../06-0115.pd. Accessed May 2, 2015.

Castles, S., Haas, H. D., & Miller, M. J. (2014). *The age of migration: International population movements in the modern world*. New York, NY: Guilford Press.

Chomsky, N., & Herman, E. S. (1979). *The Washington connection and third world fascism*. Boston, MA: South End Press.

Churchill, W. (1940) *Their finest hour*. Speech delivered to the House of Commons, June 18, 1940. Available at https://www.winstonchurchill.org/resources/speeches/1940-the-finest-hour/their-finest-hour. Accessed August 14, 2017.

Daniels, R. (2002). *Coming to America: A history of immigration and ethnicity in American life*. New York, NY: Perennial.

History.com staff (2009). *Korean War*. Available at http://www.history.com/topics/korean-war. Accessed April 28, 2015.

Hutchinson, E. P. (1981). *Legislative history of American immigration policy 1798 to 1965*. Philadelphia: University of Pennsylvania Press.

Kloby, J. (2004). *Inequality, power, and development: Issues in political sociology*. New York, NY: Humanity Books.

Kposowa, A. J. (1998). *The impact of immigration on the United States economy*. Lanham, MD: University Press of America.

Kposowa, A. J. (2006) Erosion of the rule of law as a contributing factor to civil conflict. *Police Practice & Research, 7*(1), 35–48.

National World War II Museum (2015). *By the numbers: Worldwide deaths*. Available at http://www.nationalww2museum.org/learn/education/for-students/ww2-history/ww2-by-the-numbers/world-wide-deaths.html. Accessed April 25, 2015.

Obama, B. H. (2010). *President's immigration address*. Speech delivered at American University, Washington, DC, July 1. Available at http://www.state.gov/j/prm/migration/index.htm

Obama, B. H. (2004). Speech delivered at the Democratic Party National Convention, Boston, MA, July 27, 2004. Transcript available at http://www.washingtonpost.com/wp-dyn/articles/A19751-2004Jul27.html

Parenti, M. (1993). *Inventing reality*. New York, NY: St. Martin's Press.

Pinkney, A. (2000). *Black Americans* (5th ed.). Upper Saddle River, NJ: Prentice Hall.

Rhodes, C. (1877). *Confession of faith.* Available at http://chasegalleryconnect.org/ FNC_C/Data/Brain-Neural/Political_and_Governance_Dimensions/Forms%20of% 20Government/Cecil%20Rhodes,%20'Confession%20of%20Faith'.pdf. Accessed April 6, 2015.

Snellgrove, L. E. (1974). *The modern world Since 1870.* London, UK: Longman Group.

Syrian Observatory for Human Rights [SOHR] (2015). *We will be good people.* Available at http://www.syriahr.com/en/category/news/refugees-news/. Accessed May 28, 2015.

The Mohammad Mossadegh Project (2015). *Dr. Mohammad Mossadegh biography: Prime minister of Iran, 1951–1953.* Available at http://www.mohammadmossadegh.com/biography/. Accessed May 2, 2015.

The New American Bible (1987). *Holy Bible.* Nashville, TN: Catholic Bible Press.

United Nations (2013). *Population facts no. 2013/2.* New York, NY: Department of Economic and Social Affairs, Population Division.

U.S. Bureau of the Census (1975). *Historical statistics of the United States, colonial times to 1970.* Washington, DC: Government Printing Press.

U.S. Department of State (2012). *Naturalization ceremony at the White House.* Available at http://www.state.gov/j/prm/migration/index.htm. Accessed April 20, 2015.

U.S. Department of Homeland Security (2005a). *Statistical year book 2001.* Washington, DC: U.S. Bureau of Citizenship and Immigration Services.

U.S. Department of Homeland Security (2005b). *2005 yearbook of immigration statistics.* Washington, DC: Office of Immigration Statistics.

U.S. Bureau of the Census (1975). *Historical statistics of the United States, colonial times to 1970.* Washington, DC: Government Printing Office.

U.S. Congress (1850). Chap. XLVI: 15th Cong. Sess. II, CH, 45, 46 1819. *An act regulating passenger ships and vessels. Public satutes at large of the United States of America, from the organization of the government in 1789, to March, 3, 1845.* Available at http://www. constitution.org/uslaw/sal/sal.htm. Accessed May 1, 2015.

WikiLeaks (2015). *EU defence chiefs' approved plan for military intervention against 'refugee boats' in Libya and the Mediterranean.* Available at https://www.wikileaks.org/ eu-military-refugees/. Accessed May 28, 2015.

2 | Concepts in Migration Research

The study of migration has become interdisciplinary, and various disciplines approach the topic in varying ways according to their modes of inquiry or paradigms. Migration is studied in sociology, economics, geography, history, anthropology, political science, and even law. Sociologists have traditionally investigated migration with regard to its causes, characteristics of migrants, and the effect of the migration process at both sending and receiving areas. Sociologists also consider the consequences of movement on the individuals who are involved, on those that are left behind, and how migrants are assimilated at destination. Furthermore, sociologists study migration as a process, and not just as a single isolated event.

To understand migration as a process, it is important to have a basic understanding of other concepts that are related, and the primary one is **demography**. Similar to many modern social science disciplines, the word "demography" has an ancient Greek etymology. In ancient Greek, the word δεμοσ [*demos*] stands for people, and γραφε [*graphé*] may be translated as writings, representations, or depictions. Combining the two Greek words leads us to a definition of demography as writings or representations about people. Thus, demography may be defined as the study of people, and given that historically most demographers have studied not just individual persons, the field is usually framed in many texts (e.g., Newell, 1988; Yaukey et al., 2007; Poston & Bouvier, 2010) as the study of human populations in a systematic and scientific manner. Populations are studied with regard to their size; their composition or structure, including age, sex, race/ethnicity, educational attainment and other characteristics; and change. Typically, demographers study human populations in some clearly defined spatial units, such as countries, states, counties, parishes, provinces, and so on. The idea is to know how many people are present in a given locality or unit, the characteristics of the people, especially with regard to age and sex, and how they are distributed across regions within a country or even across the globe. It is important to note that in demographic analysis, interest is often in the future or potential population. The present population is studied, but with an eye on what the future is going to look like, because planning and policies are often geared toward preparing for the future, such as educational systems, employment availability, health care, and so on. Demographers may consider, for example, the present number of people in some age group, for example, 9 to 19, within a country and ask what the size of this group is going to be in a decade. After a decade, the group will have aged by

10 years, so members will be in age group 19–29. If some educational planning was placed into effect a decade earlier, it hopefully would have been sufficient to educate those in the 9–19 age group, and by becoming young adults, aged 19–29, provision would have also been made for employment opportunities as this is the age wherein many population members might complete school and begin to form their own families.

Population size hardly ever remains static, but it undergoes dynamic processes that bring about change, and those components of change are fertility, mortality, and migration. These three are heavily studied in demography, and arguably demography would not exist without them. People are born into a population of a country, say the United States, thereby contributing to the size of the local, state, and national population. This is fertility, the process by which a population gains members through birth. Individuals inevitably also exit a population by death, and the process by which they leave a population is called mortality. The mathematical difference between births and deaths is called natural increase, that is, the way by which a population changes through the life cycle. Natural increase is calculated as $B-D$, where B stands for births, and D represents deaths within a specified period (such as number of births in 2015 and number of deaths in 2015). Population change can be either positive or negative. If the difference between births and deaths (B-D) is negative, it implies that the population of an area experienced growth or change by losing members—more people died than were born. On the other hand, if the difference between births and deaths (B-D) is positive, it means that the area in question gained population members. Specifically, the number of births exceeded the number of deaths.

The word "natural" is used to describe the kinds of change in population size just cited for the simple reason that individuals are born into a population without consultation. They have no choice regarding the families into which they wanted to be born; they were not asked about the color of skin, eyes, or hair that they prefer. They were not asked about the neighborhood or country into which they wanted to be born; they just found themselves in a population (and they could not request to be unborn!).

Similarly, and for the most part, population members are unlikely to be consulted about the time, place, and even circumstances of that inevitable exit from the population called mortality, or death. For sure, some might say a human being can influence the timing of his or her death based on health promotion or health behavior, including the lifestyle selected, such as texting while driving or crossing a major intersection. Even here, there are limitations, for a person's individual life chances are heavily influenced by structural and contextual factors. A person born into a lower-income family living in a distressed neighborhood wracked by high unemployment and who experiences daily degradations hardly has the same life chances as a counterpart born into an upper-income family with lots of available liquid wealth, and who lives in a big mansion on a hill surrounded by trees and all the comforts of modern life. For the first person, the idea of the existence of some "equal opportunity" may well be a cruel joke. But no matter how one lives, and no matter how long the life expectancy, no human in modern memory has survived to be 200 years old; there is a life cycle process of exit from a population for each member.

In addition to fertility (births) and mortality (deaths), there is a third process by which population size changes, and that is through migration, which refers to movement from one population to another, usually by crossing some administrative line. Unlike births and deaths, however, the migration process is not considered "natural" because, to a large extent, individuals have a choice about moving or staying. Options available may be limited by stages in the life cycle or by events beyond an individual's control. For example, young children are unlikely to have a say in whether they move or not; their parents make that decision. In a country experiencing civil war or an intense level of political violence, people might move from one region to another to avoid death and misery. A natural disaster, such a typhoon, earthquake, or hurricane, might displace some population members who then have to move to a safer refuge, albeit for a short duration until the crisis is over. But whether by compulsion or free choice, if individuals move from one place to another, such as from one state to another within the same country, they contribute to change in population size both at their origin (which loses population) and also at their destination (which gains population).

Of the three components of population change, migration is more difficult to conceptualize and also to measure with precision. Part of the problem is that movement between places involves an origin and a destination, a dyadic relationship. Furthermore, unlike births and deaths, which are experienced only once by an individual, migration can be experienced multiple times by the same person, either intentionally or not. This contributes to the problem inherent in calculating migration rates. One must ask whether there is correspondence between the number of people moving and those at risk of moving. For example, for calculating in-migration, the numerator is the number of people who have moved into some territory; the denominator is often the people who are already in the territory. There is a bias in this, in the sense that those already in the country were never at risk of moving in because they were already there. This issue is addressed further when calculating various measures of migration in following chapters.

Migration

Not all movements made by people are considered migration. For example, short distance commutes between cities or counties are not considered migration. Likewise, temporary changes of residence, excursions, field trips made by students, and moves for vacation purposes do not constitute migration. For a move to be considered migratory, it has to have some demographic significance. A move is considered migration if it involves a permanent change in a person's usual place of residence or place of abode that lasts for at least a year. According to the United Nations (1970, p. 1), the change of residence must entail "taking up of life in a new or different place." Typically, the individual concerned must cross a geographic or administrative boundary. In the United States, a county line is usually the smallest geographic boundary a person can cross for migratory purposes.

Migration Streams

Migration occurs in streams or flows, which may be represented as M_{ij}, where M stands for movement, or flows from an origin, $_i$ to a destination $_j$ or from place $_i$ to place $_j$. Flow of migrants between any two clearly identified places and within a defined time period is referred to as a migration stream. It is important to note that as the process of migration takes place from one origin to a given destination, there is a flow or stream occurring in the opposite direction. For instance, just as there is a flow of migrants from Los Angeles to New York City, there is a flow going from New York City to Los Angeles within the same defined time period (M_{ji}). Thus, migration is rarely a one-way process, and no matter how unattractive a place, it experiences a flow.

Internal Migration

Movement of people across geographic units within a country or territory is called internal migration. In this case, the mover is an out-migrant with regard to the origin (area of departure) and an in-migrant with reference to the place of arrival or destination, for a mover takes up two forms of status during a move. The region, city, parish, or state from which he or she is departing considers the mover an **out-migrant**, but the region, city, parish, or state into which he or she moves considers the same individual an **in-migrant**. A given state or city experiences in-migration (people moving in) while at the same time experiencing out-migration (people moving out).

Net Migration

Net migration refers to the mathematical difference between in-migrants (in-migration) and out-migrants (out-migration). It is formulated as follows: $M_{ij} - M_{ji}$. For example, if in a hypothetical scenario, the number of people who moved into Los Angeles within a year is 250,000, and the number of individuals who moved out of the city was 300,000 during the same period, the difference (250,000 − 300,000 = −50,000) is regarded as net migration. When it is negative (as in the case above), the implication is that the city lost population; in this case, it lost more people (−50,000) than it gained. A positive difference would mean the city or area gained population through migration. Although demographers often use the word "net" migration, there is no such term as net migrant.

Gross Migration

Instead of subtracting those who moved in from those who left, movers may be added to leavers. The result of this summation gives us a concept called **gross migration**, represented as $M_{ij} + M_{ji}$. Its size tells us the volume of movement within a defined territory, city, county, or state, but says nothing about direction of movement. A high number (there is no upper limit) tells us there is a lot of population movement occurring in the defined area. On the other hand, a low number yields the opposite interpretation.

Migration Efficiency

Migration efficiency describes the extent to which an area is able to attract migrants within a specified period. If a state, city, county, or parish has experienced a lot of in-migration within a period, but little or no out-migration during the same time interval, then the geographic area concerned (state, city, county, or parish) is said to be efficient in migration; its net migration will be positive. On the other hand, if an area has experienced much out-migration, but relatively little or no in-migration, it is described as being inefficient; its net migration will be negative. Migration efficiency for some spatial area is calculated by dividing the entity's net migration by its gross migration. A positive value implies efficient migration, whereas a negative value implies the opposite.

$$\text{Migration Efficiency} = \frac{\text{Net Migration}}{\text{Gross Migration}}$$

The above formula shows the contribution made by in-migrants to overall population movement. The ratio can be multiplied by 100 to make interpretation easier, whereby it would be the percentage of total migration accounted for by net migration (the difference between movers and leavers). What happens if, for a given locality, the number of in-migrants is about the same as that of out-migrants? In that situation, the area concerned is said to experience inefficient migration (Poston & Bouvier, 2010). It is easy to see from this explanation that regions, states, or cities with high values on migration efficiency are attractive to movers, and a possible reason for the attractiveness may well be availability of employment and other economic opportunities (Bogue, 1969). A state with an enduring stagnant economy and depressed wages is less likely to draw people than one with a growing economy.

Area Holding Power

This concept describes the ability of an area to hold on to its inhabitants—that is to say, those originally born in the state, city, county, or parish tend not to move out or migrate to other places in large numbers. For state level analysis, area holding power can be determined by comparing the percentage of the population born in a given state and who still live there. If a sizable proportion of the population born in a state is enumerated, say in a census as still living in that state, then it (the state in question) is described as having a high holding power. Consider the following scenario: Jack was born in California in 1980. He attended school and college in California, never moved out of California permanently (not even to Oregon, Washington, or Arizona), and in fact got married in California, and now proudly intends to eventually die in California. If a lot of people in California have a similar migration profile as Jack, then the state is able to hold on to its population, or has high holding power. States with high holding power are very likely marked by low out-migration and in-migration from other places.

A low value on area holding power reflects a region's high rate of in-migration or immigration. If more people move from outside into an area, then that reduces the percentage distribution of people born in the area. Data from population censuses or surveys can be used to calculate area holding power. In 2011, for example, Nevada, Arizona, and Colorado had relatively lower scores (on holding power) than Louisiana, Michigan, and Ohio. Data from the American Community Survey (Grieco et al., 2011) indicated that Nevada, Arizona, and Colorado ranked high in states with high levels of immigration, and this accounted for their low holding power values. Simply put, Nevada, Arizona, and Colorado have more people moving into them than the states of Louisiana, Ohio, and Michigan.

International Migration

International migration may be defined as change of usual place of residence that involves crossing an international boundary; the movement must involve taking up new abode in a country of destination different from the country of origin. An individual is considered an international migrant if he or she changes country of abode and the duration of residence in the destination country lasts for at least a year. Usual place of residence is defined by United Nations (1998, p. 9) as the country where the individual "normally spends the daily period of rest."

Internally Displaced Persons

Given so many civil wars the in the post-Soviet era, individuals are often uprooted from their region of usual or de facto residence and forced to flee to other, safer parts of their country. Those forced to flee from an area within a country to another area as a result of war, military operations (coups d'état), "death squads," or natural disasters are considered internally displaced. Depending on circumstances, they may stay with relatives or extended family members living in an area yet untouched by the war or natural calamity, or in some cases are placed in refugee camps. Wars in Sierra Leone, Liberia, Iraq, Syria, Somalia, and the Ukraine gave rise to many internally displaced people when they occurred.

Nativity Status

As used by the Census Bureau, the concept describes whether an individual was born in the United States (native-born) or born abroad (foreign-born). The native-born comprises those born in the United States or U.S. possessions, including Puerto Rico, U.S. Virgin Islands, Guam, Western Samoa, or the Commonwealth of Northern Mariana Islands. Native-born also covers an individual born abroad of American parents or parent. Foreign-born refers to anyone not a U.S. citizen at birth. Those gaining citizenship through naturalization, permanent residents of the United States, and those on temporary visas including visitors, students, crew members, and representatives of foreign governments are all in the foreign-born classification.

Legal Immigrants

This refers to those given permission to move to another country before making the move. Permission is usually given at the consular office of the embassy serving the country of citizenship or origin of the potential immigrant in the form of a permanent visa. In some cases, the immigrant arrives at his or her destination and is given time to adjust his or her status. The key is that permission is given before the move; the individual applied for and obtained a permanent visa.

In the United States, a legal immigrant is a foreigner admitted for lawful permanent residence. According to the U.S. Immigration and Nationality Act of 1952, "Immigrants are those individuals lawfully accorded the privilege of residing permanently in the United States. They may be issued immigrant visas by the Department of State overseas or adjusted to permanent resident status" upon their arrival in the United States by the U.S. Citizenship and Immigration Services. In many cases, a year of permanent residency of an immigrant may differ from the year in which he or she became a resident of the United States.

Illegal Immigrants

The concept refers to individuals or groups that make a move into another country without legal authorization prior to their arrival. In some circles, there have been concerns over whether an individual is illegal. No one is inherently legal or illegal. The labels legal or illegal do not refer to the person concerned, but rather to their status at destination; it simply has to do with whether they received permission before moving into another country or have since obtained such permission—for example, through adjustment of status.

In the category of illegal immigrants are:

1. *Unauthorized Border Crossers* or persons entering the country without inspection by immigration officials. In the jargon of immigration officials, those in this category are at times described as EWIs (entrants without inspection). Unauthorized border crossing also covers anyone who enters through sea or air border without inspection.
2. *Visa Over-stayers*: This category covers individuals who previously entered with permission but stayed past the time provided to them at entry. For example, a student given permission to stay for the duration of his or her program of study (e.g., four years), who then remains in the country past that time without authorization from U.S. Citizenship and Immigration Services, becomes a visa over-stayer.
3. The third group of illegal immigrants consists of those who enter without proper documentation. Papers presented to immigration officials may be counterfeit, altered, or borrowed.

Combined, illegal border crossers and visa over-stayers represent most of the illegal immigrant population, with estimates put at 60% and 40%, respectively (U.S. Department of Homeland Security [INS] 1999, p. 199).

The Law of Presumption in U.S. Immigration Policy

U.S. immigration laws, culminating in the Immigration and Nationality Act of 1952, presume that any foreigner (alien) coming to the United States intends to stay permanently. Perhaps this way of looking at prospective international migrants falls under what is often described as American "exceptionalism." The burden of proof resides in the prospective mover to demonstrate at a U.S. consulate abroad that his or her proposed travel does not entail living permanently in the country. The first evidence is the type of visa for which the prospective traveler applies. A person intending to stay for a temporary duration applies for a nonimmigrant visa. A nonimmigrant proves that he or she is coming for a temporary stay, such as tourism, study, or business consultation. Further evidence required depends on purpose of the trip, answers to questions on temporary visa application forms, responses to questions asked by visa officers, and documentation presented with the application form. For example, a student shows proof of acceptance at a school authorized to admit foreign students, a documented funding source for the trip, and evidence of return air ticket availability post-education and practical training. Visa officers will typically look for evidence of "grounding" at origin, which entails determination of whether the individual traveler is tied to his or her country in some fashion that he or she is very likely to return after the U.S. trip. Having a good job and being married are likely helpful variables in determining the grounding aspect, though financial assets of the traveler and one's family are likely to weigh even more in the entire process. At a consulate or a port of entry, an applicant for admission is presumed to be an alien until he or she shows evidence of citizenship. A foreigner is presumed to be an immigrant (wishes to stay permanently) until he or she proves that he or she fits into one of the nonimmigrant classifications. Overall, the presumption of the wanting-to-stay principle is a clear indication of just how extremely difficult and burdensome it is for a foreigner to travel to the United States and enter the country.

Nonimmigrant

The nonimmigrant population comprises all travelers who are not citizens of the United States and whose visit is for some specified temporary duration. Included in this category are tourists who may stay for a few days or a limited number of months, business people who might stay for less than a few weeks (depending on the nature of their business activities and their role), scholars/professors wishing to travel and engage in research or research consultation with U.S. colleagues (these fall under Temporary Visitors for Business), and students (and their immediate family members, such as children and spouses). Representatives of foreign governments accredited to foreign embassies in Washington, DC, foreign dignitaries or workers at the United Nations as per the Headquarters Agreement (along with their dependents and servers), temporary workers (and spouses and children), crewmen/women of vessels (airlines, trains, ships), performers and their immediate entourage, and members of the clergy (typically invited by a church/mosque/other religious entity) are all considered nonimmigrants unless an immigrant visa was secured abroad by a given traveler. The nonimmigrant population comprises by far the largest number of people coming to the United States in a given year, and within that group, temporary visitors for pleasure represent the most. This is evident in Figure 2.1.

FIGURE 2.1: Nonimmigrant Admissions by Class of Admission, Fiscal Year 2013

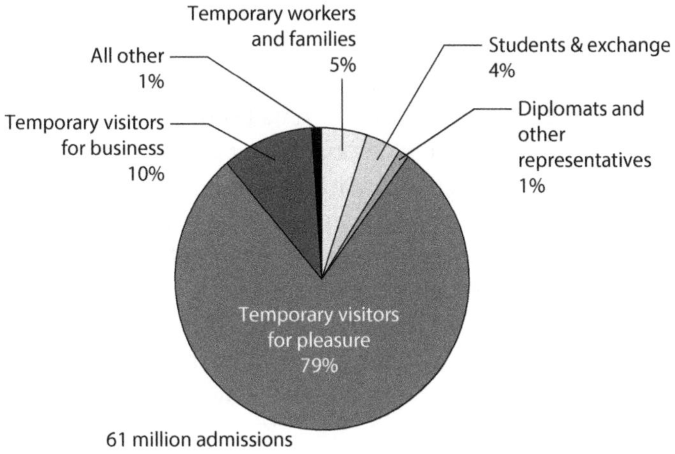

Source: Yearbook of Immigration Statistics: 2013, Table 25, U.S. Department of Homeland Security, Office of Immigration Statistics.

Of the 61 million temporary admissions in the United States in fiscal year 2013, 79% were visitors. These add substantially to the U.S. economy benefitting industries such as hotels, transportation, entertainment, amusement parks, restaurants, and other service industries. Stopping this type of immigration or substantially making it difficult for travelers would have detrimental consequences on the U.S. economy. The same holds for students. A heavy burden or impediment imposed on their entry would very likely lead to potential benefits of their admission shifting to other countries, such as Canada, the UK, and Australia. The loss would be felt by universities, colleges, college and university towns, and real estate owners.

As stated in the first chapter, immigration has become an important component of population growth in the United States and other "settler" nations (Canada, Australia, and New Zealand). Given population aging in many nations in the Global North, immigration will also most likely be embraced—albeit not so joyfully in other nations, especially in northern and western Europe, and perhaps Japan.

Population Change and Immigration

Immigration contributes to population change. One method used by demographers in demographic analysis to assess the role of migration is the employment of the balancing, or basic demographic equation, which shows the natural components of change, along with immigration. The equation is as follows:

$$P_{t-1} = P_t + B_t - D_t + I_t - O_t$$

Where: P_{t-1} refers to an estimate of the population at some later point in time (following an interval represented by $_{t-1}$). That later population is a function of an earlier population size (P_t) plus the number of births that have occurred in the interval that has elapsed (B_t) minus the number of deaths that have elapsed in the interval (D_t). If a country has closed its borders and allowed no immigration within the interval, then its estimated population size at the end of the interval would have been determined solely by natural increase (births – deaths). Assuming, however, that most nations in the modern world do not have sealed borders, but allow people to move in and even settle, net international migration is added to the balancing equation as the difference between people moving into the country (I_t) and those moving out (O_t). Net international migration affects an entire society, but since immigrants might move in larger numbers to some localities within a country, some regions, states, or counties will feel their presence more than others.

Administration of U.S. Immigration

Administration of U.S. immigration has changed hands many times since 1819 when the first immigration policies were put into force. The first serious attempt by Congress to regulate the process of immigration into the United States was with the Immigration Act of 1891, which created the Office of the Superintendent of Immigration in the Treasury Department (Department of Homeland Security [DHS], 2015a). The superintendent was tasked with overseeing a new body of immigrant inspectors stationed at the country's principal ports of entry. It was during the first decade of its existence that the Immigration Service formalized basic immigration procedures (DHS, 2015a). For example, the collection of manifests, which had been the duty of customs officials since the passage of the Act of 1819, was taken over by the new Immigration Service. Inspectors questioned new arrivals to determine their admissibility and recorded their admission or rejection on the manifest records (DHS, 2015a).

In 1893, immigration inspectors also served on Boards of Special Inquiry that closely reviewed each case that was barred from entry. On March 2, 1895, a congressional act (the Act of 1895) renamed the Office of Immigration as the *Bureau of Immigration* and changed the title of *superintendent of immigration* to *commissioner-general of immigration*. A later congressional act (June, 6, 1900) consolidated immigration enforcement by assigning enforcement of both alien contract labor laws and Chinese exclusion laws to the commissioner-general (DHS, 2015a and 2015b). The *Chinese Exclusion Act* (passed in 1882) will be covered in detail in a following chapter.

In 1903, the Bureau of Immigration moved from the Treasury Department to the newly created Department of Commerce and Labor. How were these bureaucracies financed? Until 1909, a special fund that had been created from the collection of immigrants head tax financed the Immigration Service. The fund was replaced in 1909 with an annual congressional appropriation (DHS, 2015a and 2015b).

In 1913, the Bureau of Immigration and Naturalization was split into the Bureau of Immigration and the Bureau of Naturalization. The two agencies were housed separately within the U.S. Department of Labor until reunited as the *Immigration and Naturalization Service* (INS) on June 10, 1933, via executive order (DHS, 2015b). In 1940, the Presidential Reorganization Plan No. V moved the INS from the Department of Labor to the Department of Justice, where it remained until 2002 (DHS, 2015a and 2015b).

Today, three agencies are charged with administering U.S. immigration laws, policies, and regulations. They are: (1) United States Citizenship and Immigration Services (USCIS), (2) Immigration and Customs Enforcement (ICE), and (3) Customs and Border Protection (CBP). These three operate as units or agencies within the broader bureaucracy called the Department of Homeland Security (DHS). Other federal agencies with indirect links to immigration administration include the Department of Agriculture (which examines agricultural products being brought into the country through an airport), Health and Human Services (which could potentially inspect an immigrant suspected of carrying some infectious disease), and the Department of Labor (which issues work authorization permits).

In the wake of the attacks on the United States on September 11, 2001, there were perceptions that contributing factors in those attacks were failures or lapses in immigration enforcement as some of the attackers had entered the United States legally. It was believed by some in and out of government that the existing system of allowing immigration to be handled by one agency—the Immigration and Naturalization Service (INS)—was not adequate.

Structurally, the INS also appeared to have a built-in conflict of interest that had never been addressed by policy makers. On the one hand, the agency provided benefits to would-be immigrants, such as controlling and managing change of status for those foreigners (aliens) already in the country, approving and granting work permits (in consultation with the Department of Labor), processing and approving applications for naturalization, and other benefits. At the same time, the INS was charged with determining whether individuals coming to the United States were admissible at ports of entry (which could be airports, seaports, land-border crossings by train or vehicles). The agency also policed immigration, including removal of individuals who were in the country illegally, either through visa overstays or from unauthorized entry, along with enforcement of most immigration laws.

In response to the above conflict of interest, and to reduce risk of future attacks on the United States emanating from abroad, the U.S. Congress passed the Homeland Security Act of 2002 as Public Law No. 107–296 (116 Statute 2135). Under the act, the INS was disbanded effective March 1, 2003. Its previous responsibilities, charges, and staff members were distributed to the three components of the newly formed Department of Homeland Security: Customs and Border Protection, Immigration and Customs Enforcement, and U.S. Citizenship and Immigration Services (DHS, 2015a and 2015b).

Policing duties (especially within the country), such as removal of those judged to be in the United States without authorization or to have violated other immigration regulations, were given to the Immigration and Customs Enforcement (ICE). Border protection duties were assigned to Customs and Border Protection (CBP), which manages, controls, and protects U.S. borders and between ports of entry. Typically, agents belonging to this group are found in large numbers at airports. The U.S. Citizenship and Immigration Services (USCIS) was tasked with the duty of providing benefits to immigrants or prospective ones. While there are overlaps in duties and responsibilities of these three agencies, their creation appears to have removed, at least in part, the structural conflict of interest in the former Immigration and Naturalization Service (INS). At the same time, the emergence of such a huge bureaucracy is not without its costs, and it is unknown how much U.S. taxpayers spend to fund increasing functions developed by DHS; for example, in expanding preclearance infrastructure at more airports abroad, and in some cases having a presence at foreign (friendly) airports, such as Kotoka International Airport (Ghana).

Visa and Traveler Inspection

Obtaining a U.S. visa abroad is no guarantee that a prospective traveler would enter the United States. In a sense, a visa is merely evidence of eligibility to travel to a U.S. border checkpoint or port of entry (POE). Upon arrival the prospective traveler is inspected by immigration and customs officials and, if needed, by agricultural and health officials as well, and the individual may be found inadmissible according to the various excludable categories that have accumulated into U.S. immigration laws since the 19th century, primarily section 212(a) of the Immigration and Nationality Act. Affirming the above points, the U.S. Department of State (2015, p. 1) indicates that:

> Having a U.S. visa allows you to travel to a port of entry, airport or land border crossing, and request permission of the Department of Homeland Security (DHS), Customs and Border Protection (CBP) inspector to enter the United States. While having a visa does not guarantee entry to the United States, it does indicate a consular officer at a U.S. Embassy or Consulate abroad has determined you are eligible to seek entry for that specific purpose. DHS/CBP inspectors, guardians of the nation's borders, are responsible for admission of travelers to the United States, for a specified status and period of time. DHS also has responsibility for immigration matters while you are present in the United States.

Inspection typically begins with a Customs and Border Protection (CBP) officer, and immigration regulations specify that "An officer is responsible for determining the nationality and identity of each applicant for admission and for preventing the entry of ineligible aliens, including criminals, terrorists, and drug traffickers, among others. U.S. citizens are automatically admitted upon verification of citizenship; aliens are questioned and their documents are examined to determine admissibility based on the requirements of the U.S. immigration law" (DHS, 2015b, p. 1).

The Immigration and National Act (INA) does not appear to have brought aliens within the protection of the U.S. Constitution with regard to the phrase "unreasonable" searches and seizures because it empowers immigration and customs officials (and other inspectors) to search without warrant the foreigner and personal effects of any foreigner seeking admission, when there is reason to believe that grounds for exclusion exist that would be disclosed by such search. The various grounds for exclusion or inadmissibility appear in section 212(a) of the 1952 Immigration and Nationality Act, as amended. These grounds for exclusion actually begin to be applied at U.S. consulates abroad when potential travelers apply for visas. A list of excludable or inadmissible persons are specified in great detail under the heading: INA: Act 212—General Classes of Aliens Ineligible to Receive Visas and Ineligible for Admission; Waivers of Inadmissibility at the website of United States Citizenship and Immigration Services: (USCIS, 2006; [https://www.uscis.gov/ilink/docView/SLB/HTML/SLB/0-0-0-1/0-0-0-29/0-0-0-2006.html]).

The list of persons or groups not eligible to enter or be in the United States is now incredibly long; it has grown considerably over the ages and will most likely keep growing until the end of time. Going through it gives one chills to wonder whether, in time, even angels and saints would be welcome. In recent years, [(Section 212(a)(10)(D)] the list has included "Unlawful Voters," no doubt fueled by claims of voter "fraud" heard repeatedly in some circles in the land. The section provides that any foreign national who voted in violation of any U.S. law is inadmissible. Elections for which an alien may be found inadmissible are those for the office of President, Vice President, Presidential Elector, member of the Senate, Member of the House of Representatives, Delegate from the District of Columbia, or Resident Commissioner.

As shown in Figure 2.2, immigrant visa denials have typically outpaced non-immigrant visa denials, but in 2013, for the first time, the reverse occurred, whereby those wishing to enter as nonimmigrants were denied entry at a higher rate than those applying as permanent residents.

An unavoidable question at ports of entry becomes: What happens if after all the uncomfortable experience of being searched, nothing is found to exclude the alien? Rights of the inspected for redress are not addressed in INA, but it is sensible for some grievance or complaint procedure in the event that a given traveler is manhandled in a way that seems especially discourteous, if not outrightly rude by immigration and customs officials.

Deferred Inspection
There may come up circumstance in which an immediate decision on the admissibility of a potential entrant cannot be made at a U.S. port of entry. Lack of proper documentation and errors in submitted documents—for example, in visa category and/or number—constitute a primary reason. In this case, immigration officials at a port of entry may allow the traveler to visit a site (physical location) for later

FIGURE 2.2: Aliens Denied Visas Under §212(a) Inadmissibility, Fiscal Years 1994–2013

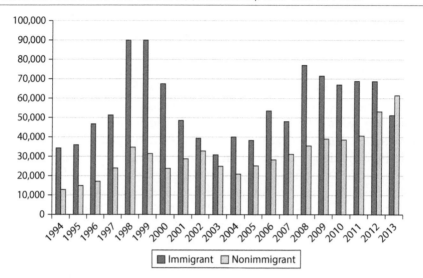

Source: U.S. Immigration Policy: Chart Book of Key Trends / William A. Kandel and Ruth Ellen Wasem, "Aliens Denied Visas 1994-2013," https://www.fas.org/sgp/crs/homesec/R42988.pdf, pp. 15. Copyright in the Public Domain.

inspection before the final decision on admissibility is made. The traveler is given what the Department of Homeland Security (2015c) calls an Order to Appear and asked to complete a form (I-546) indicating information and documents needed to resolve inconsistencies. There were 77 Deferred Inspection sites in the United States and outlying areas and possessions in 2015. The sites are typically within airports (though not always) and managed by Deferred Inspection units within U.S. Customs and Border Protection (CBP). It should be pointed out that deferred inspection is on a case-by-case basis, and the option is not available to all potential entrants (Department of Homeland Security, 2015c). Furthermore, the center to which a potential entrant is referred may be different from the city or airport where he or she landed.

Preclearance

One of the hallmarks of modern international travel is airport congestion at areas of destination, a broader consequence of the general increase in the volume of international travelers, including those for business, tourism, and education. Clearly, one reason for the congestion (aside from the increased volume of airport travelers), at both origin and destination, is heightened security due to fears or concerns about terrorists infiltrating immigration systems. Congestion may have also worsened due to perhaps exaggerated fears about trafficking of contraband. Safeguarding the need for a pleasant system of entry for typical travelers (most of the traveling public) has to be balanced with protecting against potential criminals (a minority). To the casual leisure traveler, however, since September 11, 2001, airports have not been a particularly pleasant or inviting part of travel, and at times appear to have become centers of high-tech electronic strip searching—places to avoid at all costs if possible, and places that give typical travelers high anxiety levels. Every traveler is viewed as a suspect of some sort until electronic devices or/and strip searchers prove otherwise. This is a high price the nation continues to pay for what some might view as an overreaction to the attacks of September 2001. By building "Citadel USA," the country may have inadvertently played into the hands of terrorists, for their dream likely included draining the nation of economic resources, and creating a sense of distrust or unease among the population.

To minimize congestion at airports and make it faster for travelers to go through ports of entry, Customs and Border Protection (CBP) has a preclearance system that in effect subjects a traveler to the same inspection that an arriving passenger would undergo at a U.S. port of entry, but it is performed at a foreign airport (or other designated airport or train station). Once done, travelers do not have to undergo a second CBP inspection upon arrival in the United States, though travelers pre-inspected for admissibility at non-airport sites must still undergo customs and agriculture inspections upon arrival.

At present, CBP preclearance of commercial airline passengers and their luggage—clothing, souvenirs, currency, and any other personal effects—is available at 15 locations in six foreign countries, and there are plans for expansion (U.S. Department of Homeland Security, 2015d). There are now preclearance facilities at the following sites: Calgary International Airport (Alberta, Canada); Edmonton International Airport (Alberta, Canada); Halifax Robert L. Stanfield International Airport (Nova Scotia, Canada); Montreal Trudeau International Airport (Quebec, Canada); Ottawa MacDonald-Cartier International Airport (Ontario, Canada); Vancouver International Airport (British Columbia, Canada); Winnipeg International Airport (Manitoba, Canada); Victoria (British Columbia, Canada); Bahamas, Freeport and Nassau; L. F. Wade International Airport (Bermuda); Aruba; Shannon International Airport (Ireland); Dublin Airport (Ireland); and Abu Dhabi International Airport (United Arab Emirates).

Data on Immigration

Data on immigration come from various sources, and their utility depends on which aspect of immigration a researcher is interested in studying. Some data are collected primarily for administrative purposes, so migration information is derived more as a by-product than an actual measure of population mobility or reasons for movement. For determining the volume of immigration into a country, a national population census is a relatively reliable source of immigration data if the census questionnaire has a question that asks residents to indicate their state, region, or country of birth. The format may vary from country to country depending on the administrative units. For example, Ghana is divided into 10 regions, so in the 2010 Population and Housing Census, the place of birth

FIGURE 2.3: In what region of country was [NAME] born

01	Western
02	Central
03	Greater Accra
04	Volta
05	Eastern
06	Ashanti
07	Brong Ahafo
08	Northern
09	Upper East
10	Upper West
11	Nigeria
12	Liberia
13	Sierra Leone
14	Gambia
15	Togo
16	Burkina Faso
17	Cotê d'Ivoire
18	Other ECOWAS states
19	Africa, other than ECOWAS
20	Europe
21	Americas (North, South/Caribbean)
22	Asia
23	Oceania

Source: Ghana Statistical Service (2010). Excerpt from: Census Question-naire. Copyright in the Public Domain.

question was worded as follows: **"In what region or country was [NAME] born?"** Possible responses were:

The respondent named his or her region or country of birth, and not the numbers in column 1, which were for tabulation purposes only. It can be seen from Figure 2.3 that if someone did not name one of the 10 Ghanian regions as his or her country of birth, selecting any other place automatically made that individual a foreign-born person or immigrant. The place of birth question is limited for demographic analysis as it merely distinguishes those born in the country from those born outside. There is no indication as to when a given foreigner entered the country, or whether he or she is a naturalized citizen. To augment the measure, some censuses ask for year of entry into the country and also citizenship status (whether the respondent is a citizen or not). Duration of residence in the country is either asked directly or can be derived from the year-of-entry question.

FIGURE 2.4A: Where was this person born?

A.

12 "Where was this person born?"

☐ In the United States—Print name of state

```
┌─────────────────────────────────────────────────┐
│                                                   │
│                                                   │
│                                                   │
└─────────────────────────────────────────────────┘
```

☐ Outside the United States—*Print name of foreign country, Puerto Rico, Guam, etc.*

```
┌─────────────────────────────────────────────────┐
│                                                   │
│                                                   │
│                                                   │
└─────────────────────────────────────────────────┘
```

13 "Is this person a CITIZEN of the United States?"

☐ Yes, born in the United States

☐ Yes, born in Puerto Rico, Guam, the US Virgin Islands, or Northern Marianas

☐ Yes, born abroad of American parents or parent

☐ Yes, a U.S. citizen by naturalization

☐ No, not a citizen of the United States

14 "When did this person come to live in the United States?"

Year

```
┌───────────────────┐
│                   │
│                   │
└───────────────────┘
```

Source: Excerpt from: United States Census. Copyright in the Public Domain.

The 2000 U.S. Census of Population (U.S. Department of Commerce, 2000) contained three items that could be used to determine immigration status. On the long form, questions 12, 13, and 14 inquired about immigration.

Question 14 is specific to the foreign-born, so when doing research that utilizes the item, it is often necessary to delete the native-born.

The U.S. Constitution makes provision for a decennial census of the population. Given the long duration between one census and another, however, it may be necessary to have information on newly arrived immigrants or even immigrant stock. Periodic sample surveys are taken to provide a snapshot of the population in the intercensal period, and questions from such surveys may be used to estimate immigration, depending upon the interest of the analyst. If one is interested in social and economic characteristics, for example, the American Community Survey is a relatively good source of data. Indeed, the ACS has taken over the role that used to be performed by the long form in previous censuses. The drawback of the survey (including the American Community Survey) is that

FIGURE 2.4B

B.

NATVTY   In what country (were/was) ....born? (Enter code)_____

MNTVTY   In what country was ....'s mother born? _____

FNTVTY   In what country was ....'s father born? _____

AUTOMATED SKIP PATTERN:

If NATVTY = US (1) → END sequence for this person

If NATVTY = PR (2) → or OA (3) → go to INUSYR

If MNTVTY and FNTVTY = US (1), PR (2) or OA (3) → go to INUSYR

ALL OTHERS → go to CITIZN

Source: Excerpt from: United States Census. Copyright in the Public Domain.

it does not claim to have a complete count of the population. A census may offer a complete count of the population, though subject to errors, but surveys, by their very nature, obtain samples, and numbers derived from them are estimates of population parameters. Thus, a survey, except if it is large enough, may produce weak statistical power about investigating immigration topics.

Using the Current Population Survey (U.S. Census Bureau, 1999), it is also possible to study immigrants, for example by their characteristics by looking up variables, such as CITIZN (citizen of the United States), CITTYPA (born a citizen of the United States), CITTYPB (citizen through naturalization), and INSYR (duration of U.S. residence via entering when the individual came to live in the United States). More questions are then asked about each household member, which could be used to establish generational status. There are skip patterns when not applicable to a given individual:

The next few questions ask about each household member's country of birth.

(Note: In the above, PR stands for Puerto Rico, and OA stands for outlying areas.)

For studying the health profile of immigrants, the **National Health Interview Survey** is a great place to begin as it has questions on nativity status, citizenship status, and even duration of U.S. residence. One could use it to study, for example, whether the foreign-born have a higher risk of diagnosis for certain health conditions relative to the foreign-born. In the last two decades, the National Health Interview Survey has been linked to the National Death Index (NDI) to ascertain the mortality of survey respondents. It is, therefore, possible to conduct studies seeking, for example, an assessment on whether diabetes mortality is higher or lower among the foreign-born relative to the native-born. One may also focus exclusively on the foreign-born and try to study whether the mortality from diabetes is related to duration of residence in the United States.

Other data sources for demographers and others studying immigration are administrative records produced by government agencies charged with controlling a nation's immigration laws. These include, for example, landing cards or declaration forms, typically completed by passengers before an aircraft lands at a port of entry, the number of visas issued by a country within some defined period, and passport applications made within a given period (for counting departing travelers), though nations often ask applicants to indicate countries they plan to visit. In circumstances in which there is some reliability, nations listed may give an indication of travel, though it is possible for an applicant to designate a country as an intended place of visit but never really enter the country, or in some cases he or she may change the year of the planned travel. Many countries now have systems of recording the number of foreign-born individuals in their country. Such systems include using visa applications and counting those applying for permanent residence and those applying for citizenship, but the reliability of such systems depends on how comprehensive they are in making distinctions between those entering solely for temporary purposes or for permanent settlement. The number of unauthorized individuals within a country may be especially difficult to capture with certitude as their presence is known only if apprehended by the immigration authority in the country.

The United States has tended to rely on apprehension rates as indicators of unauthorized immigration, though increases in apprehension may often be due to more aggressive policing than increases in the actual number of disallowed entrants. Censuses and surveys may be used to derive estimates of unauthorized people in a country, but care must be taken to avoid using a census or survey for such purpose, as questions on citizenship, when asked, tend to have low response rates. All individuals in a territory must also be assured that regardless of their responses in a government survey or census, their identity is never in any way compromised through inadvertent disclosure.

REFERENCES

Acosta, Y. D., de la Cruz, P. (2011). *The foreign-born population from Latin America and the Caribbean: 2010 American Community Survey briefs*. Washington, DC: United States Census Bureau, Department of Commerce, Economics and Statistics Administration.

Bogue, D. J. (1969). *Principles of demography*. New York, NY: Wiley and Sons.

Congressional Research Service (2014). *U.S. immigration policy: Chart book of key trends* (Report R42988). Washington, DC: Government Printing Office.

Ghana Statistical Service (2014). *2010 population and housing census*. Accra: Government Printing Press.

Grieco, E. M., Acosta, Y. D., de la Cruz, G. P., Gambino, C., Gryn, T., Larsen, L. J., Trevelyan, E. N., & Walters, N. P. (2011). *The foreign-born population in the United States 2010*. American Community Survey Reports, ACS-19. Washington, DC: U.S. Census Bureau, Department of Commerce.

Newell, C. (1988). *Methods and models in demography*. New York, NY: Guilford Press.

Poston, D. L. (2010). *Population and society: An introduction to demography*. New York, NY: Cambridge University Press.

Yaukey, D., Anderson, D. L., & Lundquist, J. H. (2007). *Demography: The study of human population.* Long Grove, IL: Waveland Press.

United Nations (1970). *Methods of measuring internal migration population studies 47.* New York, NY: United Nations Department of Economic and Social Affairs.

United Nations (1998). *Recommendations on statistics of international migration* (Rev. 1). New York, NY: United Nations, Department of Economic and Social Affairs.

U.S. Department of Commerce (2000). *United States census 2000.* Washington, DC: Bureau of the Census.

U.S. Census Bureau (1999). *Profile of the foreign-born population of the United States.* Current Population Reports, Special Studies, pp. 23–195. Washington, DC: Government Printing Office.

U.S. Citizenship and Immigration Services (2006). *INA: Act 212—General classes of aliens ineligible to receive visas and ineligible for admission; Waivers of inadmissibility.* Available at https://www.uscis.gov/ilink/docView/SLB/HTML/SLB/0-0-0-1/0-0-0-29/0-0-0-2006.html. Accessed August 13, 2017.

U.S. Department of Homeland Security (2015a). *1891: Immigration inspection expands.* Available at http://www.cbp.gov/about/history/1891-imigration-inspection-expands. Accessed April 6, 2015.

U.S. Department of Homeland Security (2015b). *Deferred inspection.* Available at www.cbp.gov/contact/deffered-inspection/overview-deferred/inspection. Accessed March 30, 2015.

U.S. Department of Homeland Security (2015c). *Immigration inspection program.* Available at http://www.cbp.gov/border-security/ports-entry/overview. Accessed March 30, 2015.

U.S. Department of Homeland Security (2015d). *Preclearance locations.* Available at http://www.cbp.gov/border-security/ports-entry/operations/preclearance. Accessed May 12, 2015.

U.S. Department of Homeland Security [Immigration and Naturalization Service] (1999). *Statistical yearbook of the Immigration and Naturalization Service, 1997.* Washington, DC: Government Printing Office.

U.S. Department of State (2015). *U.S. visas.* Available at http://travel.state.gov/content/visas/english/general/frequently-asked-questions/what-is-a-u-s-visa.html. Accessed April 21, 2015.

3 | Theories of Migration

The question of why people move from one place to another, from one city to another, from one village to a city, or from one country to another remains an enduring subject for explanation. Migration is a universal phenomenon that has existed from time immemorial. The volume of movement in the past 50 years, however, is without precedent in recent human memory, and it defies explanation. This chapter attempts to provide theories or explanations of migration, focusing on the process, and providing examples where possible.

One of the earliest criticisms raised against demographers in general, and migration scholars in particular, was the paucity of theories in explaining population movement. The tendency for demographers to see numbers (statistics) first along with the ready availability of administrative and census data may have created this perception in the field. One may characterize the situation as "data sets in search of research problems" or "data in search of explanations." Petersen (1958, p. 264) alluded to this problem in migration research when he wrote that "Classifications of modern migrations tend to derive from the statistics that are collected, whether or not these have any relevance to theoretical questions." A similar critique was made by Ohio State University sociologist and demographer Wen Lang Li (1983, p. 3) when he observed that resistance to generalizations was common in demography and migration research, and that investigations tend to be bound by factual data, with a temptation to distrust abstraction. Yet, few disciplines can make advances by merely relying on compiled empirical facts (statistics). Facts can be overwhelming, and without theories aimed at explaining some phenomenon, the analyst is at a loss as to what may be hidden in the data. This is especially true in the modern world with the increases in data archives and the proliferation of statistical data on both individual nations and on the globalized world. The availability of "big data" and the processing speed of modern computers often mean some lag between data and theories to help make meaning of the empirical facts before a researcher.

Indeed, a preeminent migration scholar, Ernest George Ravenstein (1885, p. 167; 1889), proposed his generalizations about migration partly in response to a remark by a critique (William Farr) that claimed migration appeared to occur without any definite theories or explanations. In an effort to amend the lack of systematic theories of migration, Ravenstein, a Fellow of the Royal Geographic Society, presented a paper on migration to the Royal Statistical Society on March 17, 1885. In his presentation, and the paper that was subsequently published in the June issue of the *Journal of the Statistical Society*, Ravenstein (1885) came up with a general set of explanations as to why people move, along with patterns of movement using data from the British census of 1881, supplemented by that of 1871. He noted that he was limiting his analyses to the United Kingdom but would consider other countries in subsequent work. His theories have formed a basis for much migration research over time, though some have often criticized him for referring to them as laws. There are those who believe that a proposition or statement is law if—and only if—it fits all facts and all the time. If exceptions can be found, then the statement is not a law. This criticism is overexaggerated by the author's critics, as Ravenstein himself admitted in the papers and in the discussions that immediately followed his presentation that his use of "laws" in explaining migration should not be construed as the way laws are employed in the physical sciences. In his second appearance before the Royal Statistical Society on April 16, 1889, he remarked in his opening statements: "Of course I am perfectly aware that our laws of population, and economic laws generally, have not the rigidity of physical laws, as they are continually being interfered with by human agency." Perhaps scholars who are uncomfortable with his use of "laws" could simply select other labels, and move on with migration research. In the pages that follow, the terms "theories" and "generalizations" are used interchangeably to describe Ravenstein's explanations of migration.

Ravenstein's Theories of Migration

Distance and Migration
The first theory proposed by Ravenstein (1885) is that there is a relationship between distance and migration. He posed the association in two ways. First, he argued that the bulk of migrants move for only a short distance, or as he put it (1885, p. 198): "The great body of our migrants only proceed a short distance." Inherent in the above is the second way that he conceived of distance and migration; that is, there is a negative association between distance and migration such that the longer the distance between two places—the origin (or place of dispersion) and the destination (or place of absorption)—the fewer the number of migrants moving between those two places. Speaking about Canadian internal migration to illustrate this association, Ravenstein (1889) added that the underlying principle in the migration process is that a substantial proportion of migrants prefers a short journey to a long one. He pointed out that in the migration process, "more enterprising long journey migrants are the exception" (1889, p. 279). Earlier, in 1885, he stated, "Migrants enumerated in a certain centre of absorption will ... grow less as distance from the centre increases" (1885, p. 198–199).

Numerous studies have been done on the distance-migration relationship, and most have found support for the position that distance retards population movement (Zipf, 1946; Ritchey, 1976; Rogers, 1967; Li, 1983; Kposowa, 1986). Using place of birth and place of enumeration matrix, Kposowa (1986, p. 68) reported that of the total 156 flows, distance was consistently associated with migration across districts in Sierra Leone. Simply put, the longer the distance between one origin and destination, the lower the migration flow (stream) between the two areas. Similarly, Li (1983) observed that the longer the distance between one Korean town and another, the fewer the migrants moving between them.

While most findings on internal migration support Ravenstein's contention that migration is reduced by distance, legitimate questions could be asked as to whether this association exists in international migration. Questions could be raised about the role of distance with regard to international migration. The answer as to whether Ravenstein's ideas are applicable to international migration should be obvious. Consider, for example, the United States. Despite huge numbers of migrants who come to the country every year, clearly streams from countries that are nearby appear to be stronger than streams from countries farther away. The introduction of the jet engine, whether in forms as the Boeing 747 or Airbus A380, may have shortened travel times compared with the period when travel was by dangerous sailboats or steam ships such as the RMS Titanic. Even here, however, the negative relationship persists. Countries closer to the United States tend to send in more migrants than those in more remote parts of the world. Mexican immigrants dominate entry streams, both of the authorized and unauthorized types. It is plausible that streams sent would have been much smaller had Mexico not been a contiguous country sharing land borders with the United States (Kposowa 1998). Similarly, there is a sizable back-and-forth movement of people between Canada and the United States. In talking about the relationship between distance and international migration, one should not be tempted to focus on effect sizes (the volume of migration); rather, the emphasis, and the one proposed by Ravenstein, is the direction of the relationship. Advances in modes of transportation have greatly reduced the great obstacle that distance once presented, but the fact remains that the longer the distance between countries, the fewer the number of travelers going between those nations.

Step or Stage Migration

This theory suggests that migration occurs in steps or stages. Migrants from rural areas or villages do not immediately move from where they are to live in large urban centers or big cities. Rather, they first move to small towns where they settle for a while before moving on to the bigger cities and eventually to major urban centers. As these initial migrants move, vacancies or gaps are left at their origin, so people from even farther away or from more remote areas rush in to fill the gaps. The migration process goes on in this manner until the entire country experiences the effect of the pull factor associated with the large urban areas of the nation. While migrants looking for work may move from parish to parish, they settle in each place for a while before moving on. Ravenstein (1885, p. 199) adds that "The inhabitants of the country immediately surrounding a town of rapid growth flock into it; the gaps thus left in the rural population are filled up by migrants from more remote districts, until the attractive force of one of our rapidly growing cities makes its influence felt, step by step, to the most remote corner of the kingdom."

While on face value the theory just cited is plausible, it has been difficult to test using empirical data. How, for instance, might a researcher determine whether the number of migrants currently living in Los Angeles from Riverside had previously lived in Needles or Victorville prior to moving to Los Angeles? How long is the lag period—that is, what length of time constitutes settling at a place in order for that locality to fit the definition of a step or stage?

If stage migration theory were correct, perhaps it might find its strongest verification in developing societies, and especially those suffering from chronic primacy problems. One could construct a place of birth and place of enumeration matrix using a population census to determine the number of migrants in cities who were either born in, or previously lived in, rural areas or smaller towns. One then calculates rates of in-migration and out-migration. Even if one were to find differential rates of in-migration into urban areas and out-migration from rural areas, it may not be accurate to infer that migrants first moved to smaller towns or cities before proceeding to larger cities. The migrants could have come directly to their present metropolitan location from a small town or rural area without going through stages. This may especially be true in the rural-urban migration process in many developing countries with primacy problems wherein one large city, typically the capital, has come to dominate the entire nation (Kposowa, 1986).

Stage migration theory is also much less applicable in the area of international migration for practical reasons. First, consider the expense involved in the modern age of travel. A migrant desiring to leave a small town in Bangladesh and settle in Chicago, Illinois, would have to be relatively wealthy to interrupt the flight from Dhaka to O'Hare Airport by settling first for a year in Leeds, England, assuming there is no direct flight from Dhaka to Chicago. There may also be visa or other travel restrictions in places along the way. For instance, some countries (such as the United Kingdom) require travelers passing through from specified nations to purchase and obtain transit visas before departing their home countries. The cost of these visas is not cheap and often appears as a blatant act of discrimination against travelers from the nations affected, almost all in the developing world. Why pay to land at an airport if you have no intention of staying in the country and are literally just passing through because there is no direct flight from your origin to your eventual destination? Unless one has relatives in transit or is wealthy enough to pay for the increasingly high cost of hotels and transport, migrating in steps at the international level is simply not a common option for most travelers. Using Korean census data, Li (1983, p. 121) found no support for stage/step migration theory. He admonished, however, that Ravenstein's theory explains "migration behavior in the intra-generational context. In a person's lifetime ... there is a possibility that the mobility process involves a step-by-step movement from the very rural to the most urban." In other words, in the course of life, a person could have been born in a rural area, and when that person reached school age, maybe the family sent him or her to live with a close relative in a small town; he or she completed high school and attended college in a city, and upon graduation got a job in a bigger city or large metro area where the individual ended up settling. This type of explanation is interesting and most likely plausible in many cases, especially in developing societies, but it is difficult to transform it into the theory that Ravenstein presented to the Royal Statistical Society in 1885 and 1889.

Streams and Counter Streams in Migration

This theory holds that each stream (current) of migration is accompanied by a compensating counter stream (current). It implies that migration flows are rarely one-way phenomena. For instance, just as there might be a flow of movers going from New York City (the origin or dispersion) to Los Angeles (the destination or absorption), there is also a flow or stream moving from Los Angeles to New York. The theory does not imply equality of flows, so it is entirely possible that of the two cities, one may pull more migrants from the other over time than the other performs in the same period. Ravenstein states that streams need not be even, adding:

> I also believe that I have proved that each main current produces a counter current of feebler strength. As I have dealt at length with this branch of my inquiry in my former paper, I need say no more about it on the present occasion (1889, p. 287).

This theory appears to have received consistent support among migration scholars and is applicable in both developed and less developed societies. In studies of interstate migration in the United States, it has been reported that each state serves both as a place that disperses migrants and also absorbs migrants (Ritchey, 1976). Some states appear to have higher pulling power than others. For example, California has in the past 20 years been a significant receiving place of immigrants and ranks as the state with the highest immigrant population, followed by New York. Data from the 2010 American Community Survey (Grieco et al., 2011) show that in 2010, 27% of California's population was foreign-born, followed by New York, which had 22%, and then New Jersey, whose foreign-born population was 21%. The U.S. average in 2010 was 13% of the population being of foreign origin (U.S. Bureau of the Census, 2013). Despite the differentials, cross-tabulation of census or ACS data reveals that if one were to select any given city, it will have a variegated distribution of the source of both immigrants and domestic movers. No matter how unattractive a state in terms of weather, economic development, and social issues, it will serve both as a place that receives migrants and also one that disperses them to other places.

Rural-Urban Differences in Migration

This theory holds that residents of towns and cities are less migratory than those of rural areas. Implied in this is that migration is largely from rural to urban areas in most societies. Thus, urbanization has increased, basically since the Industrial Revolution, as a result of rural to urban population movement. Ravenstein argued that big cities (urban areas) grow at the expense of small towns. He points out that "The question of whether our large towns grow at the expense of the rural parts of the country, even to the extent of producing a 'depopulation' of the rural parts, has recently been dealt with before this Society in an able manner. My inquiries justify me in asserting that in all settled countries the towns do increase in this way. If left to their own resources, if dependent upon natural increment only, they would increase very slowly, and in some instances they would even retrograde. Nothing can prove this more clearly than the proportion which the native town element bears to the total population of our large towns" (1889, p. 287). He recognized that while within nations migration is largely from rural to urban centers, cities fill up not solely due to local residents moving to cities. Hence, he cited data from the United States that led him to conclude: "In the United States, however, and I suppose in other newly settled countries having large agricultural resources, this tendency of the rural population towards the towns is hardly perceptible. The towns there increase largely in consequence of foreign immigration." (1889, p. 288).

Ravenstein may not have been familiar with the Great Migration of African Americans from the rural South to the urban North from the late 1880s to the early 1960s (Pinkney, 2000), which well fit into his theory. He certainly also was not to experience the White flight from urban areas to vanilla suburbs following the great African American migration. Historically, this theory appears to have received empirical support not only in Ravenstein's testing using data from several countries in the 1889 paper, but rural to urban migration has resulted in creating a world system with substantially large portions of populations in many countries situated in the urban environment. Rural to urban migration tends to be especially heightened in countries with primacy problems, where one city, usually the capital, dominates all other towns or cities within the country. Li (1983, p. 117) found that the overall out-migration rate (per thousand) from urban areas to Seoul was higher (62 per thousand) than that from rural areas to Seoul (42 per thousand); however, the out-migration rate from rural areas to other cities was higher (41.2 per thousand) than the rate from other cities to others (apart from Seoul), which was 32 per thousand. The overall picture was consistent with Ravenstein's thesis that cities had gained population at the expense of rural areas. Similarly, Kposowa (1986) used census data to conclude that most of the population movement in Sierra Leone was from rural to urban areas, with Freetown, the capital city, gaining more people than any other city in the country.

In his 1889 paper, Ravenstein concludes: "But although long-journey migrants move by preference into our large cities, still the larger share of the increment is due to an inflow of the surrounding rural population, and this accounts for the fact that even the largest cities of Europe partake of provincial characteristics. The local streams which carry the rural populations" (1889, p. 287).

Sex Differences in Migration

This theory proposes that females are more migratory than males. Ravenstein puts it in a matter-of-fact manner in his 1885 paper, "Woman is a greater migrant than man" (p. 196). It suggests, however, that this greater propensity of female migration may be more pronounced in internal migration than international movements, for in 1889, Ravenstein observed that "Females appear to predominate among short-journey migrants. I have drawn attention to exceptions to this rule, but numerically they are insignificant. On the other hand long-journey migrants appear to predominate among females born in large towns, including London; all the great Scotch towns, Paris, Vienna, and many others. Some of these ladies are no doubt carried abroad by counter currents with a view to their adorning rural homes, but many, I am sure, are sought for their accomplishments in certain branches of industry" (1889, p. 288).

Ravenstein presented data from the 1881 census that appeared to support his claim, and analyses of the data are shown in Table 3.1. An examination of the table shows that when consideration is limited to those residing in the county where they were born, there is hardly much difference between men and women. But among those residing beyond county of birth, but not beyond limits of the United Kingdom (internal migrants or short distance movers), women far outnumber men.

TABLE 3.1: Sex Differences in Migration, United Kingdom, 1885

	Number of Females to Every 100 Males among Natives of			
	England and Wales	Scotland	Ireland	United Kingdom
Residing in county where born	104	108	104	105
Residing beyond county where born, but not beyond limits of United Kingdom	112	114	116	112
Residing in other parts of the United Kingdom	81	91	92	90

Source: E.G. Ravenstein, "Sex Differences in Migration, United Kingdom, 1885," *The Laws of Migration Journal of the Statistical Society*, vol. 48, no. 2, pp. 197. Copyright in the Public Domain.

The last row shows data on those residing in other parts of the United Kingdom, an expression that Ravenstein used for long-distance movers. There it is seen that men outnumber women in population mobility.

In an apparent attempt to generalize the UK finding to other countries, Ravenstein stated in the 1889 presentation that "Females predominate among those migrants who go only short distances, and even in entire provinces, as in Schleswig-Holstein and Oldenburg, whence they are drawn to the neighbour- ing Hanse towns, in which the demand for domestic servants is considerable. Among long-journey migrants they form a decided minority, for out of 1,000 women enumerated, only 88 were found outside their native province, whilst the proportion among men similarly situated was 106" (p. 249).

The theory appeared to challenge popular assumptions at the time that men moved in larger numbers than women. It is very likely the theory applies differ- ently in different countries, and may be affected by both the population structure of a country and also individual socioeconomic status. Findings on sex differences in migration have been mixed. Earlier U.S. studies showed that males were more migratory than females (Thomas, 1958; Shryock, 1964), but the sex disparities disappear in short-distance moves. Caldwell (1969) reported that in rural-urban migration in Africa, males predominated long-distance moves, while females moved shorter distances than males. His findings supported Ravenstein's theory, but his explanation of the disparity was different, in that he placed sex differences in migration on traditional practices and expectation with regard to gender roles. The Caldwell (1969) finding supports the view that in more traditional societies, families tend to exert greater control over female decision making than on male decision making. Families may control how far they wish their daughters to move, and typically short-distance moves are preferred, but they may give more freedom to their male children, and thus for males, longer moves result. As societies undergo modernization and rapid social change, however, there may not be much difference in migration propensity of males and females or in distance covered. As more women participate in the labor force, availability of jobs becomes a determining factor in migration decision making. Accordingly, distinctions about short and long distance migration as proposed by Ravenstein (1885, 1889) become less and less relevant.

Technology and Migration

This theory argues that there is an association between the level of technological development within a country and its rate and volume of migration. Accordingly, countries ranked high on various development indicators—including infrastructure, gross domestic product (GDP), industrial output, and trade—will have higher migration rates than nations ranked low on these indicators. One of the primary reasons provided by Ravenstein for this observation was the development of transportation, especially advances in railway travel in the UK at the time. Rail travel meant that manufactured goods moved faster, and cities could trade goods they produced in exchange for goods they did not produce. Cities could specialize in products unique to them, and quickly move them to other regions that lacked such products. Going hand in hand with improvements in manufacture of machines also meant that people had to move to service the machines or work in the factories being built following the Industrial Revolution. Travel time between cities and parishes was severely reduced, so a journey that could have taken four days would take only a day or two at most. Accordingly, migration increased. Technological advances may also bring with them greater economic opportunities within a nation, and people may then move from one region of the country to another to take advantage of employment opportunities, educational opportunities, or any other opportunity that enhances life. It is in response to opportunities that migration increases. Ravenstein observed that "Wherever I was able to make a comparison I found that an increase in the means of locomotion and a development of manufactures and commerce have led to an increase of migration. In fact, you need only seek out those provinces of a country within which migration is proceeding most actively, and you will either find yourself in the great centres of human industry, or in a part of the country whose resources have only recently become available. Migration means life and progress; a sedentary population stagnation" (1889, p. 288).

This is a plausible theory that explains not only internal, but also international migration. The vast increases in global population mobility in the last five decades are most likely due, in part, to advances in technology, especially air, automobile, and rail travel. The Colonial period in what was to become the United States of America was a rather long period, but not many people came. The rigors of the sea voyage, duration of travel, and overall uncertainty about troubled waters and oceans probably kept away many who would have come had transportation systems been more reliable. With improvements in shipbuilding, rates of migration to the United States dramatically increased in the period known as the "Great Migration." Rates were to further increase in the jet age, especially with wide-bodied aircraft. Likewise, even within the United States following the Treaty of Paris, internal migration increased at a faster rate with completion of the transcontinental railway system that linked California to points east. Internal migration, especially of the interstate type, would increase again following the completion of the interstate highway system.

Material Benefits and Migration

Ravenstein recognized that migration is a complex process, and that no single reason explains why people move. Nevertheless, he argued that if you were to put side by side various known reasons for migration, movement for material gain would outnumber movements for other reasons. He pointed out that "Bad or oppressive laws, heavy taxation, an unattractive climate, uncongenial social surroundings, and even compulsion (slave trade, transportation), all have produced and are still producing currents of migration, but none of these currents can compare in volume with that which arises from the desire inherent in most men to 'better' themselves in material respects." (1889, p. 286).

The theory does not specifically state that the most important reason why people move is for economic reasons; "bettering" oneself in material respects does not automatically imply economic gain—for example, jobs, employment, money. Nevertheless, it is difficult to imagine people moving freely from one country to another to experience pain or punishment, or even doing so within a single country. Given the almost universal human desire to avoid pain and punishment, and experience happiness and satisfaction, bettering oneself in material respects could comprise any movement to enhance a person's physical quality of life, and this could entail economic, social, and even health aspects.

Time and Volume of Migration

This theory states that there is a relationship between passage of time and volume and the rate of migration. This association is most likely caused by the fact that, over time, there is greater information about potential destinations; barriers to population movement may be reduced, even by the most restrictive of countries; and in those nations with family reunification programs these become more effective because earlier movers may try to bring in family members who may not be subject to annual ceilings. Migration also increases over time for reasons having to do with diversity of areas and diversity of populations in nations around the world (Lee, 1966, pp. 52–53). Ravenstein considered increases in migration over time as a natural process, stating: "Does migration increase? I believe so! The exception in England, where the county element rose from

74.04 per cent in 1871 to 75.19 per cent in 1881, is an exception accounted for by the interference of Irish immigrants with the normal process of migration" (1889, p. 288). Echoing Ravenstein, Lee (1966, p. 53) indicated that "The volume of migration tends to increase with time for a number of reasons, among them increasing diversity of areas, increasing diversity of people, and the diminution of intervening obstacles." Indeed, it could be argued that international migration has increased over several decades due to diversity of the global population as a whole, and due to economic diversity and trade across countries. Area diversity implies the probable existence of more economic opportunities to which potential movers might be attracted, regardless of region of the world (Lee, 1966, p. 52). As many nations have moved from being mono-racial to multiracial, it is plausible that in some places racism has declined, thereby making it possible for marginalized and previously stigmatized groups to move. Diversity of people might also create racial hierarchies in some societies (even in the multiracial ones), and groups that are discriminated against might move from one part of a country (with high levels of discrimination) to those parts of the country with lower levels of discrimination. As Lee (1966, p. 53) notes, "A diversity of people inevitably implies that the social statuses of some groups will become more elevated above those of others. Discrimination among racial or ethnic groups is the rule rather than the exception, and the degree of discrimination varies from place to place, often in as extreme a manner as in the United States." Discrimination might lead to vast movements of people from areas with high discrimination and racial prejudice to those with perceived low levels of prejudice and discrimination. This is a rather ominous warning about the future of the United States. Although many people proudly talk about diversity and embracing diversity, in an age of what is termed "political correctness" or "identity politics," few debate the pros and cons of diversity. Could diversity, for example, lead to the creation of a new racial/ethnic hierarchy? A group once in the minority finds itself in the majority, with increasing power at the political, economic, and social levels. As demographics change, will the group that emerges dominant and with more power treat others equally? Will the various minority groups—Asians, Latinos, African Americans, Asian Indians, and Middle Easterners—get along in a harmonious way, or will they start fighting among one another? Are there potentials for "ethnic favoritism" in employment? If the different racial/ethnic groups failed to get along, then one could well wonder whether diversity had become a blessing for the nation or something more sinister. Diversity as a concept need not be treated as some absolute good; whether it is a blessing or something else depends on how groups and individuals embrace it. We now move on from Ravenstein to other theories of migration, some older and others newer.

Cultural Dissimilarity Theory

This theory proposes that there is a relationship between cultural dissimilarity in a country and migration flows. Kposowa (1986, p. 11) argued that in nations that are homogeneous with regard to cultural components such as language, ethnicity or race, religion, and traditions, the volume of interregional migration is higher. At the other extreme, in nations that are regionally heterogeneous in terms of ethnicity or race, language, traditions, and religion, the volume of internal migration is lower. The theory implies that migration flows are heavier from origins with the same cultural practices to destinations with similar cultures. Streams between areas with similar cultures are heavier than streams between areas with different cultures.

To test the cultural dissimilarity theory, Kposowa (1986, p. 39; 1987) mapped the 13 administrative districts of Sierra Leone and created a 13×12 migration matrix that resulted into 156 migration flows, with each district treated as both an origin and a destination based on the nation's 1974 population census. There are 18 distinct ethnic groups in Sierra Leone, each of which speaks a different language and generally has distinct cultural practices. A district was treated as being culturally similar to another district if both had the same ethnic group (in terms of language). On the other hand, any two districts were considered culturally dissimilar if they did not have the same ethnic group. As Kposowa explains, "... if most of the inhabitants of a particular district are Mende, that district is considered a predominantly Mende district. A score of zero is recorded in the data if a particular district of destination has the same predominant ethnic group as the district of origin. A score of 1 is recorded if the predominant ethnic groups in origin and destination are different." Regression analysis showed support for the cultural dissimilarity theory ($\beta = -.197$, t = -2.629). The implication was that the more different or dissimilar the origin and destination in terms of culture (indexed by language), the lower the flow of migrants between the two places. Part of the explanation for the association between culture and migration was distance, with Kposowa (1986, 1987) arguing that one reason why differences in culture would reduce migration is that the farther two places are apart in distance, the more dissimilar they would also be with regard to culture.

While the cultural dissimilarity argument may apply in a country marked by different languages, and with each language unique to each administrative unit, it remains to be seen whether it also applies to international migration. It is plausible that nations with similar languages will have higher rates of migration between them. Indeed, one of the potential obstacles to moving into a new country may well be the psychic costs of assimilation, which would include the speed of learning the language spoken in the new society, a factor that may affect employment chances. Migration from south to north was largely from colonies with former colonial ties, and such movement was to a nation with which a colony had the closest ties. Thus, France would be expected to have a greater number of migrants from former French-speaking countries in West Africa and North Africa than from English-speaking nations in West or East Africa.

Human Capital Theory

This theory focuses on individual accumulation of skills that are needed in the labor market. Hence, it is also described in migration research as neoclassical microeconomic theory. Human capital refers to a bundle of skills and abilities that individuals acquire over the life course, especially when they are young. The theory was first given prominence in the work of Schultz (1961), Sjaastad (1962), and Becker (1975). At young ages, individuals invest in themselves through formal schooling, doing internships, undergoing further training while on the job, and acquiring skills. The issue then arises as to where the person will get the best returns on investments made. According to the theory, individuals are rational actors, so they will tend to move to those locations, either domestic or international, where returns to characteristics are highest. If the prospective migrant has accumulated a high level of education and skills that are transferable to a foreign nation, and the person concludes that he or she would most likely be paid more for his or her education and skill abroad than the home country, then the migrant would more likely move to a nation where salaries or wages and benefits would be higher compared with where he or she now lives. In addition, having acquired skills, individuals move to where they can be most productive, whether internally or externally (Massey et al., 1993, p. 434).

Wage-Labor Differentials and Migration

According to the theory, migration occurs in adjustment to the supply and demand for labor. The theory states that international migration is caused by both geographic disparities in the supply of labor and also by geographic differences in the demand for labor (Massey et al., 1993). Countries in the world can be roughly divided into high wage and low wage countries, and high labor demand and low labor nations. Typically, countries undergoing economic expansion tend to have higher wage rates compared with those that are either stagnating economically or have contracting economies. Those with growing economies also have a labor surplus compared with those that are not growing, and typically situated in developing societies. Migration then tends to move from countries with low wages and a large pool of labor to those nations with high wages and scarce supply of labor (Todaro, 1969; Arango, 2000).

This theory is one of the oldest used for explaining both internal and international migration, and it has garnered some support. Free migration has typically been from less to more developed countries in the post-World War II period. Even within countries, areas with higher wage rates tend to attract more migrants than areas with lower wage rates. The large-scale migration that occurred in the United States by African Americans was, in part, a flight from racial discrimination in the South. At the same time, this movement took advantage of better paying industrial jobs in northern cities. States that have low wages, West Virginia, for instance, tend to attract fewer migrants and immigrants than those with higher wage rates. Finally, large-scale migration from Europe to the United States decelerated following economic recovery and expansion at the end of World War II. Immigration decelerated largely because wage levels in Europe and America had reached some level of equilibrium. Why, for example, would a middle-income worker with a stable job in Cologne, Germany, that probably also came with annual vacations and reliable health care wish to emigrate to the United States? Furthermore, the euro may have higher purchasing power than the U.S. dollar! Even in a period of south to south migration, movement is from countries with an overabundance of labor and low wages to those with higher wages, such as the recent movement of Black Africans from places such as Malawi, Zimbabwe, and Lesotho to South Africa.

New Household Economics Theory

The new economics theory of migration, often attributed to the works of Stark (1984), and Stark and Bloom (1985), suggests that decisions to migrate internationally are often not made by individual actors alone but by the family, within the context of what is in the best interest of the entire household or family. In a third world context, family is not limited to the nuclear one of husband, wife, and children. Rather, the extended family is considered in the theory. Family or household members act in a collective fashion not only to maximize the expected income or benefits of immigration, but to weigh and minimize the risks involved (Massey et al., 1993). Migration is a form of income or economic diversification for household members, and not just a means to dispatch people to foreign lands. Family members may even pull their financial resources to finance the migration expenses of the individual selected to move abroad. In return, the person who moves is expected to send remittances that could be used by family members at origin. The remittance can serve as crop insurance (in the event of crop failure), unemployment insurance (in the event a household member loses a job), futures markets insurance (in the event that commodity prices fluctuate in such a way that cash crops produced at home do not bring profit for the family), and investment insurance (in the event the family wishes to expand business or get involved in new business activities). According to the new economics of migration, in developed societies there are usually systems in place to mitigate risks that would arise from unemployment, crop failures experienced by farmers, or borrowing privileges from banks if someone wants to start a new business or expand an existing one. These are often either absent in third world countries or operate to the disadvantage of the poor or those without collateral, so the immigrant is expected to send money home (remittances) to assist the family and prevent total collapse should the unexpected suddenly occur (Arrago, 2000; Massey et al., 1993).

Dual Labor Market Theory

Proponents of dual labor market theory (Doeringer & Piore, 1971; Piore, 1979) argue that immigration is caused by the structure of modern industrial economies, and the way that employers act to ensure a steady supply of labor at reduced cost and enhanced profits. Immigration results not so much because of push factors in countries of origin, but due to chronic need for foreign workers to occupy jobs that would otherwise require substantially high payment if domestic workers were employed to take them. The need for foreign labor is ongoing because the economy of modern industrial societies has become increasingly bifurcated into primary and secondary sectors (Piore, 1979).

The primary sector has jobs that are stable, pays employees' salaries, offers fringe benefits, and periodic vacations. Workers also perform their duties under some degree of freedom. There is also a process in which customary rules of work and practices have been formalized through collective bargaining that benefits those already hired, and employees cannot be laid off without just cause (Duncan, 1984; Chang, 1989).

The secondary labor market is characterized by job instability and factors opposite those that exist in the primary sector. Doeringer and Piore (1971, pp. 165–166) observe that jobs in the secondary sector "tend to have low wages and fringe benefits, poor working conditions, higher turnover, little chance of advancement, and often capricious supervision." Due to these conditions, there are no incentives for individual workers to remain with a particular firm or employer for long; there are frequent job changes (Kposowa, 1998, p. 13). In earlier times, employers were able to find workers from domestic sources, but due to higher cost of living, and the temptation for employers to drive wages even further while wanting to reap more profits, it has become increasingly difficult to tap the domestic work force. But given the fact that low wage jobs are still needed in the economy, employers seek out foreign labor, and this drives international migration, especially of the unauthorized type. In time, the jobs themselves might become labeled "immigrant jobs", a process that further pulls immigrants as a result of information diffusion and social networks.

It is important to note that dual labor market does not suggest that domestic workers do not want secondary labor market jobs or that they somehow look down upon them. After all, these jobs were once performed by domestic workers, especially visible minorities, teenagers, and women in earlier periods (Massey et al., 1993, p. 443). The argument is that wages are so low, and working conditions so poor, that a native-born worker may find it difficult to support a family in these jobs. Constant exploitation by firms, low wages, lack of social mobility, and other poor conditions have combined to make the sector unattractive for native-born workers. The easier and more profitable alternative for firms is foreign (immigrant) laborers.

Military Intervention and Migration

The military intervention perspective is that wars, whether intrastate or interstate, create conditions that generate migration from the immediately affected areas or countries to foreign nations; wars produce population movement, and some lead to land seizure from the defeated. Initially, the movements are in the form of population displacement, but over time the lingering effects of conflict create refugees and other forms of emigrants. The volume of war migration is influenced by both the intensity of conflict and also its duration. Bombs dropped on civilian populations in a single night may not be enough to create a dense pool of refugees, but a protracted war with repeated bombings, explosions, shootings, and land grabs will very likely cause immense havoc that uproots large numbers of people who may seek sanctuary in other nations. Although initial exit might be temporary, if the war is prolonged or if the invading power occupies conquered territory over an extended period, temporary movers become permanent ones wherever they have resided, or they may move on to nations willing to accept them, and over time migration streams are formed. The likelihood of permanent migration increases if the invading power takes over land previously held by the vanquished. The question then becomes, what happens to the defeated, those who have been dispossessed? They most likely emigrate to other nations or become permanent or stateless refugees suffering in refugee camps.

People in the affected territories who have relatives in countries with family reunification programs will very likely be encouraged to take advantage of such programs even though they may not have wished to move under conditions of peace. Ultimately, a longer duration of war generates higher volumes of migration, and creates more lasting flows than incidence or accidental incursions. An army of occupation will give rise to more out-migration than one that does not take territory. A civil war with high intensity in terms of death counts and one that lasts long will cause more out-migration than one with fewer death counts and of short duration.

Applicability of the military intervention explanation of migration abound. Many mass movements occurred both during and after World War II, creating perhaps the greatest humanitarian crisis of the 20th century. With the outbreak of war and early German victories prior to 1943, millions of Europeans were uprooted from their homelands as one nation after another fell victim to the Nazi war machine. Some movements—up to eight million—were to Germany itself, with substantial proportions made up of slave laborers from conquered territories and prisoners of war (Kulischer, 1949, p. 168). As the tide of war changed against Germany, mass movements took place away from the country or from one major city to another. Massive aerial bombardments of German cities, many with no strategic value, in 1944 by the British Royal Air Force and the U.S. Air Force led to six million movers away from affected cities, such as Dresden and Cologne, and by the end of the war, in 1945, there were 9.5 million German refugees (Kulischer, 1949, p. 168; Shirer, 1990). In the United States, Congress passed the *Displaced Persons Act* in 1948 as a direct result of the refugee crisis created in Europe by the war in an effort to allow admissions that would otherwise have been impossible due to the 1924 national origins quota system.

The partition of India at independence offers another example of how war leads to population movement. Conflict between India and Pakistan in 1947, following the partition of India at independence from Britain, led to the migration of millions of Muslims from India to the newly created nation of Pakistan, and there was likewise movement of Hindus and Sikhs going in the opposite direction. Similarly, war between the new state of Israel and Palestine created a population movement whose consequences persist to the present day. As observed by Forman and Kedar (2003, p. 810),

> The war that erupted in Palestine in 1948 (referred to by Israelis as the "War of Independence" and by Palestinians as "the Catastrophe") was the culmination of an ethno-national conflict between Arabs and Jews. The war resulted in the establishment of Israel,

the expulsion and flight of hundreds of thousands of Palestinian refugees, the immigration of hundreds of thousands of Jews to Israel, and the reallocation of land formerly held by Arabs to Jewish groups and individuals.

What happened to the Palestinians? It is estimated that before the war, about 850,000 Palestinians lived in territory seized by Israel. By the end of the war, only 160,000 remained, and from 1946 to 1951 the Israeli Jewish population doubled, going from 608,000 to 1.4 million (Kimmerling, 1983; Government of Palestine, 1991a, 1991b). Most of this increase was due to immigration into Israel. Thus, war leads not only to emigration from the source of conflict, but also migration to the conflict zone depending on the nature of the conflict, the victor, the vanquished, and policies adopted or implemented by the conquerors regarding the defeated.

World Systems and Migration

The world systems perspective traces migration to developments in the world economic, especially the trade and market system since colonialism (Wallerstein 1974). With the advent of colonial expansion, Europeans or other foreign powers entered less developed societies and created sources of raw materials, mainly in the form of primary products that were exploited and shipped back to the mother country. In the course of their entry into those societies, they introduced much instability, some of which affected the cultures of indigenous populations. For example, societies that had been based on communal ownership of property were influenced to adopt private ownership. Instead of cooperation, competition was encouraged, which in turn led to individualism and the drive for consumption and capitalist accumulation. A net effect of penetration of third world societies by foreign powers was to make people migration prone (Massey et al., 1993, p. 444).

In the process of entering foreign cultures, colonial countries created ideological, educational, and political linkages between colonies and the foreign power (Massey et al., 1993; Arango, 2000). Thus, even after independence the economies and state structures of the new states were inextricably tied to that of the former colonial power. For example, colonies that had been under British rule used English as their official language and their main trading partner was Great Britain. The educational system was also, at least initially, British. So were the political systems—the Westminster-style parliament in Whitehall, for example. Similarly, nations that had emerged from French rule employed French, had France as their major trading partner, even used currency created for them by France, and adopted government systems based on the National Assembly system in Paris. Thus, nations experienced immigration largely from those countries with which they had the most severe and long-lasting contacts during the colonial era. A person completing high school in Ghana and wishing to emigrate would most likely think first of Britain as the destination. Likewise, someone in Algeria, Morocco, or Senegal wishing to move abroad would most likely think first of France as a potential destination.

Alongside the division of the world global system into periphery, semi periphery, and core status, there has also emerged neoliberal economic policies whereby nations in the periphery depend largely on core states for their survival. Agricultural production in the periphery has been diverted from producing subsistence crops to cash crops, as these are the ones needed in the core for manufacturing purposes. One result is the increase in peripheral nations of food insecurity (Alderman et al., 2014, p. 1); countries that were once exporters of subsistence crops, such as rice, suddenly find themselves having to import rice to sustain their inhabitants because their focus had long changed from rice production to diamond digging or coffee production.

Neoliberal policies have further led to situations wherein economic outcomes of entire nations in the periphery are determined by policies set far away in global cities—e.g., New York, London, Paris, Milan, Frankfurt, Sydney, and Osaka (Castells, 1989; Sassen, 1991)—with a highly educated workforce that has to be serviced, and foreign workers are often needed for them because the domestic population is unwilling to perform the labor at prevailing low wages (Massey et al., 1993, p. 447). In addition, monetary policies that affect the periphery countries are dictated by financial institutions, such as the World Bank and the International Monetary Fund, which often demand major economic structural adjustments as stipulation for nations to obtain loans. Often described as the "Washington Consensus," neoliberal adjustments might include demands that countries allow key sectors (such as water, health, transportation, communications, and electricity) to be privatized (Harvey, 2007, p. 2). Currency devaluations may also be required, a process that causes instability within the country as it often comes with inflationary tendencies disliked by residents. Ironically, at times, countries that seem to do relatively well in terms of economic growth, at least on the surface or in gross national product, are those that are heavily indebted to international financiers, a phenomenon that has been characterized in the African context as dependent development (Bradshaw, 1985; Bradshaw & Tshandu, 1990).

Strongly linked to neoliberalism is that as more and more nations have been brought into the global monetary and capitalist system, inequality has intensified both within and across countries. Some multinational corporations have also relocated to developing countries in search of increasingly more profits at the expense of local populations in dire need for jobs at any wage. As global inequality has increased, and as foreign capital penetration has also increased, so has international migration.

Migration theory has traveled a far and diverse path from the original comment made by William Farr in the 19th century that migration appeared to have no common trajectory guided by theory. Ravenstein's response to this critique was the development of a preliminary set of migration theories, such as those that approach population mobility based on the relationship of time and density of flows. Later and more contemporary theories looked at cultural disparities, individual-level or state-level needs, military intervention, and consequences of national incorporation into the global capitalist (market) system. While the question of why people move from one location to another cannot be definitely answered by one theory, the theories presented provide a framework from which an immigration scholar can examine migration flows and add to the growing literature on international population movements.

REFERENCES

Arango, J. (2000). Explaining migration. *International Social Science Journal*, 52, 283–296.

Becker, G. S. (1975). *Human capital.* New York, NY: Columbia University Press.

Bradshaw, Y. W. (1985) Dependent development in black Africa: A cross-national study. *American Sociological Review, 50*(2), 195–207.

Bradshaw, Y. W., & Tshandu, Z. (1990). Foreign capital penetration, state intervention, and development in sub-Saharan Africa. *International Studies Quarterly, 34*(2), 229–251.

Caldwell, J. C. (1969). *African rural-urban migration: The movement to Ghana's towns.* Canberra, AU: Australia National University Press.

Castells, M. (1989). *The Informational city: Information technology, economic restructuring and the urban-regional process.* Oxford, UK: Basil Blackwell.

Chang, C. F. (1989). *Resource or vulnerabilities? The structural determinants of economic returns in American manufacturing, 1950–1980* (Doctoral dissertation). Department of Sociology, Ohio State University, Columbus.

Doeringer, P., & Piore, M. (1971). *International labor markets and manpower analysis.* Lexington, MA: Heath Lexington Books.

Duncan, G. J. (1984). *Years of poverty, years of plenty: The changing economic fortunes of American workers and their families.* Ann Arbor: Institute for Social Research, University of Michigan.

Forman, G., & Kedar, A. S. (2003). From Arab land to "Israel lands": The legal dispossession of the Palestinians displaced by Israel in the wake of 1948. *Environment and Planning D: Society and Space*, 22, 809–830.

Government of Palestine (1991a). *A survey of Palestine (Jerusalem).* Washington, DC: Institute of Palestine Studies; first published in 1946.

Government of Palestine (1991b). *Supplement to survey of Palestine (Jerusalem).* Washington, DC: Institute of Palestine Studies; first published in 1947.

Grieco, E. M., Acosta, Y. D., de la Cruz, G. P., Gambino, C., Gryn, T., Larsen, L. J., Trevelyan, E. N., & Walters, N. P. (2011). *The foreign-born population in the United States 2010.* American Community Survey Reports, ACS-19. Washington, DC: U.S. Census Bureau, Department of Commerce.

Harvey, D. (2007). *A brief history of neoliberalism.* Oxford, UK: Oxford University Press.

Kimmerling B. (1983). *Zionism and territory: The socio-territorial dimensions of Zionist politics.* Berkeley, CA: Institute of International Studies.

Kposowa, A. J. (1986). *The relationship between opportunities and interregional migration in Sierra Leone* (Master's thesis). Department of Sociology, University of Cincinnati, OH.

Kposowa, A. J. (1987). The effects of opportunities and cultural differences on interregional migration in Sierra Leone. *African Urban Quarterly, 2*(4), 378–396.

Kposowa, A. J. (1998). *The impact of immigration on the United States economy.* Lanham, MD: University Press of America.

Kulischer, E. U. (1949). Displaced persons in the modern world. *Annals of the American Academy of Political and Social Science*, 262, 166–177.

Lee, E. S. (1966). A theory of migration. *Demography*, 3, 47–59.

Li, W. L. (1983). *The measurement and analysis of internal migration.* Lanham, MD: University Press of America.

Massey, D. A., Arango, J., Hugo, G., Kouaouci, A., Pellegrino, A., & Taylor, J. E. (1993). Theories of international migration: A review and appraisal. *Population and Development Review, 19*(3), 431–466.

Petersen, W. (1958). A general typology of migration. *American Sociological Review, 23*(3), 256–266.

Piore, M. J. (1979). *Birds of passage: Migrant labor and industrial societies.* Cambridge, UK: Cambridge University Press.

Ravenstein, E. G. (1885). The laws of migration. *Journal of the Royal Statistical Society,* 48, 167–277.

Ravenstein, E. G. (1889). The laws of migration. *Journal of the Royal Statistical Society,* 52, 241–305.

Ritchey, P. N. (1976). Explanations of migration. *Annual Review of Sociology,* 2, 363–404.

Rogers, A. (1967). A regression analysis of interregional migration in California. *Review of Economics and Statistics,* 49, 262–267.

Sassen, S. (1991). *The global city: New York, London, Tokyo.* Princeton, NJ: Princeton University Press.

Shirer, W. L. (1990). *The rise and fall of the Third Reich: A history of Nazi Germany.* New York, NY: Touchstone.

Shryock, H. S. (1964). *Population mobility within the United States* (Vol. 1). Chicago, IL: Community and Family Study Center, University of Chicago.

Schultz, T. W. (1961). Investment in human capital. *American Economic Review,* 2, 1–17.

Sjaastad, L. A. (1962). The costs and returns of human migration. *Journal of Political Economy,* 705, 80–93.

Stark, O. (1984). Migration decision making: A review article. *Journal of Development Economics,* 14, 251–259.

Stark, O., & Bloom, D. E. (1985). The new economics of labor migration. *American Economic Review,* 75, 173–178.

Stark, O. (1991). *The migration of labor.* Cambridge, MA: Basil Blackwell.

Thomas, D. S. (1958). Age and economic differentials in interstate migration. *Population Index,* 24, 313–325.

Todaro, M. P. (1969). A model of labor migration and urban unemployment in less developed countries. *American Economic Review,* 59, 138–148.

United Nations (2013). The number of international migrants worldwide reaches 232 million. *Population Facts,* No. 2013/2, September 2013. Department of Economic and Social Affairs, Population Division.

U.S. Bureau of the Census (2013). *The 2009–2013 American Community Survey.* Washington, DC: Department of Commerce.

Wallerstein, I. (1974). *The modern world-system I: Capitalist agriculture and the origins of the European world-economy in the sixteenth century.* New York, NY: Academic Press.

World Health Organization (2015). The World Food Summit of 1996. Available at http://www.who.int/trade/glossary/story028/en/. Accessed May 25, 2015.

Zipf, G. K. (1946). The P1P2/D hypothesis on the intercity movement of persons. *American Sociological Review,* 2, 677–626.

4 | Survey of U.S. Immigration

There are generally four methods that nations select in the administration of immigration: unrestricted, qualitative, quantitative, and restricted policies. A country could have a policy of **unrestricted immigration**, whereby there are no controls on the number of persons entering, and there are no restrictions whatsoever on the composition of entrants. In short, there is no exclusion. Perhaps the closest to this in the modern era is the immigration policy in 26 European countries that form the Schengen (named after a small village in Luxembourg) passport free zone. The affected countries are Austria, Belgium, Czech Republic, Denmark, Estonia, Finland, France, Germany, Greece, Hungary, Iceland, Italy, Latvia, Liechtenstein, Lithuania, Luxembourg, Malta, Netherlands, Norway, Poland, Portugal, Slovakia, Slovenia, Spain, Sweden, and Switzerland. These nations have entered into a mutual agreement (since 1985) whereby each country eliminated immigration checks (passport controls) at its internal (joint) frontiers. In a desire to implement or respect the right to free movement of people enshrined in the Universal Declaration of Human Rights, citizens of the member states are free to travel in and out of the Schengen zone without impediments, such as passports, visas, and customs inspections (European Commission, 2015). It is important to be aware that there are limitations to Schengen. In an emergency, a member state may impose travel checks for some duration, but it must not be for purposes of restricting free movement, and the country should also inform other Schengen nations. Police may do what are called spot checks, but again these should not be for purposes of immigration control. There are checks at external borders, and visas and passports are required for travelers from non-Schengen zone countries (except those that are European Union members). The Schengen policy is not completely unrestricted in the sense that free movement applies to only member states of the zone. In 2014 and throughout 2016, these countries were heavily challenged by the influx of migrants crossing into Europe across the Mediterranean from war-torn countries such as Syria, Afghanistan, Iraq, and Libya. After initially stating that it would welcome all Syrian refugees, even Germany was forced to take emergency measures of border control as a result of the unprecedented movement of people heading to the country.

The second immigration policy option for states is **qualitative control** (Harper & Chase, 1961, p. 5). This approach restricts the type of immigrants entering a country, and it is typically enforced through indicating categories or characteristics of people who are barred from entry. Laws are passed via national legislative bodies indicating the specific conditions, which, if present, would deny entry or visa issuance to an individual. Qualitative control is also invoked if a nation decides, for example, that it will only take in individuals with high human capital, or only those with certain skills. Thus, qualitative control can either exclude individuals not wanted in the country, or it can focus on bringing specific groups that are preferred. Canada's point system is a form of qualitative control in that scores are given based on specific qualities, often related to Canadian labor market needs for high-skilled workers. Japan has had the lowest number of immigrants as share of population among all industrial nations since World War II. From 1950 to 1988, foreigners comprised 0.6 percent of the population, and in 2007 that number had risen to only 1.7 percent (Adolino & Blake, 2011, p. 118). The country's insistence on maintaining population homogeneity, despite an aging population and labor shortages, largely explains resistance to immigration. Japan's qualitative control of immigration is perhaps best summarized by Adolino & Blake (2011, p. 119): "Today, government policy is centered on the acceptance of a limited number of foreign workers in highly skilled occupations, control of illegal immigration, and caution with respect to the admission of low-skilled workers."

The third method employed by sovereign states to administer immigration is **quantitative control** (Harper & Chase, 1961, p. 4). In this regard, a country may limit the number of people entering within a defined period, such as a year. An example of quantitative control is a quota system, whereby a certain percentage of immigrants from another country is permitted, often by law, or a numerical ceiling is imposed beyond which no one (from a specified country) is allowed to enter.

The final method used to administer immigration is a **total ban** on all movement, and the country is described as being closed. Its population growth can be affected by only natural increase. It is difficult to conceive of a modern state that has this policy, but some countries have controls that are so restrictive that they come very close to a ban. Japan, for instance, has been very resistant to opening up to mass migration, and has had a long period of very restrictive immigration. During its long history, the United States has allowed unrestricted immigration, qualitative immigration, and quantitative immigration. In the pages that follow, we will see why and how the above forms of immigration control came about, and where the nation stands today.

The Founding Documents and Immigration

THE DECLARATION OF INDEPENDENCE

IN CONGRESS, July 4, 1776.

The unanimous Declaration of the thirteen united States of America,

We hold these truths to be self-evident, that all men are created equal, that they are endowed by their Creator with certain unalienable Rights, that among these are Life, Liberty and the pursuit of Happiness.—That to secure these rights, Governments are instituted among Men, deriving their just powers from the consent of the governed,—That whenever any Form of Government becomes destructive of these ends, it is the Right of the People to alter or to abolish it, and to institute new Government, laying its foundation on such principles and organizing its powers in such form, as to them shall seem most likely to effect their Safety and Happiness. Prudence, indeed, will dictate that Governments long established should not be changed for light and transient causes; and accordingly all experience hath shewn, that mankind are more disposed to suffer, while evils are sufferable, than to right themselves by abolishing the forms to which they are accustomed. But when a long train of abuses and usurpations, pursuing invariably the same Object evinces a design to reduce them under absolute Despotism, it is their right, it is their duty, to throw off such Government, and to provide new Guards for their future security.—Such has been the patient sufferance of these Colonies; and such is now the necessity which constrains them to alter their former Systems of Government. The history of the present King of Great Britain is a history of repeated injuries and usurpations, all having in direct object the establishment of an absolute Tyranny over these States. To prove this, let Facts be submitted to a candid world.

He has refused his Assent to Laws, the most wholesome and necessary for the public good. He has forbidden his Governors to pass Laws of immediate and pressing importance, unless suspended in their operation till his Assent should be obtained; and when so suspended, he has utterly neglected to attend to them. He has refused to pass other Laws for the accommodation of large districts of people, unless those people would relinquish the right of Representation in the Legislature, a right inestimable to them and formidable to tyrants only.

He has called together legislative bodies at places unusual, uncomfortable, and distant from the depository of their public Records, for the sole purpose of fatiguing them into compliance with his measures. He has dissolved Representative Houses repeatedly, for opposing with manly firmness his invasions on the rights of the people. He has refused for a long time, after such dissolutions, to cause others to be elected; whereby the Legislative powers, incapable of Annihilation, have returned to the People at large for their exercise; the State remaining in the mean time exposed to all the dangers of invasion from without, and convulsions within.

He has endeavoured to prevent the population of these States; for that purpose obstructing the Laws for Naturalization of Foreigners; refusing to pass others to encourage their migrations hither, and raising the conditions of new Appropriations of Lands.

He has excited domestic insurrections amongst us, and has endeavoured to bring on the inhabitants of our frontiers, the merciless Indian Savages, whose known rule of warfare, is an undistinguished destruction of all ages, sexes and conditions.

In every stage of these Oppressions We have Petitioned for Redress in the most humble terms: Our repeated Petitions have been answered only by repeated injury. A Prince whose character is thus marked by every act which may define a Tyrant, is unfit to be the ruler of a free people.

Nor have We been wanting in attentions to our British brethren. We have warned them from time to time of attempts by their legislature to extend an unwarrantable jurisdiction over us. We have reminded them of the circumstances of our emigration and settlement here. We have appealed to their native justice and magnanimity, and we have conjured them by the ties of our common kindred to disavow these usurpations, which, would inevitably interrupt our connections and correspondence. They too have been deaf to the voice of justice and of consanguinity. We must, therefore, acquiesce in the necessity, which denounces our Separation, and hold them, as we hold the rest of mankind, Enemies in War, in Peace Friends.

We, therefore, the Representatives of the united States of America, in General Congress, Assembled, appealing to the Supreme Judge of the world for the rectitude of our intentions, do, in the Name, and by Authority of the good People of these Colonies, solemnly publish and declare, That these United Colonies are, and of Right ought to be Free and Independent States; that they are Absolved from all Allegiance to the British Crown, and that all political connection between them and the State of Great Britain, is and ought to be totally dissolved; and that as Free and Independent States, they have full Power to levy War, conclude Peace, contract Alliances, establish Commerce, and to do all other Acts and Things which Independent States may of right do. And for the support of this Declaration, with a firm reliance on the protection of divine Providence, we mutually pledge to each other our Lives, our Fortunes and our sacred Honor.

Source: U.S. National Archives (2015).

Some portions of the above document have bearings on immigration. For example, Jefferson writes, "The history of the present King of Great Britain is a history of repeated injuries and usurpations, all having in direct object the establishment of an absolute Tyranny over these States. To prove this, let Facts be submitted to a candid world." He then goes into his bill of particulars, or specific charges or allegations against the king that the signatories felt justified the 13 colonies breaking away from Britain, and becoming independent. Among the charges is the following: "He has endeavoured to prevent the population of these States; for that purpose obstructing the Laws for Naturalization of Foreigners; refusing to pass others to encourage their migrations hither, and raising the conditions of new Appropriations of Lands." In other words, one of the charges levied against the "present King of Great Britain," and used as justification for the colonies breaking ties, was that the king had engaged in behaviors that slowed emigration from England and its isles into the colonies. He was accused of manipulating laws, which had the effect of obstructing naturalization of new arrivals. The king was also accused of not approving new appropriations (of people) to move to the American colonies and, above all, his intention, as alleged, was to prevent increasing the population of the colonies.

It is evident from the Declaration of Independence that the framers were in favor of immigration. The same document, however, reveals a disturbing picture of their perceptions of race, and what they envisaged the new country to be. It was alleged the king "... has excited domestic insurrections amongst us, and has endeavoured to bring on the inhabitants of our frontiers, the merciless Indian Savages, whose known rule of warfare, is an undistinguished destruction of all ages, sexes and conditions." The same people who were writing the lofty words "that all men are created equal, that they are endowed by their Creator with certain unalienable Rights, that among these are Life, Liberty and the pursuit of Happiness" were suddenly describing Indians (the native population) as savages, and presumably belonging to some subhuman inferior race. The inhabitants of their frontiers were White, and the king was accused of letting the Indians (the "savages") encroach on the frontiers and kill Whites. While Thomas Jefferson and those who signed the Declaration of Independence appeared to favor immigration, it is clear that their racial preference was White people, who they expected to continue coming from Great Britain.

We next have a look at the Constitution. It is a much longer document than the Declaration of Independence, so beyond the preamble, only those sections that are pertinent to immigration are reproduced below.

The Constitution

THE CONSTITUTION OF THE UNITED STATES

We the People of the United States, in Order to form a more perfect Union, establish Justice, insure domestic Tranquility, provide for the common defence, promote the general Welfare, and secure the Blessings of Liberty to ourselves

Excerpt from: The Constitution of the United States. Copyright in the Public Domain.

and our Posterity, do ordain and establish this Constitution for the United States of America.

Article I

Section 2. No person shall be a Representative who shall not have attained the age of twenty-five years, and been seven years a citizen of the United States, and who shall not, when elected be an inhabitant of that State in which he shall be chosen.

Representatives and direct taxes shall be apportioned among the several States which may be included within this Union, according to their respective numbers, which shall be determined by adding to the whole number of free persons, including those bound to service for a term of years, and excluding Indians not taxed, three fifths of all other persons. The actual enumeration shall be made within three years after the first meeting of the Congress of the United States, and within every subsequent term of ten years, in such manner as they shall by law direct.

Section 8. The Congress shall have power... [3] To regulate commerce with foreign nations, and among the several States, and with the Indian tribes; [4] *To establish an uniform rule of naturalization*, and uniform laws on the subject of bankruptcies throughout the United States;

Section 9. The *migration* or importation of such persons as any of the States now existing shall think proper to admit shall not be prohibited by the Congress prior to the year one thousand eight hundred and eight, but a tax or duty may be imposed on such importation, not exceeding ten dollars for each person.

Article II

Section 1. [5] No person except a natural-born citizen, or citizen of the United States at the time of the adoption of this Constitution, shall be eligible to the office of President.

Source: U.S. National Archives (2015).

The clause, *"To establish an uniform rule of naturalization,"* implies that the framers expected immigration to continue, for who else was going to be naturalized if there were no foreigners entering the new nation? If they wanted no immigration, they would have put it into the document, but they did not. At the same time, the Constitution is otherwise silent about immigration. The word itself does not appear anywhere in the original, except in connection with the slave trade, which the document specifically endorsed by allowing it to continue until 1808, as seen in Article I, Section 9, Clause 1. Not only was slavery to continue ("the migration of all other persons"), but the government was given the right to levy a tax (not to exceed $10) on each imported slave. This is not surprising, given that some of the Founding Fathers, including Jefferson, were slave owners. George Washington himself, the country's first president, is said to have owned well over 100 slaves laboring on his Mount Vernon estate or at other places in which he lived, such as New York and Philadelphia (Lawler, 1995, p. 1), and he signed the *Fugitive Slave Act* in 1793, in compliance with Article IV, Section 2 of the Constitution, which states: "No person held to Service or Labour in one State, under the Laws thereof, escaping into another, shall, in Consequence of any Law or Regulation therein, be discharged from such service or Labour, but shall be delivered up on Claim of the Party to whom such Service or Labour may be due." By these words, a slaveholder had the legal right to recapture his runaway slave. The Fugitive Slave Act furnished the framework by which the recapture would take place by making it a federal crime to assist a runaway slave or prevent his or her recapture. The use of the expression "other persons" in the Constitution is also revealing in that the Founding Fathers could not bring themselves to using the word "slaves"; it would have looked especially shameful and scandalous to later generations in a document they knew would last into perpetuity.

In Article II, Section 1, Clause 5, the Framers made distinctions between native-born and foreign-born, indicating that only native-born could hold the highest office in the land. One implication of this is that except for the office specified, all others were open to immigrants (foreign-born persons).

The Constitution's silence on immigration would have a lasting effect on the administration of U.S. policy. It meant that future immigration would be determined by Congress, and throughout the history of the nation, the political climate existing at the time has influenced decisions on who was welcome or, more appropriately, not welcome. This became evident when Congress first met in 1790 and passed the Act of March 26, 1790. As the Constitution had mandated, the law was aptly titled *An Act to Establish a Uniform Rule of Naturalization*.

ACT OF MARCH 16, 1790: AN ACT TO ESTABLISH A UNIFORM RULE OF NATURALIZATION

Section 1: Be it enacted by the Senate and House of Representatives of the United States of America in Congress assembled, That any alien, being a free white person, who shall have resided within the limits and under the jurisdiction of the United States for the term of two years, may be admitted to become a citizen thereof, on application to any common court of record, in any one of the states wherein he shall have resided for the term of one year at least, and making proof to the satisfaction of such court, that he is a person of good character, and taking the oath of affirmation prescribed by law, to support the constitution of the United States, which oath of affirmation such court shall administer; and the clerk of such court shall record such application, and the proceedings thereon; and thereupon such person shall be considered as a citizen of the United States. And the children of such persons so naturalized, dwelling within the United States, being under the age of twenty-one years at the time of such naturalization, shall also be considered as citizens of the United States. And the children of citizens of the United States, that may be born beyond the sea, or out of the limits of the United States, shall be considered as natural born citizens; Provided, That the right of citizenship shall not descend to persons whose fathers have never been resident in the United States; Provided also, That no person heretofore proscribed by any state, shall be admitted a citizen as aforesaid, except by an act of the legislature in the state in which such person was proscribed.

Source: U.S. Congress (1790). Public Statutes at Large of the United States (1 Stat. 103).

The law is notable for two main reasons. First, it was a very generous statute, and in retrospect perhaps the most generous immigration law ever passed in the history of the United States. A person had to reside in the United States for only two years and was then eligible to become a citizen. The second important aspect of the Act was that it injected race into U.S. immigration debate and policy, and that has been a persistent feature since 1790. The expression "free white person" meant that the generosity in the law depended on your skin color; by using the word "white" (which at the time implied someone from northern and western Europe) the act deliberately excluded African slaves and their descendants from citizenship. It was not forward-looking enough to consider other racial groups, such as Asians who may someday wish to come to the United States. Quite disturbingly, it ignored the citizenship status of Indians (Native Americans) on whose land and continent the new republic had been established. Presumably, if Congress shall have power to regulate commerce with foreign nations, and among the several states, and with the Indian tribes, then members of the tribes in question must be foreign; they are not "free white" persons, and thus not citizens. Such was the position taken later, in 1831, when the Supreme Court played on words in its ruling in the *Cherokee Nation v. State of Georgia* case:

> Though the Indians are acknowledged to have an unquestionable, and heretofore, unquestioned right to the lands they occupy until that right shall be extinguished by a voluntary cession to our government, yet it may well be doubted whether those tribes which reside within the acknowledged boundaries of the United States can, with strict accuracy, be denominated foreign nations. They may more correctly, perhaps, be denominated domestic dependent nations. They occupy a territory to which we assert a title independent of their will, which must take effect in point of possession when their right of possession ceases. Meanwhile, they are in a state of pupilage. Their relation to the United States resembles that of

a ward to his guardian. They look to our Government for protection, rely upon its kindness and its power, appeal to it for relief to their wants, and address the President as their Great Father (*U.S. Supreme Court, 1831*).[1]

Some broad racism appears to have existed among the framers and early White settlers, and this must have influenced what they wrote or failed to write in the founding documents and early legislation, such as the Act of 1790. In his *Observations Concerning the Increase of Mankind*, Benjamin Franklin (1755, p. 224) brought out the prevailing White racial superiority complex when he wrote:

> Why should the Palatine Boors be suffered to swarm into our Settlements, and by herding together establish their Language and Manners to the Exclusion of ours? Why should Pennsylvania, founded by the English, become a Colony of Aliens, who will shortly be so numerous as to Germanize us instead of our Anglifying them, and will never adopt our Language or customs, any more than they can acquire our Complexion. "Which leads me to add one Remark: That the Number of purely white People in the World is proportionately very small. All Africa is black or tawney. Asia chiefly tawney. America (exclusive of the new Comers) wholly so. And in Europe, the Spaniards, Italians, French, Russians and Swedes, are generally of what we call a swarthy Complexion; as are Germans also, the Saxons only accepted, who with the English, make the principal Body of White People on the Face of the Earth. I could wish their numbers were increased. ... Why should we in the Sight of Superior Beings, darken its people? Why increase the Sons of Africa, by Planting them in America, where we have so fair an Opportunity, by excluding all Blacks and Tawneys, of increasing the lovely White and Red? But perhaps I am partial to the Complexion of my Country, for such Kind of Partiality is Natural to Mankind.

Source: Benjamin Franklin (1755, p. 224).[2]

Evidence of racism, especially against Blacks, is seen in Thomas Jefferson's writings, notably his *Notes on the State of Virginia*. In the treatise, Jefferson (1785) claimed that Blacks were inferior to Whites in areas of beauty, reasoning, and intelligence. Fearful of a race war should Blacks ever seek revenge on Whites for their mistreatment under slavery, Jefferson was among the earliest of the Founding Fathers to argue for mass expulsion of Blacks from America to Africa, regardless of their place of birth. The American Colonization Society was founded in 1816/1817 precisely for this purpose: repatriation of Africans

---

1   Excerpt from: Cherokee Nation v. State of Georgia. Copyright in the Public Domain.

2   Benjamin Franklin, Observations Concerning the Increase of Mankind. Copyright in the Public Domain.

to Africa so that they do not take revenge on the White population in America following the end of the slave trade. In 1822, the society succeeded in establishing a colony for freed African slaves on territory around the Montserrado River in West Africa, naming the capital Monrovia, and the territory Liberia, which declared independence in 1847.

Jefferson remarked in his *Notes on the State of Virginia* that Blacks and Whites could not live together, as there was so much incompatibility that the two races would destroy each other in an inevitable race war as Blacks, he believed, would surely wish to take revenge for all the insults, humiliations, degradations, and other horrors that White people had visited upon them. In Jefferson's views, one begins to see the seeds of Black-White racial segregation and outright Black racial hatred planted in American culture and psyche at the earliest times in the country's history, two phenomena that have haunted the country from Jefferson's days to the present.

Recall that the Constitution had mandated that slavery—that is, new importation of slaves—would end no sooner than 1808. Jefferson, a big slave master, was to become president in 1801. On Blacks, he observed, among many things in his *Notes on the State of Virginia*, that:

> ... They have less hair on the face and body. They secrete less by the kidnies, and more by the glands of the skin, which gives them a very strong and disagreeable odour. This greater degree of transpiration renders them more tolerant of heat, and less so of cold, than the whites. ... They seem to require less sleep. A black, after hard labour through the day, will be induced by the slightest amusements to sit up till midnight, or later, though knowing he must be out with the first dawn of the morning. ... Comparing them by their faculties of memory, reason, and imagination, it appears to me, that in memory they are equal to the whites; in reason much inferior, as I think one could scarcely be found capable of tracing and comprehending the investigations of Euclid; and that in imagination they are dull, tasteless, and anomalous ... I advance it therefore as a suspicion only, that the blacks, whether originally a distinct race, or made distinct by time and circumstances, are inferior to the whites in the endowments both of body and mind (*Jefferson, 1785, Query XIV*).

The hypocrisy and arrogance of some of the Framers is difficult to comprehend, for how could one reconcile Jefferson's vile language against Blacks with the claim that "All men are created equal, that they are endowed by their Creator with certain unalienable Rights ..."? They may as well have written that "all men are created equal except Blacks"! In moments of racial crises, such as the August 12, 2017, violent demonstrations in Charlottesville, Virginia, revisionists of American history are tempted to think that the notion of White supremacy began with the Civil War. This is not correct at all. It is inconceivable that people such as Confederate President Jefferson Davis, and his top military commanders General Robert E. Lee and General Thomas J. "Stonewall" Jackson, believed in racial equality, but to limit the origins of White supremacist ideology to them and the Confederacy has the risk of absolving the Founding Fathers of their complicity in planting the seeds of White racial superiority in the United States long before the Civil War, in their actions, in their spoken words, and in what they wrote.

Personal Letters

Apart from the Declaration of Independence and the Constitution, some personal letters written by the Founding Fathers also provide evidence that they were for the most part not anti-immigration, but they expected immigration to continue. One example is George Washington's (1783) letter to Joshua Holmes, and meant to be read to the "Members of the volunteer Associations & other Inhabitants of the Kingdom of Ireland who have lately arrived in the City of New York," in which he wrote:

> It was not an uninteresting consideration, to learn, that the Kingdom of Ireland, by a bold and manly conduct had obtained the redress of many of its grievances; and it is much to be wished that the blessings of equal Liberty and unrestrained Commerce may yet prevail. ... The bosom of America is open to receive not only the Opulent and respected Stranger, but the oppressed and persecuted of all Nations and Religions; whom we shall welcome to a participation of all our rights and privileges, if by decency and propriety of conduct they appear to merit the enjoyment (*New York, December 2, 1783*).

In a letter to Hugh White, Thomas Jefferson (1801) writes:

> Born in other countries, yet believing you could be happy in this, our laws acknowledge, as they should so, your right to join us in society, conforming, as I doubt not you will do, to our established rules. That these rules shall be as equal as prudential considerations will admit, will certainly be the aim of our legislatures, general and particular (*May 2, 1801*).

Perhaps some euphoria came upon the Framers following the Declaration of Independence and the adoption of the Constitution, creating some feelings that predisposed them to have a pro-immigration position. With the passage of time, however, conflicts emerged, and the early consensus on immigration began to break down. We now examine circumstances and events that broke the pro-immigration consensus and called into question the sincerity with which they had written letters, along with their adherence to the Constitution itself, at least in the first decade of the nation's existence.

Political Divisions and Breakdown in Immigration Consensus

From the organization of the U.S. government in 1789 to 1801, immigration policy was greatly influenced by a seemingly unbridgeable gulf between two political camps in the country, the Federalists, led by Alexander Hamilton and

John Adams on the one hand, and the Democratic-Republicans led by James Madison and Thomas Jefferson on the other. The issues on which the two groups differed ranged from the mundane and minor, such as which title the president of the United States should have, or the alleged monarchical tendencies of John Adams, to the more serious, including freedom of speech and civil liberties, and the nature of government. While the Federalists, for example, supported a strong central government, Democratic-Republicans favored a decentralized popular government (Stone, 2004, p. 25). Whereas Federalists believed that a ruling elite was needed for national survival, and feared that uncontrolled democracy might lead to anarchy, Democratic-Republicans (Jeffersonians) favored a government directly answerable to the will of the people, without mediation by some ruling class (Stone, 2004). They were also distrustful of moneyed interests, such as big landowners, bankers, financiers, merchants, and shipping companies, and were concerned about the future of democracy should such groups have influence on government and public officials.

The two groups differed sharply on immigration, with Federalists viewing the rapidly increasing foreign-born population in the United States as the greatest internal threat facing the country. New immigrants were coming primarily from France, Ireland, and Germany—and, upon their arrival, tended to favor Democratic-Republicans. In addition, after gaining naturalization, they tended to vote against Federalist candidates (Daniels, 2002). Wealthier ones among them would buy printing presses or become editors and pamphleteers, and some would write articles critical of John Adams and his Federalist administration. Federalists viewed the new immigrants as a threat to their party and control of the government, and a source of future growth for Democratic-Republicans (Stone, 2004; Daniels, 2002). Accordingly, something must be done to stem the tide, and so, in 1795, the Federalist-controlled Congress repealed the Act of 1790 and passed a new naturalization statute. It is highly likely that Federalists feared Jefferson would run for president in the 1796 election, and passing this act may have been designed to derail his chances of winning by reducing his voter support base. More recently arrived immigrants would not have been naturalized in time to vote for Jefferson and his Democratic-Republicans.

ACT OF JANUARY 29, 1795: AN ACT TO ESTABLISH A UNIFORM RULE OF NATURALIZATION; AND TO REPEAL THE ACT HERETOFORE PASSED ON THAT SUBJECT

Section 1: Be it enacted by the Senate and House of Representatives of the United States of America in Congress assembled, That any alien, being a free white person, may be admitted a citizen of the United States, or any of them, on the following conditions, and not otherwise—

... He shall at the time of his application to be admitted, declare on oath or affirmation, before some one of the courts aforesaid, that he has resided within the United States, five years at least; that he will support the constitution of the United States; and that he doth absolutely and entirely renounce and abjure all allegiance and fidelity to every foreign prince, potentate, state or sovereignty whatever, and particularly by name, the prince, potentate, state or sovereignty whereof he was before a citizen or subject; which proceedings shall be recorded by the clerk of the court.

... The court admitting such alien, shall be satisfied that he has resided within the limits and under the jurisdiction of the United States five years; and it shall further appear to their satisfaction, that during that time, he has behaved as a man of good moral character, attached to the principles of the constitution of the United States, and well disposed in the good order and happiness of the same.

... In case the alien applying to be admitted to citizenship shall have borne any hereditary title, or been of any of the orders of nobility, in the kingdom or state from which he came, he shall, in addition to the above requisites, make an express renunciation of his title or order of nobility, in the court to which his application shall be made; which renunciation shall be recorded in the said court ...

Section 4: And be it further enacted, That the act intituled "An act to establish an uniform rule of naturalization," passed the twenty-sixth day of March, one thousand seven hundred and ninety, be, and the same is hereby repealed.

Source: U.S. Congress (1795). Public Statutes at Large of the United States.

As may be seen, the new statute raised the residency requirement for naturalization from two to five years. Concerns about new immigrants fleeing revolutionary or tyrannical governments and potentially destabilizing the United States should they become citizens are reflected in the law's repeated references to words such as "foreign prince," "potentate," "state or sovereignty," and demands for "renunciation and abjuration of all allegiance and fidelity to every foreign prince, potentate, state or sovereignty."

The Alien and Sedition Acts of 1798
Specific political reasons or motivations behind passage of the Act of 1798 and a series of three other laws that same year are debatable. There is, however, broad consensus that an underlying reason was the polarization between Federalists and Democratic-Republicans, and the resulting anti-foreign sentiments that descended on the 5th Congress between 1797 and 1799, a time frame that coincided with the administration of President John Adams, and a period that Jefferson is said to have described as a "reign of witches" (Monticello.org, 2015).

There were both domestic political reasons, and a significant international reason for the sudden rise in anti-foreign feelings in Congress.

Many Americans were initially supportive of the French Revolution that broke out on Bastille Day, July 14, 1789. It was felt by some that the revolutionary slogans of *"liberté, fraternité, égalité"* were somewhat in line with America's own democratic values. After all, America had won its independence through revolution, and France had supported that endeavor, though ironically under a monarchy at the time. American public opinion, however, was tempered by the excesses of the revolutionaries and the Reign of Terror (1793–1798). It began with the execution of the former king, Louis XVI, on January 21, 1793, followed by that of his wife, Marie Antoinette, on October 16, 1793. It is estimated that between September 1793 and July 1794, the French revolutionaries arrested more than 200,000 and executed thousands, largely members of the aristocracy (Humphrey, 2003, p. 263). Despite their slogans of liberty, equality, and fraternity, the revolutionaries appeared bent on de-Christianizing France and suppressing all forms of dissent. Afraid that the revolution might spread to other nations led by crowned heads, a pro-monarchist coalition—England, Spain, Austria, the Netherlands, and Prussia—declared war on France (Stone, 2004, p. 21). This coalition was defeated in 1794, and three years later Napoleon had seized Belgium, Germany's Rhineland, and most of Italy; England also appeared to be in trouble with the French army about to cross the English Channel. American politicians found themselves with a problem over how to respond to the war in Europe, and which side to take, that of England or that of France. Fissures emerged largely along party lines with many in the Federalist camp urging action on the side of England, while Democratic-Republicans urged restraint. Fears were expressed largely by Federalists that the French might invade the United States, and part of their response was to seek radicals at home that they claimed might engage in sabotage. It started a classic and recurring theme in American history, politicians using crises to advance some hidden agenda, exaggerating dangers to the republic, creating mass hysteria, punishing their perceived domestic enemies, often immigrants, and sacrificing civil liberties at the altar of national security.

In 1778, France and the United States had signed a treaty wherein both sides had pledged to come to the aid of each other in the event of war. Yet when war broke out between Britain and France in 1793, the United States maintained neutrality in violation of the treaty, with George Washington arguing that the United States was not strong enough to become embroiled in a Franco-British war (Humphrey, 2003, p. 303). The French felt betrayed by the Americans, especially when U.S. leaders signed a separate treaty (Jay Treaty) with Great Britain in 1795 that ensured the United States would not go to war against Britain. France responded by attacking American ships, starting a period known as the "Quasi-War" that lasted briefly, from 1796 to 1798. From June 1796 to June 1797, France seized 316 American ships on the high seas, and promised to keep doing so until U.S. support for Britain ceased (Stone, 2004, p. 21).

Relations between France and the United States suffered a hit with the XYZ Affair of 1798. In an attempt to de-escalate rising tensions between the two nations, President Adams sent three special envoys to Paris in the autumn of 1797 to negotiate a way of withdrawing the United States from the 1778 treaty with France. Upon their arrival in France, the three emissaries were presented terms of negotiation, which though normal in European diplomacy at the time horrified the Americans (Humphrey, 2003, p. 313). To allow negotiations to begin, France asked for a loan of $12 million, and a $250,000 bribe to be given to the French foreign minister, Charles Maurice de Talleyrand-Périgord. The American emissaries viewed the French demands as extortion, and instead of continuing with negotiations, at least two of them decided to return to the United States. Largely to protect the identity of the French negotiators, President Adams used the letters X, Y, and Z in reporting the matter to Congress, and hence the entire incident came to be known as the XYZ Affair (Humphrey, 2003, p. 313).

News of the XYZ Affair made many Americans angry, and Federalists in Congress demanded retribution (war) because France had presumably insulted American pride. Newspapers of the day took sides, often consistent with the views of the political party with which they were aligned. Federalist-aligned newspapers chastised the French with some calling for war in defense of American honor (Stone, 2004, p. 30; Humphrey, 2003, p. 313). Democratic-Republican papers tended to minimize the XYZ incident, suggesting that diplomatic efforts had not been pushed hard enough. As war fever gripped the nation, Federalists imagined disloyalty lurking everywhere on the domestic front, and to them only the foreign-born could be disloyal. Fear of immigrants, their tendency to side with Democratic-Republicans, and the potential harm they could visit upon the United States caused the Federalist-dominated Congress to amend the Naturalization Act of 1795, and pass a far more intrusive statute, the Act of June 18, 1798. It was the first in a series of laws that would push civil liberties to their limits, with anti-foreign (alien) tones.

NATURALIZATION ACT OF JUNE 18, 1798

SECTION 1: *Be it enacted by the Senate and House of Representatives of the United States of America in Congress assembled,* That no alien shall be admitted to become a citizen of the United States, or of any state, unless in the manner prescribed by the act, intituled "An act to establish an uniform rule of naturalization; and to repeal the act heretofore passed on that subject," he shall have declared his intention to become a citizen of the United States, five years, at least, before his admission, and shall, at the time of his application to be admitted, declare and prove, to the satisfaction of the court having jurisdiction in the case, that he has resided within the United States fourteen years, at least, and within the state or territory where, or for which such court is at the time held, five years, at least, besides conforming to the other residence within the United States, and five years in the state, where he applies; besides otherwise conforming to the former act, declarations, renunciations and proofs, by the said act required, anything residence therein to the contrary hereof notwithstanding: *Provided*, that any alien, who was residing within the limits, and under the jurisdiction of the United States, before the twenty-ninth day of January, one thousand seven hundred and ninety-five, may, within one year after the passing of this act—and any alien who shall have made the declaration of his intention to become a citizen of the United States, in conformity to the provisions of the act, intituled "An act to establish an uniform rule of naturalization, and to repeal the act heretofore passed on that subject," may, within four years after having made the declaration aforesaid, be admitted to become a citizen, in the manner prescribed by the said act, upon his making proof that he has resided five years, at least, within the limits, and under the jurisdiction of the United States: *And provided also*, that no alien, who shall be a native, citizen, denizen or subject of any nation or state with whom the United States shall be at war, at the time of his application, shall be then admitted to become a citizen of the United States.

SEC. 2. *And be it further enacted*, That it shall be the duty of the clerk, or other recording officer of the court before whom a declaration has been, or shall be made, by any alien, of his intention to become a citizen of the United States, to certify and transmit to the office of the Secretary of State of the United States, to be there filed and recorded, an abstract of such declaration, in which, when hereafter made, shall be a suitable description of the name, age, nation, residence and occupation, for the time being, of the alien; such certificate to be made in all cases, where the declaration has been or shall be made, before the passing of this act, within three months thereafter; and in all other cases, within two months after the declaration shall be received by the court. And in all cases hereafter arising, there shall be paid to the clerk, or recording officer as aforesaid, to defray the expense of such abstract and certificate, a fee of two dollars; and the clerk or officer to whom such fee shall be paid or tendered, who shall refuse or neglect to make and certify an abstract, as aforesaid, shall forfeit and pay the sum of ten dollars.

SEC. 3. *And be it further enacted*, That in all cases of naturalization heretofore permitted or which shall be permitted, under the laws of the United States, a certificate shall be made to, and filed in the office of the Secretary of State, containing a copy of the record respecting the alien, and the decree or order of admission by the court before whom the proceedings thereto have been, or shall be had: And it shall be the duty of the clerk or other recording officer of such court, to make and transmit such certificate, in all cases which have already occurred, within three months after the passing of this act; and in all future cases, within two months from and after the naturalization of an alien shall be granted by any court competent thereto: in all future cases, there shall be paid to such clerk or recording officer the sum of two dollars, as a fee for such certificate, before the naturalization prayed for, shall be allowed. And the clerk or recording officer, whose duty it shall be, to make and transmit the certificate aforesaid, who shall be convicted of a wilful neglect therein, shall forfeit and pay the sum of ten dollars, for each and every offence.

Sec. 4. *And be it further enacted*, That all white persons, aliens, (accredited foreign ministers, consuls, or agents, their families and domestics, excepted) who, after the passing of this act, shall continue to reside, or who shall arrive, or come to reside in any port or place within the territory of the United States, shall be reported, if free, and of the age of twenty-one years, by themselves, or being under the age of twenty-one years, or holden in service, by their parent, guardian, master or mistress in whose care they shall be, to the clerk of the district court of the district, if living within ten miles of the port or place, in which their residence or arrival shall be, and otherwise, to the collector of such port or place, or some officer or other person there, or nearest thereto, who shall be authorized by the President of the United States, to register aliens: And report, as aforesaid, shall be made in all cases of residence, within six months from and after the passing of this act, and in all after cases, within forty-eight hours after the first arrival or coming into the territory of the United States, and shall ascertain the sex, place of birth, age, nation, place of allegiance or citizenship, condition or occupation, and place of actual or intended residence within the United States, of the alien or aliens reported, and by whom the report is made. And it shall be the duty of the clerk, or other officer, or person authorized, who shall receive such report, to record the same in a book to be kept for that purpose, and to grant to the person making the report, and to each individual concerned therein, whenever required, a certificate of such report and registry; and whenever such report and registry shall be made to, and by any officer or person authorized, as aforesaid, other than the clerk of the district court, it shall be the duty of such officer, or other person, to certify and transmit, within three months thereafter, a transcript of such registry, to the said clerk of the district court of the district in which the same shall happen; who shall file the same in his office, and shall enter and transcribe the same in a book to be kept by him for that purpose. And the clerk, officer or other person authorized to register aliens, shall be entitled to receive, for each report and registry of one individual or family of individuals, the sum of fifty cents, and for every certificate of a report and registry the sum of fifty cents, to be paid by the person making or requiring the same, respectively …

Sec. 6. *And be it further enacted*, That in respect to every alien, who shall come to reside within the United States after the passing of this act, the time of the registry of such alien shall be taken to be the time when the term of residence within the limits, and under the jurisdiction of the United States, shall have commenced, in case of an application by such alien, to be admitted a citizen of the United States; and a certificate of such registry shall be required, in proof of the term of residence, by the court to whom such application shall and may be made.

Sec. 7. *And be it further enacted*, That all and singular the penalties established by this act, shall and may be recovered in the name, and to the use of any person, who will inform and sue of the same, before any judge, justice, or court, having jurisdiction in such case, and to the amount of such penalty, respectively.

Approved, June 18, 1798

Source: U.S. Congress (1798a). Public Statutes at Large of the United States.

The residency requirement for naturalization had already been raised by the Federalists from two (as in 1790) to five years (in 1795). The new legislation raised it to 14 years, the highest level ever in U.S. history. This was more than just out of concern about war with France, but the legislation appeared to target newcomers for their tendency to join the Democratic-Republicans upon naturalization and vote against Federalists. Now, if it took more than a decade for newcomers to achieve citizenship, it would be easier for Federalists to hold onto power. The new act instituted a registry for "aliens," which was to be delivered to the secretary of state. What was cleverly omitted was that the registry could be used in an emergency to track aliens, and possibly have them arrested, imprisoned, or even deported.

Finally, the Act of 1798 stipulated that before naturalization, an alien must declare intent to do so at least five years prior. Incoming aliens were also to report their whereabouts to officials within 48 hours of arrival into the United States, and various fees that had not been levied before were introduced into immigration policy.

With xenophobia still raging in the country, notably on the Federalist side, and the alleged potential for immigrants to endanger the United States, Congress on June 25, 1798, passed *An Act Concerning Aliens*. The law's title itself made it clear what the intended targets were: foreigners (or *aliens*, as new entrants increasingly came to be described).

The law empowered the president (during peace time), acting solely on his own at any time, to order out of the United States, or cause to be deported, any aliens he deemed to be dangerous to the peace and safety of the country. Reasons could include suspicion of treason, spying, or anything else that the president felt. If the alien failed to leave and stayed in the United States, the president had the right to have him or her imprisoned for *three years*, and never allowed to become a citizen of the United States. The president could issue a license to such an alien, granting him or her temporary residency in the United States. The act further required that ships entering U.S. ports declare any aliens they might have on board. There was to be no judicial review of the president's orders, since in Section 4, circuit and district courts were ordered to be cognizant of all behaviors that violated the law and were to carry out the orders of the president. In effect, foreigners (aliens) were stripped of basic due process protections and placed outside the limits of the U.S. Constitution.

The act uses some very terrifying language that betrays the paranoia and xenophobia about immigrants, such as "treasonable or secret machinations." Some language is downright humiliating, if not insulting for foreigners.

That it shall be lawful for any alien who may be ordered to be removed from the United States, by virtue of this act, to take with him such part of his goods, chattels, or other property, as he may find convenient; and all property left in the United States, by any alien who may be removed as aforesaid, shall be and remain subject to his order and disposal, in the same manner as if this act had not been passed.

Apparently, if the president expelled an alien, that person was allowed to take with him or her property acquired in the United States, presumably including houses, horses, and cattle. By passing this act, Congress began a gradual process of concentrating power in the hands of the president, who could act without any checks and balances.

AN ACT CONCERNING ALIENS

June 25, 1798

SECTION 1. Be it enacted by the Senate and House of Representatives of the United States of America, in Congress assembled, That it shall be lawful for the President of the United States, at any time during the continuance of this act, to order all such aliens as he shall judge dangerous to the peace and safety of the United States, or shall have reasonable grounds to suspect are concerned in any treasonable or secret machinations against the government thereof, to depart out of the territory of the United States within such time as shall be expressed in such order; which order shall be served on such alien, by delivering him a copy thereof, or leaving the same at his usual abode, and returned to the office of the Secretary of State, by the marshal, or other person, to whom the same shall be directed. And in case any alien, so ordered to depart, shall be found at large within the United States after the time limited in such order for his departure, and not having obtained a license from the President to reside therein, or having obtained such license, shall not have conformed thereto, every such alien shall, on conviction thereof, be imprisoned for a term not exceeding three years, and shall never after be admitted to become a citizen of the United States: Provided always, and be it further enacted, That if any alien so ordered to depart shall prove, to the satisfaction of the President, by evidence, to be taken before such person or persons as the President shall direct, who are for that purpose hereby authorized to administer oaths, that no injury or danger to the United States will arise from suffering such alien to reside therein, the President may grant a license to such alien to remain within the United States for such time as he shall judge proper, and at such place as he may designate. And the President may also require of such alien to enter into a bond to the United States, in such penal sum as he may direct, with one or more sufficient sureties, to the satisfaction of the person authorized by the President to take the same, conditioned for the good behaviour of such alien during his residence in the United States, and not violating his license, which license the President may revoke whenever he shall think proper.

SECT. 2. And be it further enacted, That it shall be lawful for the President of the United States, whenever he may deem it necessary for the public safety, to order to be removed out of the territory thereof any alien who may or shall be in prison in pursuance of this act; and to cause to be arrested and sent out of the United States such of those aliens as shall have been ordered to depart therefrom, and shall not have obtained a license as aforesaid, in all cases where, in the opinion of the President, the public safety requires a speedy removal. And if any alien so removed or sent out of the United States by the President shall voluntarily return thereto, unless by permission of the President of the United States, such alien, on conviction thereof, shall be imprisoned so long as, in the opinion of the President, the public safety may require.

SECT. 3. And be it further enacted, That every master or commander of any ship or vessel which shall come into any port of the United States after the first day of July next shall, immediately on his arrival, make report in writing to the collector or other chief officer of the customs of such port, of all aliens, if any on board his vessel, specifying their names, age, the place of nativity, the country from which they shall have come, the nation to which they belong and owe allegiance, their occupation, and a description of their persons, as far as he shall be informed thereof, and on failure, every such master and commander shall forfeit and pay three hundred dollars, for the payment whereof, on default of such master or commander, such vessel shall also be holden, and may by such collector or other officer of the customs be detained. And it shall be the duty of such collector or other officer of the customs, forthwith to transmit to the office of the Department of State true copies of all such returns.

SECT. 4. And be it further enacted, That the Circuit and District Courts of the United States shall respectively have cognizance of all crimes and offences against this act. And all marshals and other officers of the United States are required to execute all precepts and orders of the President of the United States, issued in pursuance or by virtue of this act.

SECT. 5. And be it further enacted, That it shall be lawful for any alien who may be ordered to be removed from the United States, by virtue of this act, to take with him such part of his goods, chattels, or other property, as he may find convenient; and all property left in the United States, by any alien who may be removed as aforesaid, shall be and remain subject to his order and disposal, in the same manner as if this act had not been passed.

SECT. 6. And be it further enacted, That this act shall continue and be in force for and during the term of two years from the passing thereof.

Approved June 25, 1798

Source: U.S. Congress (1798b). Public Statutes at Large of the United States.

Luckily for immigrants and for the United States, the above act had a sunset clause in Section 6 that might have been put there by design to coincide with the election of 1800, which is when the Federalists must have feared they were going to lose due to their consistent overreach about immigration and warmongering. Despite the expiry of the act, it set a dangerous precedent that could be used by future presidents, through Congress, to demand far-ranging powers to enforce U.S. immigration.

The third anti-immigration act passed in that one session of the same Congress, in 1798, was the Alien Enemies Act, approved on July 6. It was motivated by fears about a potential shooting war with France and concerns about the role of foreigners, especially those from France. It empowered the president, during wartime, to imprison aliens from a foreign nation with which the United States was at war, and to have them deported.

THE ALIEN ENEMIES ACT

(July 6, 1798)

SECTION 1. Be it enacted by the Senate and House of Representatives of the United States of America, in Congress assembled, That whenever there shall be a declared war between the United States and any foreign nation or government, or any Invasion or predatory incursion shall be perpetrated, attempted, or threatened against the territory of the United States, by any foreign nation or government, and the President of the United States shall make public proclamation of the event, all natives, citizens, denizens, or subjects of the hostile nation or government, being males of the age of fourteen years and upwards, who shall be within the United States, and not actually naturalized, shall be liable to be apprehended, restrained, secured and removed, as alien enemies. And the President of the United States shall be, and he is hereby authorized, in any event, as aforesaid, by his proclamation thereof, or other public act, to direct the conduct to be observed, on the part of the United States, towards the aliens who shall become liable, as aforesaid; the manner and degree of the restraint to which they shall be subject, and in what cases, and upon what security their residence shall be permitted, and to provide for the removal of those, who, not being permitted to reside within the United States, shall refuse or neglect to depart therefrom; and to establish any other regulations which shall be found necessary in the premises and for the public safety:... the President of the United States may ascertain and declare such reasonable time as may be consistent with the public safety, and according to the dictates of humanity and national hospitality.

Approved July 6, 1798

Source: U.S. Congress (1798c). Public Statutes at Large of the United States.

Excerpt from: The Alien Enemies Act (July 6, 1798). Copyright in the Public Domain.

Since the law lacked a sunset clause, it found its way into the present U.S. Code. The precedent it set would be used later in U.S. history to imprison some Japanese aliens (and even citizens) on the West Coast during World War II, and to detain so-called "enemy combatants" following the September 11, 2001, attacks on the United States, and its later invasions of Afghanistan and Iraq.

The Sedition Act of July 14, 1798

The previous three laws passed in 1798 targeted foreigners for domestic political reasons, including suppression of their votes because, upon naturalization, they tended to cast them for Democratic-Republicans. With impending war with France, some of them were also viewed as potentially disloyal to the United States, and so extraordinary powers were given to the president to imprison, fine, or deport as he saw fit any person he perceived to be a threat to the peace and safety of the United States. Given that the laws were focused on "aliens," no citizen ever suffered from them. The Sedition Act was a different story, in that it targeted everyone regardless of nativity status, or citizenship status. Why was this particular act passed, and what were the consequences for the United States?

The reasons are complex, but they again dwell on the relationship between the two political camps in the country at the time regarding political ideology, views about France and fears about the French revolutionary spirit spreading to America, and suspicions that there were sympathizers of the French within the United States. Perhaps the single, most important reason involved different views or interpretations of the First Amendment to the Constitution. The Federalist camp did not believe that freedom of speech or expression was absolute; it appeared to have held the position that civil liberties and press freedom could be curtailed or even revoked if the government believed it was necessary. In other words, Federalists were less tolerant of political dissent.

A common feature in American politics from 1796 to 1801 was that newspaper editors, pamphleteers, and gazetteers of the day took political ideological sides. Some backed Federalists, while others supported the political views of Democratic-Republicans. Federalist newspapers and gazetteers tended to criticize Jefferson and his Democratic-Republicans, especially their alleged sympathies with France. Democratic-Republican-leaning newspapers were staunch critics of John Adams, his policies, and the laws he appeared to champion. Adams appeared to take media criticisms personally, considering them libelous. Perhaps his most vociferous critic was Benjamin Franklin Bache, editor of the *Aurora* newspaper published in Philadelphia three times a week from 1797 to 1800 (Library of Congress, 2015). Bache had started his critical publishing even before John Adams became president, a reporting that was at times interpreted by Adams and even Washington before him as too personal. It is conceivable that Democratic-Republican media criticisms of George Washington may have played some role in him not seeking a third term, as even in retirement he spoke bitterly about the attacks he had received from Benjamin Franklin Bache (Humphrey, 2003).

The Bill of Rights was ratified in 1791, and Amendment I provided that "Congress shall make no laws respecting an establishment of religion, or prohibiting the free exercise thereof; or abridging the freedom of speech, or of the press; or the right of the people peaceably to assemble, and to petition the Government for a redress of grievances." Yet barely seven years later, Federalists violated this amendment in their Sedition Act. It is not an exaggeration to claim that at least from the passage of the Act in 1798 until Thomas Jefferson took the oath of office in 1801, the United States for a brief period became a quasi-totalitarian state. Congress had overstepped its bounds and concentrated too much power in the hands of the president who, acting alone, could determine who constituted a threat to the peace and safety of the United States, and order that person to be deported if he or she were a foreigner. He could order alien enemies to be imprisoned and deported if the United States were at war with the alien's country. The president now had the power to impose heavy fines and imprisonment on anyone for writing, speaking, or publishing anything of a false, malicious, or scandalous nature about himself, the U.S. government, members of Congress, or other government officials. Who had the right to determine what was "scandalous" or "malicious"? Could there be alternative interpretations of an event? Long live the republic, and long live free speech!

THE SEDITION ACT

"An act for the punishment of certain crimes against the United States."

Section 1. *Be it enacted by the Senate and House of Representatives of the United States of America, in Congress assembled*, That if any persons shall unlawfully combine or conspire together, with intent to oppose any measure or measures of the government of the United States, which are or shall be directed by proper authority, or to impede the operation of any law of the United States, or to intimidate or prevent any person holding a place or office in or under the government of the United States, from undertaking, performing or executing his trust or duty; and if any person or persons, with intent as aforesaid, shall counsel, advise or attempt to procure any insurrection, riot, unlawful assembly, or combination, whether such conspiracy, threatening, counsel, advice, or attempt shall have the proposed effect or not, he or they shall be deemed guilty of a high misdemeanor, and on conviction, before any court of the United States having jurisdiction thereof; shall be punished by a fine not exceeding five thousand dollars, and by imprisonment during a term not less than six months nor exceeding five years; and further, at the discretion of the court may be holden to find sureties for his good behaviour in such sum, and for such time, as the said court may direct.

Sec. 2. *And be it further enacted*, That if any person shall write, print, utter or publish, or shall cause or procure to be written, printed, uttered or published, or shall knowingly and willingly assist or aid in writing, printing, uttering or publishing any false, scandalous and malicious writing or writings against the government of the United States, or either house of the Congress of the United States, or the President of the United States, with intent to defame the said government, or either house of the said Congress, or the said President, or to bring them, or either of them, into contempt or disrepute; or to excite against them, or either or any of them, the hatred of the good people of the United States, or to stir up sedition within the United States, or to excite any unlawful combinations therein, for opposing or resisting any law of the United States, or any act of the President of the United States, done in pursuance of any such law, or of the powers in him vested by the constitution of the United States, or to resist, oppose, or defeat any such law or act, or to aid, encourage or abet any hostile designs of any foreign nation against the United States, their people or government, then such person, being thereof convicted before any court of the United States having jurisdiction thereof, shall be punished by a fine not exceeding two thousand dollars, and by imprisonment not exceeding two years.

SEC. 3. *And be it further enacted and declared*, That if any person shall be prosecuted under this act, for the writing or publishing any libel aforesaid, it shall be lawful for the defendant, upon the trial of the cause, to give in evidence in his defence, the truth of the matter contained in the publication charged as a libel. And the jury who shall try the cause, shall have a right to determine the law and the fact, under the direction of the court, as in other cases.

SEC. 4. *And be it further enacted*, That this act shall continue and be in force until the third day of March, one thousand eight hundred and one, and no longer: *Provided*, that the expiration of the act shall not prevent or defeat a prosecution and punishment of any offence against the law, during the time it shall be in force.

APPROVED, July 14, 1798.

Source: U.S. Congress (1798d). Public Statutes at Large of the United States.

Curiously, the Sedition Act was written in such a manner that it was to expire on the 3rd day of March, 1801, suggesting that President Adams had demanded this particular act as a way to silence dissent, punish and humiliate his critics, and barricade himself from Democratic-Republican media attacks. He became too unpopular as more and more Americans learned about the impending Sedition Act, and he must have known that he was not going to win the 1800 election. The act was a last-ditch effort to hold on to power with some peace of mind, while taking revenge on his enemies in the press, including the notable Benjamin Franklin Bache.

As we have seen in this chapter, the U.S. Constitution placed formulation of immigration policy under the control of Congress. That body's authority to formulate immigration policy is in the commerce clause (Article 1, Section 8, Clause 3), which states that Congress shall have power to "regulate commerce with foreign nations, and among the several states, and with the Indian tribes." Throughout most of their history, the courts have stayed on the sidelines and given Congress the prerogative over immigration, including over who is allowed to come into the country, who is banned from coming and for how long, who may naturalize, and length of residency for citizenship. Thus, even when some of the most pernicious anti-immigration laws are passed, immigrants have relatively little legal recourse to seek redress. The laws examined in this chapter show emerging patterns, and later chapters will illustrate more about the punitive administration of immigration, and how this has affected immigrants over the years. Early fights over immigration were not about race; indeed, the Alien and Sedition Acts had no racial component. The battle lines were about ideological divides. But given that race was injected into immigration in 1790 by the reference to "free white persons," groups perceived as different and not White would bear the brunt of punitive polices as we move on.

REFERENCES

Blake, J. R., & Blake, C. H. (2011). *Comparing public policies: Issues and choices in industrialized countries.* Washington, DC: CQ Press.

European Commission (2015). *Migration and home affairs.* Available at http://ec.europa.eu/dgs/home-affairs/index_en.htm. Accessed September 16, 2015.

Franklin, B. (1755). *Observations concerning the increase of mankind, peopling of countries, etc.* Boston, MA: S. Kneeland.

Harper, E. J., & Chase, R. F. (1961). *Immigration laws of the United States* (3rd ed.). Indianapolis, IN: Bobbs-Merrill.

Humphrey, C. S. (2003). *The revolutionary era: Primary documents on events from 1776 to 1800.* London, UK: Greenwood Press.

Jefferson, T. (1801). Letter to Hugh White, May 2, 1801. Available at http://westillholdthese-truths.org/quotes/category/immigration

Jefferson, T. (1785). *Notes on the state of Virginia.* Available at Electronic Text Center, University of Virginia, http://web.archive.org/web/20110208122414/http://etext.lib.virginia.edu/toc/modeng/public/JefVirg.html. Accessed August 14, 2017.

Lawler, E. (1995). *President's house slavery: By the numbers.* Available at http://www.ushistory.org/Presidentshouse/slaves/numbers.htm

Library of Congress (2015). *About Bache's Philadelphia Aurora. (Philadelphia [Pa.]) 1797–1800.* Available at http://chroniclingamerica.loc.gov/lccn/sn84026172/

Monticello.org (2015). *Election of 1800.* Available at https://www.monticello.org/site/research-and-collections/election-1800. Accessed September 21, 2015.

Stone, G. R. (2004). *Perilous times: Free speech in wartime from the Sedition Act of 1798 to the war on terrorism.* New York, NY: W. W. Norton.

U.S. Congress. (1790). *Public statutes at large of the United States, from the organization of the government in 1789 to March 3, 1845* (Vol. 1). Available at http://www.loc.gov/law/help/statutes-at-large/index.php

U.S. Congress. (1795). *Public statutes at large of the United States, from the organization of the government in 1789 to March 3, 1845. 1.* Available at http://www.loc.gov/law/help/statutes-at-large/index.php

U.S. Congress. (1798a). *Public statutes at large of the United States, from the organization of the government in 1789 to March 3, 1845. 1.* Available at http://www.loc.gov/law/help/statutes-at-large/index.php

U.S. Congress. (1798b). *Public statutes at large of the United States, from the organization of the government in 1789 to March 3, 1845. 1.* Available at http://www.loc.gov/law/help/statutes-at-large/index.php

U.S. Congress. (1798c). *Public statutes at large of the United States, from the organization of the government in 1789 to March 3, 1845. 1.* Available at http://www.loc.gov/law/help/statutes-at-large/index.php

U.S. Congress. (1798d). *Public statutes at large of the United States, from the organization of the government in 1789 to March 3, 1845. 1.* Available at http://www.loc.gov/law/help/statutes-at-large/index.php

U.S. National Archives (2015). Declaration of Independence. Available at http://www.archives.gov/exhibits/charters/declaration_transcript.html. Accessed September 18, 2015.

U.S. Supreme Court (1831). Cherokee Nation v. Georgia, 30 U.S. 5 Pet. 1 1. Available at https://supreme.justia.com/cases/federal/us/30/1/case.html

Washington, G. (1783). Letter to the members of the volunteer Associations & other Inhabitants of the Kingdom of Ireland who have lately arrived in the City of New York, December 2, 1783. In *The Writings of George Washington*, edited by John C. Fitzpatrick (Vol. *27*), p. 254 (1938).

5 | U.S. Immigration, 1820 to 1907

When Jefferson took over as president in 1801, the new Congress reversed the Federalist's Immigration Act of 1798, but instead of moving the period of residence to two years (as passed by the First Congress), it stopped at five years (as of the Act of 1795). The five-year residency requirement today can be traced all the way back to that period in American history. As we saw in Chapter 1, in the early days of the establishment of the United States, immigration was welcome. Earlier laws concentrated on naturalization: After arrival, how should newcomers behave? How long should they be in the country before becoming citizens? Will they uphold the Constitution? There were no federal regulations on admission into the country regarding to such issues as how many people to admit, or from which region individuals may come. There were no quantitative or qualitative controls or other means test, so to speak. Despite the lack of strict regulation, not all new entrants were welcome, and by the beginning of the 1820s, winds of nativism and xenophobia had begun to blow across the land. The first targets of nativists were Roman Catholics, especially Irish Catholics who had resumed coming to the country in large numbers following the conclusion of the War of 1812, and who had started entering in even larger numbers in the 1840s to escape the scourge of famine. As shown in Figure 1, the number of immigrants from Ireland and also Germany increased considerably from 1820 to 1860.

It can be seen from Figure 5.1 that although European immigration to the United States was on an upward slide, two countries of concern to the Know Nothing party were experiencing especially higher increases in the number of people admitted. Ireland had 3,614 immigrants in 1820, a number that was nearly 47% of all entrants from Europe (7690). In the 1821 to 1830 period, out of 98,797 European immigrants, the share due to Ireland was 50,724, representing 51.3%. The percentage of European immigrants from Ireland was 41.8 in the decade 1831–1840; from 1841 to 1850, it stood at nearly 48.9%, and in the decade before the Civil War (and the downfall of the Know Nothings), it was 37.3%. German immigration also rose consistently from 1820 to 1860, but its share of the overall European rate was below that of Ireland until the immediate decade Civil War when it slightly exceeded the Irish rate (38.8%).

Overall immigration to the United States began rising sharply after 1820 because, as was pointed out in Chapter 1, Congress passed the Steerage Act in 1819, to become effective as of January 1820. Thus, masters of ships could

FIGURE 5.1: Immigrants Admitted by Selected Country of Last Residence in Europe, Fiscal Years 1820–1860

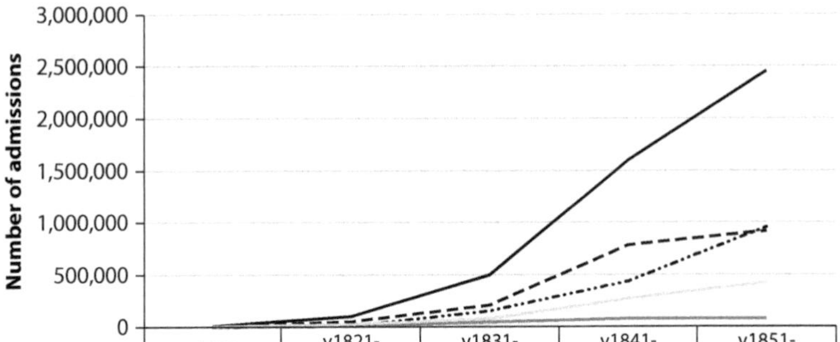

	y1820	y1821-1830	y1831-1840	y1841-1850	y1851-1860
—— All Europe	7690	98797	495681	1597442	2452577
—— France	371	8497	45575	77262	76358
- — - Ireland	3614	50724	207381	780719	914119
······· Germany	968	6761	152454	434626	951667
——— United Kingdom	2410	25079	75810	267044	423974

Source: Immigration and Naturalization Service, "Immigrants Admitted by Selected Country of Last Residence in Europe, Fiscal Years 1820-1860," *2000 Statistical Yearbook of the Immigration and Naturalization Service*, pp. 21. Copyright in the Public Domain.

not overload their vessels as they had previously done. More provisions were mandated during the voyage, as per the act, and on the whole, more passengers survived. Finally, the number of steam ships increased as competition across the Atlantic for immigrant transportation increased. Oppressive situations in some European nations (including the failure of the potato crop and accompanying famine in Ireland and elsewhere) and political upheavals in Germany all contributed to the rise in immigrants. The rise in overall immigration is illustrated in Figure 5.2.

In the decade 1820 to 1830, only 151,824 people worldwide entered the United States, but predominantly from Europe. In the 1831–1840 period, 599,125 people came. That number jumped to 1,713,251 in 1841–1850, and in 1851–1860, there was a record 2,598,214 entrants. The drop after 1861 was most likely due to the Civil War.

Apart from their Catholicism, Irish immigrants arriving during this period (following 1820) also tended to be poor. Indeed, many had had their trips subsidized by Irish landlords or the British government (Daniels, 2004, p. 9). The combination of Catholicism and poverty made the Irish especially easy targets for nativism and nativist organizations. Nativism, described by Higham (1988, p. 4) as "intense opposition to an internal minority on grounds of its foreign i.e. 'un-American' connections," was not new in the United States. Benjamin Franklin's (1751) comments about "Palatine boors" suggest that anti-foreign feelings and prejudice predate the official founding of the United States. The anti-Catholic movements by nativist organizations and groups in the 1820s through the immediate pre-Civil War era (targeting Irish and later German Catholic immigrants) appear to have started a lasting pattern of xenophobia that typically takes the

FIGURE 5.2: Immigration to the United States, 1820–1870

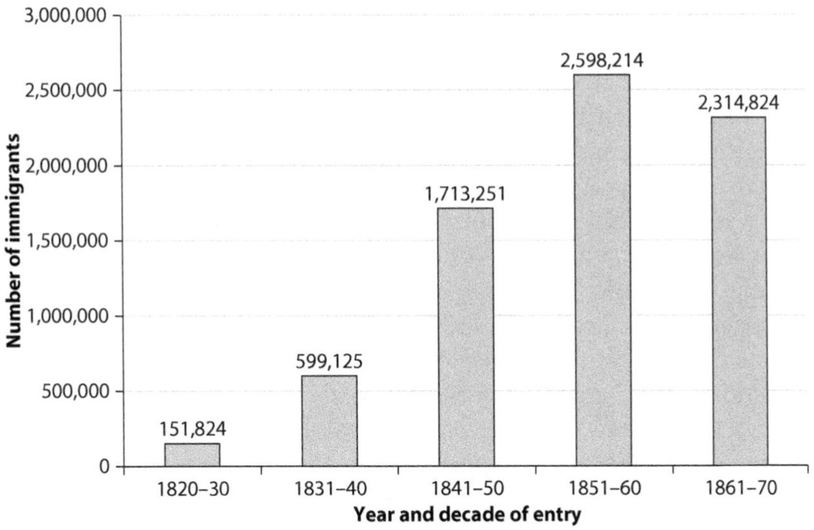

Source: Immigration and Naturalization Service, "Immigration to the United States, 1820-1870," *2000 Statistical Yearbook of the Immigration and Naturalization Service.* Copyright in the Public Domain.

form of complaining and stereotyping of immigrants, blaming them for every ill, including diseases and economic problems, and seeking national (racial) purification. As Daniels (2004, p. 8) points out, the complaints are the same: immigrants pose a threat; they do not speak English; they have strange and bad habits; they do not assimilate but tend to stick together; they are unpatriotic; they are un-American; they work for low wages and cause unemployment for the native-born. The only things that change in this litany of complaints are the groups entering the country.

The Passenger Cases and Nativism

To address the increasing cost of caring for immigrants landing on their shores, and perhaps to reduce immigration, Massachusetts and New York had imposed dollar amounts for each immigrant landing in Boston and New York, respectively. New York charged $1.50 for each cabin passenger, $1 for steerage passengers, while Massachusetts charged $2 for each immigrant. These costs were to be paid by masters of ships or immigrant ship owners (Daniels, 2002, p. 269). The charges were hailed by anti-immigration groups as ship owners invariably passed on the cost to passengers, which had the cumulative effect of slowing immigration by increasing the cost of passage and thereby reducing the number of passengers. Ship owners, however, believed the costs reduced profit due to higher ticket prices and fewer immigrants who could afford to pay and travel. Although the charges appear minimal by today's standards, ship owners filed lawsuits challenging the constitutionality of the taxes. The suits made their way to the U.S. Supreme Court, which consolidated them into what became known as the *Passenger Cases.* The court ruled in 1849 that it was unconstitutional for states (Massachusetts and

New York) to regulate immigration. That right, the court reasoned, had been ceded exclusively to Congress under the commerce clause of the Constitution in Article I, Section 9: "Congress shall have power to regulate commerce with foreign nations and among the several states ..."

The Supreme Court ruling in the Passenger Cases had the unintended consequence of uniting and galvanizing the anti-Catholic nativist movement. Chief among the nativist groups at the time was the American or Know Nothing party (Daniels 2002, p. 229). The organization had evolved from an assorted number of xenophobic groups within the Order of the Star Spangled Banner, principally located in New York, but lacking unity. The only thing that seemed to hold them together was a common dislike of Catholics and the foreign-born. The Supreme Court ruling had the effect of uniting them in some common cause: Force Congress to change laws or pass new ones on the foreign-born. The Know Nothings, for instance, wanted a constitutional amendment on the foreign-born that would limit them to only menial jobs and forbid them to hold major offices in the United States. It wanted the residence requirement raised from five to 21 years, thereby outperforming what the Federalists had accomplished (14 years) in their 1798 Naturalization Act. Disenfranchisement of the foreign-born, despite its potentially dangerous repercussions, was also a desire of theirs. Disenfranchisement of people is never a great idea because it prevents the affected group from quicker assimilation. If a group moves into another country, and that group is not allowed to participate in the political process, ultimately there is a risk that the immigrant group might feel alienated from the land. They may have nothing to lose should they participate in the event of some revolution or other political crisis. This is one reason why letting even undocumented people stay indefinitely without providing them some pathway to become citizens might create a potential danger for any country. Yet the Know Nothings were too blind in their opposition to foreigners to consider the consequences of creating a layer of stateless or second-class citizenry. Finally, the Know Nothings sought a ban on admitting into the United States paupers, criminals, idiots, lunatics, insane persons, and the blind (Daniels 2002, p. 270).

The Turn of Catholics

Nativism in the 1820s to 1850s had intellectual underpinnings, for even some who were considered "prominent" Americans showed deep-seated prejudices in their writings. In 1835, Samuel B. F. Morse penned a strongly worded anti-Catholic treatise, titled *A Foreign Conspiracy Against the Liberties of the United States*. In this book, among many other false assertions, Morse claimed the Irish were illiterate and incapable of forming independent opinions. In short, they took their marching orders from Rome, from the Pope. In the minds of Morse and other similarly prejudiced Americans, the Irish were especially unfit to be in America because they were Roman Catholic. Expressions of "non-Popery" were used often by people such as Morse and Protestant divines who claimed Catholics could not be trusted, did not believe in republican principles, and that their loyalties lay with their priests, bishops, archbishops, and the Pope, and were therefore a threat to the United States. The fact that the Mass and many liturgical rites were performed in Latin (which few Protestants understood) added to claims that Catholics were somewhat conspiratorial, for why not speak in a language that native-born Americans understood. Unfortunately, many Americans believed Morse (1835) when he warned falsely that the Pope planned to move the Vatican to the Mississippi River Valley. None questioned the logistics of moving the entire Vatican, including the Sistine Chapel, Saint Peter's Basilica itself, and the Curia, or why such a move would be necessary in the first place and why to Mississippi.

As a result of writings by people such as Morse, and also sermons by Protestant pastors and street corner divines, mob violence against Catholic priests and Catholic institutions was commonplace in the 1830s through the 1850s. The first major incidence of violence was the burning down of the Ursuline Convent on the outskirts of Boston on August 11, 1834. It has been reported that from 1834 through the 1850s, violence against Catholic institutions was so rampant that insurance companies often refused to insure them (Daniels, 2002, p. 266). The rhetoric and anti-foreign ideology of the Know Nothings is well documented, as in this manifesto attributed to Southern Baptist Minister James Robinson Graves that appeared in 1854 in the *Tennessee Baptist* (which he edited):

> Nothing is more evident than that our political parties have become sadly, deplorably corrupt ... Congress has become a most shameful and disgraceful scene of drunkenness, riot, and caucusing for the Presidency, and the minor offices of the government. The foreign element is increasing in fearful ratio. Nearly one million per annum of foreign Catholics and German infidels—who, though opposed in all else, are agreed in the subversion of our free institutions—are pouring in upon us, and the tide is increasing. These foreigners have already commenced their warfare upon the use of the Bible in our public schools—against our free school system—against our Sabbath—against our laws. They boldly threaten our constitution, through profligacy of our politicians; and we see our candidates for political preferment pandering more and more to the Catholic and foreign influence.
>
> We see from the last census that the majority of our civil and municipal offices of this government are today in the hands of Catholics and foreigners: an overwhelming majority of our army and navy are foreign Catholics. They hear the editors of Catholic papers, who are endorsed by their Archbishops, threatening in these words: "If Catholics ever gain an immense numerical majority, religious freedom in this country is at end." So say our enemies, So we believe (*Overdyke, 1950, p. 67*).[1]

---

1   Excerpt from: James Robinson Graves, *Tennessee Baptist*. Copyright in the Public Domain.

In his book, *The Protestant Crusade, 1800 to 1860*, Ray Billington (1938, p. 309) describes in chilling terms how Protestant Know-Nothings treated Catholics and Catholic institutions:

> Frequently crowds of excited Protestants, whipped to angry resentment by the exhortations of some wandering orator, rushed directly to a Catholic church, bent on its destruction. A dozen churches were burned during the middle 1850s; countless more were attacked, their crosses stolen, their altars violated, and their windows broken. At Sidney, Ohio, and at Dorchester, Massachusetts, Catholic houses of worship were blown to pieces with gunpowder. ... In New York City a mob laid siege to the prominent cathedral of St. Peter and St. Paul, and only the arrival of the police saved the building. In Maine Catholics who had had one church destroyed were prevented from laying the cornerstone of a new one by hostile Protestants, and statues of priests were torn down or desecrated.

There have survived various accounts of priests being harassed, beaten, and nearly killed. One such priest was John Bapst, whose experiences in Maine in 1854 have been recounted by Baillargeon (1950) and Daniels (2002, p. 268):

> Since the 4th of July I have not considered myself safe to walk the streets after sunset. Twice within the past month I have been stoned by young men. If I chance to be abroad when the public schools are dismissed, I am hissed and insulted with vile language; and those repeated from children have been encouraged by the smiles and silence of passersby. The windows of the church have frequently been broken—the panels of the church door stove in, and last week a large rock entered my chamber unceremoniously about 11 o'clock at night.

In some ways, it appeared in the 1820s through the 1850s that unsettled disputes between Protestantism and Catholicism, especially in matters of doctrine in the aftermath of Martin Luther's revolt in the 16th century, and that of King Henry VIII that same century, needed to be resolved, and the battleground had shifted from Europe to the United States. Hence, one of the organizations singled out for ridicule by Protestants was no other than the Society of Jesus (the Jesuits). The Jesuit order had risen in direct response to the Protestant Reformation with the specific aim of fighting falsehoods about the Catholic Church, teaching true Catholic dogma, and ultimately standing up to defend the Pope. In Protestant America in the early to mid-19th century, Jesuits were looked on with disfavor by nativists; they were presumably the means by which American Protestantism would be overtaken by Rome.

Catholics in some ways also contributed to prejudice against them by provoking Protestant mistrust. The church hierarchy at times acted arrogantly and failed to be prudent. One notable instance of this was a sermon delivered by the archbishop of New York at Saint Patrick's Cathedral in the fall of 1850. In it, the archbishop seemed to deliberately offend Protestants by equating Protestant-ism with paganism, noting the decline of Protestantism in Europe. Observed Archbishop Hughes:

> There is no secret about this. The object we hope to accomplish in time, is to convert all Pagan nations, and all Protestant nations, even England with her proud Parliament and imperial sovereign. There is no secrecy in all this. It is the commission of God to his church, and not a human project ... Protestantism pretends to have discovered a great secret. Protestantism startles our eastern borders occasion-ally on the intention of the Pope with regard to the Valley of the Mississippi, and dreams that it has made a wonderful discovery. ... Everybody should know it. Everybody should know that we have for our mission to convert the world—including the inhabitants of the United States,—the people of the cities, and the people of the country, the officers of the navy and the marines, commanders of the army, the Legislatures, the Senate, the Cabinet, the President, and all (*Billington, 1938, p. 291*).

Despite the tradition that the Catholic Church has always had an evangelical mission of conversion, the open admission at this time and place was most likely unwise because it offered ammunition to conspiracy theories circulating earlier (by people such as Samuel F. B. Morse) that Catholics could not be trusted and the Pope might move to America—to Mississippi—and from there assume control of the United States. Some in the Catholic hierarchy failed to realize that relations between church and state in Europe were much different in the United States. Whereas, in some heavily Catholic countries the crowned heads were closer to the church and had much more respect for the Pope, the situation was extremely different in America. Not only did there seem to be separation between church and state, but relations between the two were not as close as in Europe, say in England. Furthermore, the awe European nations had for the Holy See was not shared in "Protestant America," and in the early days Catholics formed a minority group among the various Christian denominations. Thus, in some instances, as in the case of Archbishop Hughes, some priests, bishops, and archbishops spoke or behaved as if the Catholic Church in America had similar status as in Catholic Europe. Given the different contexts, perhaps church leaders in America should have been more diplomatic, though it will never be known whether that would have necessarily assuaged the wrath of some Protestants or even nativists. Cer-tainly, though, delivering a sermon stating the aim of the church is conversion of all Protestant nations and pagan countries was an open invitation to attacks. After all, the United States at the time, for all intents and purposes, was heavily Protestant, though Protestantism had not been declared an official religion. For example, the Protestant Bible was read in public schools—and Catholic children were forced to read it, much to the displeasure of Catholic parents and priests. Catholic requests for state funding of parochial schools were repeatedly rebuffed by state legislatures and used as further weapon by Protestants in their crusade against Catholics.

Trusteeism and the Visit of Gaetano Bedini

One issue that proved contentious in the back-and-forth debates between Protestants (especially nativists) and the Catholic Church was trusteeism, that is, should church property be owned by clergymen (the hierarchy) or by trustees (lay members of the church)? Who was to have the deed? For many Protestants, having church property in the hands of the clergy amounted to giving in to Rome, and they saw it as allowing the Roman church to own American lands. To Protestants, the clergy owning property was viewed as a foreign power (the Pope) owning chunks of American real estate and many legislatures were soon to pass laws against clergy ownership. Nativists used the trustee issue as another excuse to attack the Catholic Church as a nondemocratic institution that did not allow individuals to control their own church property, one more evidence that "Popery" intended to subvert American institutions.

It was in the midst of the trusteeism controversy that Apostolic Delegate Monsignor Gaetano Bedini paid a visit to America in 1853. He had come as a Papal Nuncio, visiting the U.S. church, and imparting apostolic blessings on the church in the various dioceses he visited. The visit turned out to be disastrous for the Catholic Church and ill-timed because even before the archbishop landed in America, nativist papers and propagandists published articles (despite no hard evidence) claiming that Bedini had been personally involved in suppressing Italian uprisings against the Italian monarchy in 1848 and 1849, and that he had been involved in the deaths of 100 Italian patriots (Billington, 1938, p. 301). Violent protests and rioting accompanied Bedini wherever he went in the United States, with mobs trying to burn him in effigy, while others tried to hang or otherwise kill him, with the worst incident taking place in Cincinnati, Ohio. Bellington (1938, p. 303) observes that "On the night that Bedini arrived some 2,000 citizens marched through the streets carrying an effigy of the priest, a gallows, and banners which proclaimed: 'DOWN WITH BEDINI,' 'NO PRIESTS, NO KINGS, NO POPERY,' 'THE GALLOWS BIRD BEDINI,' AND 'DOWN WITH THE RAVEN BUTCHER.'"

The entire Cincinnati episode turned public opinion against the apostolic delegate across the nation and upon his departure from New York City back to Italy, the mob lying in wait at the dock to attack him was so immense that he had to be smuggled aboard his ship after it was well into a safer area away from the harbor (Bellington, 1938).

The Fall of the Know Nothings

The first phase of nativism was not to subside until the demise of the Know Nothings in 1856, following their controversial decision to insert a statement into their party platform urging Congress to pass no laws against slavery. Their fixation on Catholic immigrants and persecuting priests and nuns had blinded them to the fact that a far greater danger facing the very existence of the country was not from foreigners or the Pope, but from native-born Whites in the country (especially in the South), and their insistence on maintaining slavery. In the election of 1860 Abraham Lincoln prevailed over candidates put forth by both the Know Nothings and the Democrats. Lincoln won, and the Know Nothings ceased to be a potent force, with the Civil War about to rock the country. Their anti-Catholic and anti-immigration positions would find their second coming or resurrection later in their successor, the Ku Klux Klan.

Qualitative Restrictionism

The U.S. immigration system largely operates on a policy of "admission by exclusion." The focus in laws is not on who may come, but who may not, or should not even bother to apply for permission to come. The policy of excluding groups and entire categories of individuals appears to have started with the Act of March 3, 1875 (18 Stat. 477), which forbade the entry of criminals and prostitutes. Section 5 of the legislation states:

> That it shall be unlawful for aliens of the following classes to immigrate into the United States, namely, persons who are undergoing a sentence for conviction in their own country for felonious crimes other than political or growing out of or the result of such political offenses, or whose sentence has been remitted on condition of their emigration, and women 'imported for the purposes of prostitution.' Every vessel arriving in the United States may be inspected under the direction of the collector of the port at which it arrives, if he shall have reason to believe that any such obnoxious persons are on board; and the officer making such inspection shall certify the result thereof to the master or other person in charge of such vessel, designating in such certificate the person or persons, if any there be, ascertained by him to be of either of the classes whose importation is hereby forbidden. When such inspection is required by the collector as aforesaid, it shall be unlawful, without his permission, for any alien to leave any such vessel arriving in the United States from a foreign country until the inspection shall have been had and the result certified as herein provided; and at no time thereafter shall any alien certified to by the inspecting officer as being of either of the classes whose immigration is forbidden by this section, be allowed to land in the United States, except in obedience to a judicial process issued pursuant to law.

The list of excludable categories was soon to grow. On May 6, 1882, Congress passed a series of statutes that came to be known as the *Chinese Exclusion Act* (22 Stat. 58). The movement to exclude Chinese (specifically Chinese laborers) was a gradual process that started on the Western seaboard of the United States, notably in California, through a strange intersection of racial hatred, economic competition, and political opportunism. Chinese workers had been invited to work on railroad construction by the Central Pacific Rail Company as early as 1865, and they were viewed as hard working, dependable, able to live cheaply, and accept lower wages than comparable White workers. In 1865 there were about 50,000 Chinese in California, predominantly male and young, and the state even acknowledged benefitting from the estimated $14 million that they spent annually in the form of taxes, fees, and other charges (Hing, 2004, p. 29). Initial positive sentiments soon turned to resentment as Whites, mainly Irish immigrants, began to view the Chinese as labor market competitors and threats, especially regarding their ability to work for lower wages. The depression that hit the United States in the 1870s did not help in this regard because many Whites (Irish immigrants) in California began scapegoating the Chinese for the economic precariousness brought about by the depression. The Irish (through their Workingmen's Party), along with local politicians who saw opportunities to advance careers, engaged in a series of actions that eventually led to a referendum on excluding Chinese from California and amending the state constitution to bar Chinese from many areas of economic and social life. It is a rather unfortunate paradox in human social behavior that a group that once experienced persecution, upon gaining freedom or some advantage often resorts to persecuting some other vulnerable group. The Irish had been subjected to harassment and violence by the Know Nothings on the Eastern seaboard; they had been objects of xenophobia and hate because of their religion and their perceived poverty. With the demise of their former persecutors, the Know Nothings, the once persecuted and deprived Irish were doing to the Chinese what the Know Nothings had once done to them. What a turn of events. In any case, the referendum to bar Chinese from various offices of government passed by a majority, with 154,638 favoring exclusion and 883 opposing the measure (Hutchinson, 1981, p. 75). The state constitution was revised accordingly, and Article 19 concentrated almost entirely on a new reality for Chinese workers. Note the rather insulting language in nearly every section.

CONSTITUTION OF THE STATE OF CALIFORNIA ARTICLE XIX CHINESE

(Repealed November 4, 1952)

SECTION 1. The Legislature shall prescribe all necessary regulations for the protection of the State, and the counties, cities, and towns thereof, from the burdens and evils arising from the presence of aliens who are or may become vagrants, paupers, mendicants, criminals, or invalids afflicted with contagious or infectious diseases, and from aliens otherwise dangerous or detrimental to the well-being or peace of the State, and to impose conditions upon which persons may reside in the State, and to provide the means and mode of their removal from the State, upon failure or refusal to comply with such conditions; provided, that nothing contained in this section shall be construed to impair or limit the power of the Legislature to pass such police laws or other regulations as it may deem necessary.

SECTION 2. No corporation now existing or hereafter formed under the laws of this State, shall, after the adoption of this Constitution, employ directly or indirectly, in any capacity, any Chinese or Mongolian. The Legislature shall pass such laws as may be necessary to enforce this provision.

SECTION 3. No Chinese shall be employed on any State, county, municipal, or other public work, except in punishment for crime.

SECTION 4. The presence of foreigners ineligible to become citizens of the United States is declared to be dangerous to the well-being of the State, and the Legislature shall discourage their immigration by all the means within its power. Asiatic coolieism is a form of human slavery, and is forever prohibited in this State, and all contracts for coolie labor shall be void. All companies or corporations, whether formed in this country or any foreign country, for the importation of such labor, shall be subject to such penalties as the Legislature may prescribe. The Legislature shall delegate all necessary power to the incorporated cities and towns of this State for the removal of Chinese without the limits of such cities and towns, or for their location within prescribed portions of those limits, and it shall also provide the necessary legislation to prohibit the introduction into this State of Chinese after the adoption of this Constitution. This section shall be enforced by appropriate legislation.

Source: State of California (1879).

Soon after passage of the exclusion referendum in California, congressional representatives from the state and neighboring ones on the West Coast began to lobby Congress to do for the country what state legislators had done for California, that is, push for national exclusion. It would be a mistake, however, to cast all blame for federal exclusion of Chinese on the state of California or even on purely economic motives with regard to protecting domestic workers. Congressional representatives and even governors from states including Washington, Oregon, and Nevada had all pushed for some sort of Chinese exclusion (Hutchinson, 1981, p. 72). Furthermore, the historical records show that even before California acted, politicians on both sides (Republicans and Democrats) and from regions outside the west were using Chinese immigration as a political issue to gain votes. In the election of 1876 the Republican Party platform stated, in a clear reference to Chinese immigrants, that "It is the immediate duty of congress fully to investigate the effects of the immigration and importation of Mongolians on the moral and material interests of the country" (Republican Party Platform, 1876). The Democratic Party's platform in that same election was just as unforgiving, if not more pernicious, for it urged reform of the Burlingame Treaty that the United States had signed in 1868 respecting the rights of free Chinese immigration by blaming Republicans for the treaty:

> Reform is necessary to correct the omissions of a Republican Congress and the errors of our treaties and our diplomacy, which has ... exposed our brethren of the Pacific coast to the incursions of a race not sprung from the same great parent stock, and in fact now by law denied citizenship through naturalization as being unaccustomed to the traditions of a progressive civilization, one exercised in liberty under equal laws; and we denounce the policy which thus discards the liberty-loving German and tolerates the revival of the coolie-trade in Mongolian women for immoral purposes, and Mongolian men held to perform servile labor contracts, and demand such modification of the treaty with the Chinese Empire, or such legislation within constitutional limitations, as shall prevent further importation or immigration of the Mongolian race (*Democratic Party Platform, 1876*).

No party had clean hands in the dirty deed; politicians at the national level from both the right and the left (Republicans and Democrats) manipulated Chinese immigration to gain votes or promote other agenda (Gyory, 1998). Soon after California voted for exclusion, Congress started on a path that would lead to restriction of Chinese immigration. On February 22, 1879, it passed the *15 Passenger Act* (of 1879) that limited to 15 the number of Chinese passengers on any vessel bound for American ports—a move clearly meant to limit Chinese immigration, and which was in violation of the free movement provisions in the 1868 Burlingame Treaty. In the run-up to federal exclusion, petitions to restrict or ban Chinese immigration had come in from states such as Alabama, Indiana, Iowa, Maryland, Massachusetts, Minnesota, Missouri, New York, Ohio, Pennsylvania, West Virginia, and Wisconsin. None of these states had been affected by the presence of Chinese people. More strangely, even a church group, the Methodist Church, had joined the list of civic organizations calling for restrictions on Chinese immigration (Hutchinson, 1981, p. 81). Why would a religious organization be calling for the exclusion of a race of humans? The full text of federal exclusion act is shown here. Note the focus on Chinese laborers (both skilled and unskilled). Although diplomats, students, and visitors were exempt, Chinese immigration declined shortly after its passage.

CHINESE EXCLUSION ACT: MAY 6, 1882

An Act to Execute Certain Treaty Stipulations Relating to Chinese

Whereas, in the opinion of the Government of the United States the coming of Chinese laborers to this country endangers the good order of certain localities within the territory thereof: Therefore,

Be it enacted by the Senate and House of Representatives of the United States of America in Congress assembled, That from and after the expiration of ninety days next after the passage of this act, and until the expiration of ten years next after the passage of this act, the coming of Chinese laborers to the United States be, and the same is hereby, suspended; and during such suspension it shall not be lawful for any Chinese laborer to come, or having so come after the expiration of said ninety days, to remain within the United States.

SEC. 2. That the master of any vessel who shall knowingly bring within the United States on such vessel, and land or permit to be landed, any Chinese laborer, from any foreign port or place, shall be deemed guilty of a misdemeanor, and on conviction thereof shall be punished by a fine of not more than $500 for each and every such Chinese laborer so brought, and may be also imprisoned for a term not exceeding one year.

SEC. 3. That the two foregoing sections shall not apply to Chinese laborers who were in the United States on the 17th day of November, 1880, or who shall have come into the same before the expiration of ninety days next after the passage of this act.

SEC. 4. That for the purpose of properly identifying Chinese laborers who were in the United States on the 17th day of November, 1880, or who shall have come into the same before the expiration of ninety days next after the passage of this act, and in order to furnish them with the proper evidence of their right to go from and come to the United States of their free will and accord, as provided by the treaty between the United States and China dated November 17, 1880, the collector of customs of the district from which any such Chinese laborer shall depart from the United States shall, in person or by deputy, go on board each vessel having on board any such Chinese laborer and cleared or about to sail from his district for a foreign port, and on such vessel make a list of all such Chinese laborers, which shall be entered in registry-books to be kept for that purpose, in which shall be stated the name, age, occupation, last place of residence, physical marks or peculiarities, and all facts necessary for the identification of each of such Chinese laborers, which books shall be safely kept in the custom-house; and every such Chinese laborer so departing from the United States shall be entitled to, and shall receive, free of any charge or cost upon application therefor, from the collector or his deputy, at the time such list is taken a certificate, signed by the collector or his deputy and attested by his seal of office, in such form as the Secretary of the Treasury shall prescribe, which certificate shall contain a statement of the name, age, occupation, last place of residence, personal description, and facts of identification of the Chinese laborer to whom the certificate is issued, corresponding with the said list and registry in all particulars.

SEC. 5. That any Chinese laborer mentioned in section four of this act being in the United States, and desiring to depart from the United States by land, shall have the right to demand and receive, free of charge or cost, a certificate of identification similar to that provided for in section four of this act to be issued to such Chinese laborers as may desire to leave the United States by water; and it is hereby made the duty of the collector of customs of the district next adjoining the foreign country to which said Chinese laborer desires to go to issue such certificate, free of charge or cost, upon application by such Chinese laborer, and to enter the same upon registry-books to be kept by him for the purpose, as provided for in section four of this act.

SEC. 6. That in order to the faithful execution of articles one and two of the treaty in this act before mentioned, every Chinese person other than a laborer who may be entitled by said treaty and this act to come within the United States, and who shall be about to come to the United States, shall be identified as so entitled by the Chinese Government in each case, such identity to be evidenced by a certificate issued under the authority of said government, which certificate shall be in the English language or (if not in the English language) accompanied by a translation into English, stating such right to come, and which certificate shall state the name, title, or official rank, if any, the age, height, and all physical peculiarities, former and present occupation or profession, and place of residence in China of the person to whom the certificate is issued and that such person is entitled conformably to the treaty in this act mentioned to come within the United States.

SEC. 7. That any person who shall knowingly and falsely alter or substitute any name for the name written in such certificate or forge any such certificate, or knowingly utter any forged or fraudulent certificate, or falsely personate any person named in any such certificate, shall be deemed guilty of a misdemeanor; and upon conviction thereof shall be fined in a sum not exceeding $1,000, and imprisoned in a penitentiary for a term of not more than five years.

SEC. 8. That the master of any vessel arriving in the United States from any foreign port or place shall, at the same time he delivers a manifest of the cargo, and if there be no cargo, then at the time of making a report, of the entry of the vessel pursuant to law, in addition to the other matter required to be reported, and before landing, or permitting to land, any Chinese passengers, deliver and report to the collector of customs of the district in which such vessels shall have arrived a separate list of all Chinese passengers taken on board his vessel at any foreign port or place, and all such passengers on board the vessel at that time.

SEC. 9. That before any Chinese passengers are landed from any such vessel, the collector, or his deputy, shall proceed to examine such passengers, comparing the certificates with the list and with the passengers; and no passenger shall be allowed to land in the United States from such vessel in violation of law.

SEC. 11. That any person who shall knowingly bring into or cause to be brought into the United States by land, or who shall knowingly aid or abet the same, or aid or abet the landing in the United States from any vessel of any Chinese person not lawfully entitled to enter the United states, shall be deemed guilty of a misdemeanor, and shall, on conviction thereof, be fined in a sum not exceeding $1,000, and imprisoned for a term not exceeding one year.

SEC. 12. That no Chinese person shall be permitted to enter the United States by land without producing to the proper officer of customs the certificate in this act required of Chinese persons seeking to land from a vessel.

SEC. 13. That this act shall not apply to diplomatic and other officers of the Chinese Government traveling upon the business of that government, whose credentials shall be taken as equivalent to the certificate in this act mentioned, and shall exempt them and their body and household servants from the provisions of this act as to other Chinese persons.

SEC. 14. That hereafter no State court or court of the United States shall admit Chinese to citizenship; and all laws in conflict with this act are hereby repealed.

SEC. 15. That the words "Chinese laborers," wherever used in this act, shall be construed to mean both skilled and unskilled laborers and Chinese employed in mining.

Approved, May 6, 1882.

Source: U.S. Congress (1882a; 1882b). Statutes at Large. 22 Stat. 58.

The Chinese Exclusion Act was not a total ban on Chinese immigrants entering the United States; it was initially aimed at Chinese laborers. For example, students could come, along with visitors or others wanting to come, in the language of the Act, for "curiosity." Chinese already in the United States could travel and return provided they showed some certificate to consular officials in China. It was repeatedly reauthorized each time it neared expiration until 1943 when it was repealed. There are debates as to why it was repealed. Perhaps some believe that America made a mistake, or that it had suddenly realized a great friend in the people of China. A more honest reason for the repeal of the Exclusion Act was wartime expediency. The United States had been attacked by armed forces of the Japanese Imperial Government at Pearl Harbor, Hawaii, in 1941, a move that brought America into war with the Axis Powers (Germany, Italy, and Japan). In the Pacific theater, the war was ferocious, and at one point, U.S. forces had had to leave their colonial possession, the Philippines, in view of the Japanese onslaught. Problems arose as to how the U.S. Air Force would prosecute the war, given the takeover of key U.S. bases in Asia, including the Philippines. U.S. aircraft on bombing raids over Japan were unable to return to refueling stations on aircraft carriers or land bases in the United States (or even Guam). Recognition of this difficulty forced the United States to change its immigration policy regarding China since it wanted to use Chinese air fields to refuel American aircraft. This strategic wartime necessity, more than anything else, most likely influenced change in U.S. immigration policy, for how else would the United States have approached Chiang Kai-Shek's Kuomintang (Nationalist) government diplomatically for use of military bases with the infamous Exclusion Act still in force? It was also recognized by U.S. policy makers that the enemy (Japan) might use the Exclusion Act as propaganda to prevent or undermine any American-Chinese alliance against Japan for the duration of World War II.

The Exclusion Act was a turning point in U.S. immigration history and policy because it set a very dangerous precedent in excluding newcomers due to race. It would be emulated in varying ways to pass laws that came dangerously close to barring groups due to their race/ethnicity. At times, groups were mentioned by name. For instance, in the 63rd Congress (1913–1915), the Senate passed a bill excluding "all members of the African or black race." This African or Black exclusion bill (of January 2, 1915) would have become law had it not been vetoed by President Wilson (Hutchinson, 1981, p. 163). The veto was not due to attempts at African exclusion, but the literacy test requirement in the bill, along with its denial of political asylum. This was not the first time members of Congress had tried to add Blacks (whether from Africa or the Caribbean) to their excludable categories. At other times, groups were targeted for exclusion without mentioning them by name, as occurred in the National Origins Acts of 1921 and 1924. Congress recognized the ethnically prejudiced origins of the Exclusion Act in its June 18, 2012, resolution (H. Res. 683) expressing regret over its passage: "That the House of Representatives regrets the passage of legislation that adversely affected people of Chinese origin in the United States because of their ethnicity" (U.S. Congress, 2012).

After passage of the Chinese Exclusion Act of May 6, 1882 (22 Stat. 58), it was clear that the United States had entered into a new phase of restrictionism, but it was still based on qualitative, not numeric, control. The list of excludable categories expanded, never to decrease. A major step in that direction was passage of the Immigration Act of March 3, 1891. It was the first comprehensive law aimed at placing federal control of immigration.

The 1891 Immigration Act created the Office of the Superintendent of Immigration in the Treasury Department. The superintendent oversaw a new corps of immigrant inspectors stationed at the country's principal ports of entry. During its first decade, the Immigration Service formalized basic immigration procedures. The service began collecting arrival manifests (also frequently called passenger lists or immigration arrival records) from each incoming ship, a former duty of customs officials since 1820. Inspectors then questioned arrivals about their admissibility and noted their admission or rejection on the manifest records.

Starting in 1893, inspectors also served on boards of special inquiry that closely reviewed each exclusion case. A congressional act of March 2, 1895, renamed the Office of Immigration as the Bureau of Immigration, and changed the title of superintendent of immigration to commissioner-general of immigration. Congress added to its list of excludables, which now included those most likely to become public charges, persons suffering from certain contagious diseases, persons convicted of felonious offenses in their home countries, those convicted of other crimes or misdemeanors, polygamists, and aliens assisted by others in payment of passage. The act prohibited the encouragement of immigration through advertisements. The ban on polygamists was an apparent reference to Brigham Young and his followers in Utah. It may have also been directed at Muslims of the Ottoman Empire (Abrams, 2005).

A later congressional act of June 6, 1900, consolidated immigration enforcement by assigning enforcement of both alien contract labor laws and Chinese exclusion laws to the commissioner-general. In 1903, the Bureau of Immigration moved from the Treasury Department to the newly created Department of Commerce and Labor. A fund created from collection of immigrants' head tax (initially set at 50 cents) financed the Immigration Service until 1909, when Congress replaced the fund with an annual appropriation. It was also in 1903 that Congress set a new precedent in the Act of March 3, 1903 (32 Stat. 1213). It added to the list of excludables—and in so doing, for the first time aliens were to be inadmissible for proscribed political opinion. It specified that "Anarchists, or persons who believe in, or advocate, the overthrow by force or violence the government of the United States, or of all government, or of all forms of law, or the assassination of public officials" were inadmissible. The assassination of President William McKinley in 1901 in Buffalo, New York, by avowed anarchist Leon Czolgosz played some role in Congress adding anarchists to the expanding list of excludables (www.history.com, 2016). Major immigration legislation was the Act of February 20, 1907 (34 Stat. 898). It consolidated earlier immigration laws and for the first time, aliens coming to the United States would be classified as immigrant or nonimmigrant on the basis of their intention for temporary or permanent stays. It increased the immigrant head tax to $4. To the excludable classes were now added imbeciles, feeble-minded persons, those with physical or mental defects that may affect their ability to earn a living, persons with tuberculosis, children not accompanied by their parents, individuals who had committed crimes due to moral turpitude, and women coming to the United States for immoral purposes. In earlier immigration laws, and even subsequent ones later, Congress seemed to be rather preoccupied with sex, and thus, excluding persons or groups coming for "lewd or immoral purposes," "prostitution," "polygamy," "women coming for immoral acts," or "sexual deviates." It is unclear the reason for this rather bizarre preoccupation with immigrant sexual behavior; perhaps it had to do with the "Puritan" origins of the country's early founders, or whether there was a belief that some perfect country comprising perfect humans could be created on Earth and in North America.

In 1913, the Bureau of Immigration and Naturalization split into the Bureau of Immigration and the Bureau of Naturalization. The two bureaus coexisted separately within the new U.S. Department of Labor until reunited as the Immigration and Naturalization Service (INS) by executive order on June 10, 1933. In 1940, Presidential Reorganization Plan No. V moved the Immigration and Naturalization Service from the Department of Labor to the Department of Justice. There it would stay until the attacks of September 11, 2001 when, in the aftermath, Congress passed new legislation disbanding INS and consolidating previous immigration enforcement and administration to the newly created Department of Homeland Security (U.S. Department of Homeland Security 2016).

REFERENCES

Abrams, Kerry (2005). Polygamy, prostitution, and the federalization of immigration law. *Columbia Law Review 105*(3):641–716.

Baillargeon, A. O. (1950). *Father John Bapst and the Know-Nothing movement in Maine.* (Master's thesis, Ottawa University). Available at https://www.ruor.uottawa.ca/bitstream/10393/21764/1/EC55330.PDF. Retrieved November 15, 2015.

Billington, R. A. (1938/1952). *The Protestant crusade, 1800 to 1860: A study of the origins of American nativism.* New York, NY: Rinehart.

Democratic Party Platforms (1876). Democratic Party platform of 1876, June 22, 1876. Online by Gerhard Peters and John T. Woolley, *The American Presidency Project.* http://www.presidency.ucsb.edu/ws/?pid=29581. Retrieved March 4, 2016.

Daniels, R. (2002). *Coming to America: A history of immigration and ethnicity in early American life.* New York, NY: Perennial.

Daniels, R. (2004). *Guarding the golden door: American immigration policy and immigrants since 1882* New York, NY: Hill and Wang.

Gyory, A. (1998). *Closing the gate: Race, politics, and the Chinese exclusion act.* Raleigh: University of North Carolina Press.

Higham, J. (1988). *Strangers in the land: Patterns of American nativism, 1860 to 1925* (2nd ed.). New Brunswick, NJ: Rutgers University Press.

Hing, B. O. (2004). *Defining America through immigration policy.* Philadelphia, PA: Temple University Press.

Hutchinson, E. P. (1981). *Legislative history of American immigration policy, 1798–1965.* Philadelphia: University of Pennsylvania Press.

Morse, S. F. B. (1835). *Foreign conspiracy against the liberties of the United States.* New York, NY: Leavitt, Lord.

Overdyke, W. D. (1950). *The Know-Nothing party in the South.* Binghamton, NY: Louisiana State University Press.

Republican Party Platforms (1876). Republican Party Platform of 1876, June 14, 1876. Online by Gerhard Peters and John T. Woolley, *The American Presidency Project.* http://www.presidency.ucsb.edu/ws/?pid=29624. Retrieved March 4, 2016.

State of California (1879). *Constitution of the state of California.* http://archives.cdn.sos.ca.gov/collections/1879/archive/1879-constitution.pdf. Retrieved February 15, 2016.

U.S. Congress (1875). *The act of March 3, 1875 (18 Stat. 477) statutes-at-large of the United States.* Available at http://www.constitution.org/uslaw/sal/018_statutes_at_large.pdf. Retrieved February 14, 2016.

U.S. Congress (1882a) *The act of May 6, 1882 (22 Stat. 58) statutes-at-large of the United States.* Available at http://www.loc.gov/law/help/statutes-at-large/47th-congress/session-1/c47s1ch126.pdf. Retrieved February 15, 2016.

U.S. Congress (1882b). Chinese Exclusion Act. Available at http://avalon.law.yale.edu/19th_century/chinese_exclusion_act.asp. New Haven, CT: Lillian Goldman Law Library. Retrieved February 22, 2016.

U.S. Congress (2012) Congressional Bills 112th Cong. [H. Res. 683 Engrossed in House (EH)] H. Res. 683. Washington, DC: Government Printing Office. Available at https://www.gpo.gov/fdsys/pkg/BILLS-112hres683eh/html/BILLS-112hres683eh.htm

U.S. Department of Homeland Security (2016). *Immigration inspection expands.* Available at http://www.cbp.gov/about/history/1891-imigration-inspection-expands. Retrieved March 5, 2016.

U.S. Immigration and Naturalization Service (2002). *2000 statistical yearbook of the immigration and naturalization service.* Washington, DC: U.S. Government Printing Office, 2002. Available at http://www.dhs.gov/publication/2000-statistical-yearbook. Retrieved February 14, 2016.

Www.history.com (2016). *President McKinley is shot.* Available at http://www.history.com/this-day-in-history/president-william-mckinley-is-shot. Retrieved March 5, 2016.

6

U.S. Immigration, Eugenics, and the Progressive Era

B y the beginning of the 20th century, immigration, which had largely been unregulated at the founding of the United States, had undergone transformation. It was now being highly regulated, and qualitative controls had begun to be implemented in the sense that immigrants could be excluded based on various grounds. The start of the 20th century was to usher in not only continuing control of entrants, but also an era of very restrictive policies both qualitatively and quantitatively. In this chapter, we examine reasons behind this new form of restrictionism and nativism, precedents set, and their lasting implications for U.S. immigration.

To determine social factors that led to increasingly more immigration restriction, it is important not to overlook results of the population census and the change in the source countries. The 1890s had witnessed massive immigration influx. Between 1820 and 1860, 95% of new immigrants to the United States came from northwestern Europe. In the era of the Great Migration (1861–1900), 68% of new entrants were from northwestern Europe, a major drop from the decade earlier. During the same period, (1861–1900), 33% of immigrants were from southern and eastern Europe (U.S. Department of Homeland Security, 2006). In fact, in the 1900 to 1920 decade, the percentage of new arrivals from southern and eastern Europe (44%) exceeded the percentage of immigrants from northern and western Europe (41%). Such statistics these did not go unnoticed by those who had somehow assumed that the immigrant stock already in the country should remain composed of western and northern Europeans.

As shown in Table 6.1, immigration had been rising considerably in the United States as steamships got bigger and competition increased. Other factors contributing to rather rapid increases in immigration included poverty in Europe, rapid industrialization in the United States, which created more economic opportunities to attract foreigners, and much-improved communication, including mail and telegraph. While 9.7% of the 1850 U.S. population was foreign-born, by 1910, 14.7% was foreign-born (Batchelor, 2004). A look at Table 6.1 shows that the number for the 1901–1910 decade was especially high, and appears to have sounded an alarm to would-be restrictionists.

TABLE 6.1: Immigration to the United States, Fiscal Years, 1881–1920

Decade	1881–1890	1891–1900	1901–1910	1911–1920
All countries	5,246,613	3,687,564	8,795,386	5,735,811

Source: U.S. Department of Homeland Security (2006). *2004 Yearbook of Immigration Statistics,* Table 2.

Although immigration had been rising ever since 1820, it had largely come from traditional favorite sources: United Kingdom, Scandinavia, Germany, and later Ireland. The decennial population census was showing that immigrant stock from western and northern Europe could be superseded by the rising wave from southern and eastern Europe. As far as descendants of the Anglo-Saxons were considered, people from these regions (southern and eastern Europe) were not true White, but belonged to some inferior (Slavic) race, the type Benjamin Franklin had once described as having a "swarthy" complexion. A look at Table 6.2 illustrates just what frightened descendants of western European immigrants. Note that in 1851–1860, less than 1% of immigrants came from southern and eastern Europe and immigrant streams were dominated by those from western Europe. The number of immigrants from eastern Europe gradually rose and in 1891–1900, it surpassed entrants from traditional source countries for the first time. The disparity in source countries continued to widen, and this was one reason why restrictionist movements began to arise in the early part of the 20th century to urge congressional action. Unlike the qualitative regimes that existed previously, the move to combat immigration of "undesirable" races became a full-blown effort that eventually led to numerical restrictions for the first time in American history.

TABLE 6.2: Immigration by Region of Last Residence, 1851 to 1920

Decade	Total immigration	From northern/ western Europe (%)	From southern/ eastern Europe (%)
1851–1860	2,598,824	93.6	0.8
1861–1870	2,314,824	87.8	1.4
1881–1890	5,246,613	72.0	18.3
1891–1900	3,687,564	44.6	51.9
1901–1910	8,795,386	21.7	70.8
1911–1920	5,735,811	17.4	58.9

Source: U.S. Department of Homeland Security (2006). *2004 Yearbook of Immigration Statistics,* Table 2. (Percent calculations by author.)

In addition to immigration statistics, the 1890 census provided evidence showing the "racial" composition of the U.S. population was changing. The percentage of the population that could trace their origins to northern and western Europe had declined, while that from other regions was on the increase. The term "race" in this period was not limited to African American, White, Asian, or familiar configurations today; Slavic people and Jews were considered races, though "White" in appearance, they were of lower level. Race was also not a social construction as many sociologists argue today; it was believed to be real and had basis in biology and genes. Perception of a hierarchy within the White race had been developed by Madison Grant in his book, *The Passing of the Great Race*, published in 1916. Within the White race, those at the top of the hierarchy were Nordics; below them were Alpines, and at the bottom were Mediterranean. The Nordics were, of course, the superior race. According to Grant, the United States had been founded by Nordics (those from northern and western Europe, including, predictably, British and Scandinavians) and the country should be preserved for them and their posterity. Although largely ignored by scholars of race, it is relatively easy to see the early beginnings of presumed Nordic superiority and "master race" arguments in the writings of Grant, a theme that would later be developed in more detail by Adolf Hitler in his *Mein Kampf*, published in 1925; the Nazi leader, who had knowledge of what was taking place on the racial purification scene in America, only had to replace Nordic with Aryan. A logical outgrowth of Grant's Nordic race superiority arguments, along with those of other leading racists of the period, was that immigrants outside the Nordic race were inferior, and there should be no race mixing. The highest quality Americans (Nordics) should not intermix with lower White races (especially Jews) that were now immigrating in large numbers, as intermixing would bring about mongrelization, a process that would contaminate and lead to the destruction of the superior race. Grant's position on immigrants and the danger of race mixing is aptly summarized by Higham (1955): "In the early days, the American population was purely Nordic, but now the swarms of Alpine, Mediterranean, and Jewish hybrids threaten to extinguish the old stock unless it reasserts its class and racial pride by shutting them out" (p. 157). The racial ideology of the day was given boost by a burgeoning eugenics movement with its quest for racial purification. We turn next to this sordid, but relatively hidden, aspect of American history, and how it influenced changes in U.S. immigration policy for a very long time.

The Eugenics Movement and Immigration

The origin of the eugenics concept is usually traced to Francis Galton, an English intellectual who lived from 1822 to 1911. Galton had been interested in the characteristics of England's upper-class members (what made them be in the upper class). Among his conclusions was that they had superior intelligence, but ignoring environmental factors, Galton made a leap that the alleged superior intelligence of his upper-class subjects was inherited genetically. Accordingly, the intelligence and what he perceived as other positive characteristics of that group could be passed on through generations (Norgard, 2008). He called for a selective breeding program for humans to presumably increase the "positive" gene pool, arguing it would be quite practicable to produce a highly gifted race of men by judicious marriages during several consecutive generations just as it was possible to obtain by careful selection a permanent breed of dogs or horses gifted with peculiar powers of running, or of doing anything else (Galton, 1869).

Potentially troubling as Galton's ideas were, they would soon find fertile ground in the United States, a land where it was, and perhaps still is, relatively easy to spread any theory alleging the superiority of one group and the inferiority of others. The vehicle by which Galton's arguments were brought to the United States was Charles Davenport, a biologist, and in 1910, he founded the Eugenics Record Office (ERO) at Cold Spring Harbor Laboratory on Long Island with the expressed objective of improving the natural, physical, mental, and temperamental qualities of the human family (Norrgard, 2008). Davenport and colleagues at the Eugenics Record Office focused on finding data to prove the inheritability of physical, mental, and moral traits. As Bouche and Rivard (2014) observe, "They were particularly interested in the inheritance of 'undesirable' traits, such as pauperism, mental disability, dwarfism, promiscuity, and criminality." They wanted laws to target the sterilization of the "socially inadequate"—those supported in institutions or maintained wholly or in part at public expense. Such a law would encompass the "feebleminded, insane, criminalistic, epileptic, inebriate, diseased, blind, deaf; deformed; and dependent" including "orphans, never-do-wells, tramps, the homeless and paupers" (Lombardo, 2008, 2016).

Later, as various U.S. state legislatures and many U.S. academics from prestigious universities (including the University of California, Chicago, Harvard, Columbia, Cornell, Stanford, Northwestern, New York, et al.) embraced eugenics, and as grant funding became readily available to teach and study this "new" area through the Rockefeller Foundation, the inheritability list expanded to include imbecility, feeblemindedness, and being a moron. Soon, courses in eugenics were taught at 376 U.S. universities and colleges. Eugenics courses were covered in disciplines in the social sciences (for example, sociology at the University of California at Berkeley and New York University), biological sciences (for example, biology at Bates College, Maine), or as stand-alone courses in places such as Northwestern University, Princeton, and numerous other schools. From 1914 to 1924 eugenics courses were reaching nearly 20,000 students annually (Black, 2012, p. 75). Psychologists, ever eager to develop tests for measuring even the most dubious of concepts, were in the forefront of eugenics movement in their quest for creating tests aimed at measuring people's "intelligence" and thus coming with some number below which individuals could be classified as "morons," "imbeciles," or "idiots." Tests such as Intelligence Quotient (IQ) and later Scholastic Aptitude Test (SAT)—still widely used today, though perhaps with modifications—both owe their origins to psychologists with strong belief in eugenics and the racial superiority of Nordics (Black, 2012, p. 82). Kaelber (2012) has described American eugenics in the following words:

> American eugenics refers inter alia to compulsory sterilization laws adopted by over 30 states that led to more than 60,000 sterilizations of disabled individuals. Many of these individuals were sterilized because of a disability: they were mentally disabled or ill,

or belonged to socially disadvantaged groups living on the margins of society. American eugenic laws and practices implemented in the first decades of the twentieth century influenced the much larger National Socialist compulsory sterilization program, which between 1934 and 1945 led to approximately 350,000 compulsory sterilizations and was a stepping stone to the Holocaust (*Kaelber, 2012, p. 1*).

The National Socialist program alluded to by Kaelber was the Nazi program in Germany, which took its model from the United States. For how else to explain Hitler's remarks in *Mein Kampf* (1925, p. 439–440) that "There is today one state in which at least weak beginnings toward a better conception are noticeable. Of course, it is not our model German Republic, but the American Union, in which an effort is made to consult reason at least partially. By refusing immigration on principle to elements in poor health, by simply excluding certain races from naturalization, it professes in slow beginnings a view which is peculiar to the folkish state concept." History is full of very uncomfortable truths but pretending that terrible events never occurred in one's country, and failing to acknowledge them, does a great disservice for the advancement of knowledge and truth. The Germans probably would have gone ahead with their own sterilization programs without the Americans' full throttle ahead with some pseudo-scientific racial purification agenda, but to hear the Nazi leader profess as strange the exclusion of races from naturalization (which the National Origins laws effectively did in the 1920s) was somber, especially for revisionists in history who point to Nazi behavior as some unique aberration that all began and ended in some faraway European country called Germany. Thus, even after the details of the Nazi sterilization program and the horrors of the Hitler regime became more widely known after the war, sterilizations in some American states did not stop; some states continued to sterilize residents well into the 1970s, and as noted previously, Oregon would not cease until 1981.

The main goal of eugenicists in the United States was to uplift the White race and maintain White racial purity. Thus, individuals deemed to belong to inferior races were not allowed to immigrate, and those already in the land who were considered inferior, imbecile, feebleminded, idiots, morons, epileptics, or otherwise unfit were to be prevented from having children through forced state sterilizations. Eugenics in America (and in Nazi Germany later) was a war on the weak in search of the fittest, a master race. The idea of public gas chambers was discussed by some as a way to eliminate the unfit, but the several states that passed eugenics laws (at least 30 of them) settled for a more cost-effective method—sterilization of both men and women deemed to be deficient, largely to ensure that the weakest members of society, including the poor and disabled, would not be allowed to propagate more of their own.

Many women, and feminists in particular, were loud cheerleaders of eugenics, and in the South, especially, they lobbied actively for eugenics laws. Many feminists supported the eugenics cause, including Margaret Sanger, the birth control crusader who gave a lecture at Vassar College about the urgency of reducing what she described as the growing multiplication of the unfit and undesirable (Cohen, 2016, p. 57).

The impetus for the eugenics movement in the United States in the 1920s was collective anxiety and fear among white Anglo-Saxon Protestant middle- and upper-class Americans that the nation—their country—was changing in racial, ethnic, and even religious composition because of rising immigration (Cohen, 2016). The eugenics movement provided two solutions to the racial problem: to restrict immigration, so that no more "defective" races entered; and to take care of those already in the United States deemed unfit by making sure that they did not procreate. In terms of restricting immigration, targets included Italians, Jews, Asians, and other "inferior" races that could pose a threat to Anglo-Saxon White racial purity. Eugenicists, aided and abetted by biologists, psychologists, anthropologists, physicians, lawyers, and academics in general, argued that groups marked for exclusion from the United States had extraordinarily high levels of physical and mental hereditary defects that were degrading the U.S. Anglo-Saxon gene pool. It was suggested, for instance, through questionable "intelligence" testing, that between 40% and 50% of Jewish immigrants entering the country through Ellis Island were mentally defective (Cohen, 2016, p. 5).

In 1907, Indiana passed the first compulsory eugenics law in the country, and it was followed shortly by California (1909), followed in turn by others such as Alabama, Arizona, Connecticut, Delaware, Georgia, Idaho, Indiana, Iowa, Kansas, Maine, Michigan, Minnesota, Mississippi, Montana, Nebraska, New Hampshire, North Carolina, North Dakota, Oklahoma, Oregon, South Carolina, Utah, Vermont, West Virginia, and Wisconsin (Jerome Law Library, 1963). In all, at least 30 states had forced sterilization statutes after 1907.

Virginia, though cautious at first in its approach to eugenics, was to later become a notorious state for forced sterilizations, especially in Lynchburg. On March, 20, 1924, the state legislature passed the Eugenical Sterilization Act (Landman, 1932), which stipulated that people confined to state institutions "afflicted with hereditary forms of insanity that are recurrent, idiocy, imbecility, feeble-mindedness or epilepsy" could be sterilized (Landman, 1932, p. 84). The state's focus on racial purity was also evident when on March, 20, 1924, it passed the Racial Integrity Act, which made it "unlawful for any white person in [Virginia] to marry any [person] save a white person" (Lombardo, 2008, p. 100). Virginia's sterilization program appears to have been among the longest in the United States, going from 1924 until 1979, surpassed only by Oregon, which had its last forced sterilization in 1981. Despite passage of its sterilization law in 1924, no eugenicist sterilization occurred in Virginia until 1927 (Largent, 2008, p. 80). The state decided to wait until its law could be tested and upheld in court, and that occurred in 1927. According to Cohen (2016, p.1), the number of forced sterilizations of "unfit" people in Virginia between 1927 and 1979 was 7,450, while Dorr (2006, p. 382) provides a higher estimate of 8,300. Of those sterilized, 50% were judged to be "mentally ill"; the other 50% were deemed to be "mentally deficient" and women represented about 62% of total sterilizations. Many of the sterilizations occurred in the *Virginia Colony for Epileptics and Feebleminded* in Lynchburg, the hotbed of sterilizations, which may well have been described as "Sterilization City, USA" during that period for the sheer number of forced sterilizations that took place in the city. Only the "progressive" state of California appears to have outdone Virginia in its drive to achieve race betterment by preventing "defective" people from breeding.

The number of people sterilized in California between passage of its eugenics sterilization law (1909) until 1964 has been placed at 20,108 (Kaelber, 2012). California carried out the highest number of sterilizations in the country, about 30% of the national figure. The gender distribution was about equal. Of those sterilized, nearly 60% were considered mentally ill and more than 35% were considered mentally deficient. Men and women of Mexican origin represented between 7% and 8% of those sterilized (Stern, 2005, p. 111). Although African Americans comprised 1% of California's population, they accounted for 4% of the sterilizations (Stern, 2005, p. 111). Due to the sensitive nature of sterilization, many states have been reluctant to admit their eugenicist past and open their archives for scrutiny, and California is one such state. It is, therefore, important for scholars of immigration to be aware that the total known number of sterilizations may be conservative compared with the actual number (Stern, 2011, p. 97). As in most other states, eugenicists in California saw in sterilization a tool with many applications, all of which were applied to prevent the procreation of individuals with undesirable traits, including mental illness, mental retardation, physical or mental deficiencies, "promiscuity," overcrowding of state institutions, and to alleviate fiscal constraints on the state (Bruinius, 2006, p. 211).

At the national level, eugenics was a successful movement, in part because of general institutional failure or betrayal. The main institutions were medicine, academia, law, the legislative branch of the federal government, and the judiciary, including the U.S. Supreme Court, and even the executive branch of the government. Instead of being on the side of the disadvantaged, these institutions used their power against the vulnerable.

In the medical field, physicians throughout the United States played a leading role in advocating for eugenic sterilization, promoting it, and lending their expertise to the cause of the movement (Cohen, 2016). As for the Executive Branch of the federal government, some presidents were either racists, secret eugenicists, or outright supporters. Theodore Roosevelt, the nation's 26th president, who took office on September, 14, 1901, following McKinley's assassination, was an unabashed proponent of eugenics. In a letter to biologist Charles Davenport on January 3, 1913, Roosevelt expressed his views about eugenics:

> ... You say that these people are not themselves responsible, that it is "society" that is responsible. I agree with you if you mean, as I suppose you do, that society has no business to permit degenerates to reproduce their kind. It is really extraordinary that our people refuse to apply to human beings such elementary knowledge as every successful farmer is obliged to apply to his own stock breeding. Any group of farmers, who permitted their best stock not to breed, and let all the increase come from the worst stock, would be treated as fit inmates for an asylum. Yet we fail to understand that

such conduct is rational compared to the conduct of a nation which permits unlimited breeding from the worst stocks, physically and morally, while it encourages or connives at the cold selfishness or the twisted sentimentality as a result of which the men and women ought to marry, and if married have large families, remain celebates or have no children or only one or two. Some day we will realize that the prime duty the inescapable duty of the good citizen of the right type is to leave his or her blood behind him in the world; and that we have no business to permit the perpetuation of citizens of the wrong type.

Franklin D. Roosevelt, the much beloved savior of American capitalism for bringing the country out of the Great Depression, ordered the forced relocation/ evacuation/imprisonment of more than 100,000 Japanese Americans in the aftermath of the attacks on Pearl Harbor, Hawaii, in 1941; no similar provision was made for German Americans even though Germany had started World War II and German panzer divisions were marching through Europe. It is conceivable that the forced relocation of Japanese was predicated in part on racial bigotry as Roosevelt, a secret adherent of eugenics, believed in the racial inferiority of Japanese, and by extension Asians.

The U.S. Congress did its own part, which often included holding hearings at which eugenic "experts" testified, laying out the biological deficiencies of various groups by national origin, and the dangers such groups posed to the survival of the pure, unadulterated American Anglo-Saxon race, especially if they were allowed to immigrate to the United States. It was the result of congressional hearings that calls began for passage of immigration laws that set the precedent for numerical controls based on national origin.

On the whole, the judiciary, especially the Supreme Court, failed the weak, and often sided with the powerful, as it has often found itself on the wrong side of justice and history, breaking hearts and hopes. Perhaps the most cited example of such bias and failure, which revealed in retrospect the probable pro-eugenic sympathies of the courts, was the infamous ruling in *Buck v. Bell* in which the Supreme Court upheld the constitutionality of Virginia's Eugenical Sterilization Act of 1924, forcing Carrie Buck to be sterilized against her will on grounds brought by the *Virginia Colony for the Epileptic and Feeble-Minded* (representing the state) that she was feebleminded, imbecile, and sexually promiscuous—none of which were true. It was alleged that these traits ran through the family, and if Carrie gave birth (she had been raped and impregnated by a relative of her foster family, which kept this a secret to protect the family's reputation) the child would very likely be feebleminded just as Carrie and her mother, who also had been detained in the colony. Indeed, it was claimed in court that Carrie was an illegitimate child, although a marriage certificate to the contrary existed (Claude Moore Health Sciences Library, 2004). But lawyers, including Carrie's court-appointed "defense" attorney in collusion, suppressed this information. Carrie received no defense; she was effectively maligned, used, and betrayed by the state of Virginia in its effort to test whether its newly passed eugenical law would be upheld in court, thereby giving it a green light to embark on full-blown sterilization of allegedly "defective" individuals without restraint. This is exactly what occurred in 1927, and as can be seen in the following quotation, Oliver Wendell Holmes, Jr., who rendered the majority opinion, had no qualms about eugenics; he was a eugenicist himself and he opined as follows:

> We have seen more than once that the public welfare may call upon the best citizens for their lives. It would be strange if it could not call upon those who already sap the strength of the State for these lesser sacrifices, often not felt to be such by those concerned, in order to prevent our being swamped with incompetence. It is better for all the world if, instead of waiting to execute degenerate offspring for crime or to let them starve for their imbecility, society can prevent those who are manifestly unfit from continuing their kind. The principle that sustains compulsory vaccination is broad enough to cover cutting the Fallopian tubes. ... Three generations of imbeciles are enough (*U.S. Supreme Court, 1927*).

The three generations of imbeciles presumably consisted of Carrie, her mother, and Carrie's daughter, Vivian, whose first-grade reports showed her getting an "A" in deportment and earning a spot on the honor roll, hardly a child that fit the "imbecile" image invoked by Wendell Holmes. It was an 8–1 majority decision with the lone dissent coming from the only Catholic on the bench. All institutions failed the weak (the imbeciles, mentally deficient, prostitutes, morons, the disabled, and so on who were marked for sterilization)—except the Catholic Church, which opposed eugenics consistently and at every turn. Not only did the church view it as against moral law, but against natural law, for who decides which life is inferior or superior? By approving sterilizations of imbeciles, mentally deficient, prostitutes, morons, and disabled individuals, the Supreme Court aided and abetted those states that had passed laws that in effect denied the civil rights of individuals and groups concerned. Amendment XIV of the U.S. Constitution stipulates that no person shall be denied "equal protection of the laws." It is difficult to make a case that the sterilized were accorded such protection.

Laying the Foundation for Numerical Restrictions

The period covering the 1890s to the 1920s is usually described as the Progressive Era in the United States, so-called because of rapid social change, in part brought about by industrialization, unionization, social movements, social activism, and demands for elimination of corruption from politics (Caswell, 2001). Many reforms were made, including creation of the Pure Food and Drug Act, the Clayton Anti-Trust Act, the Federal Reserve Act, and the Meat Inspection Act. Passage of Amendment XVI of the Constitution in 1913 granted Congress the power to levy taxes on income, and Amendment XIX (1920) granted voting rights to women with the language: "The right of citizens of the United States to vote shall not be denied or abridged by the United States or by any State on account of sex."

Not all reforms appear progressive by today's standards. For example, it was during this "progressive" era in 1919 that Amendment XVIII was passed in language very inexplicable today. Section 1 of the amendment stated that "After one year from the ratification of this article the manufacture, sale, or transportation of intoxicating liquors within, the importation thereof into, or the exportation thereof from the United States and all territory subject to the jurisdiction thereof for beverage purposes is hereby prohibited." Although ostensibly justified at the time as an act to protect women from their "alcoholic" husbands and significant others, and to increase productivity at work, it appears that the amendment was also in reaction to the perceived "drunkenness" of immigrants entering the United States at the time. This perception doubtless was a primary reason why the Ku Klux Klan forcefully advocated for Prohibition. The amendment led to bootlegging, creation of underground bars (speakeasies), and the eventual emergence of what sociologists would characterize as organized crime. In short, Prohibition was a total failure with harmful societal consequences, teaching one lesson that was never really learned by the nation's political elites: Not all personal or social behavior that offends some group or groups should be proscribed or criminalized; individuals need not necessarily be protected from themselves by government. The country's declared and continuing war on drugs is testament of lessons never learned, for how high would the incarceration rate have to rise, and how much money have to be spent on prisons and law enforcement before corrective action is taken? To the members of the Women's Christian Temperance Movement, the Klan, and others who pushed for Prohibition and the creation of some more "orderly" (Christian) society, perhaps educational and public health efforts would have worked better in reducing the consumption of alcohol.

On the surface, despite progressive politics in this period, the United States at the end of the 19th century and the beginning of the 20th century, though prosperous, appeared to be a nation deeply divided along political, economic, and religious lines. These divisions saw the realignment of strange bedfellows opposed to immigration, the influence of the political power of the Ku Klux Klan, and the eventual passage of the restrictive immigration laws of 1921 and 1924.

On the political front, the first warning for the coming of restrictive immigration began with what became known in history as the Red Scare, a nationwide fear of Bolsheviks, communists, socialists, anarchists, and other dissidents deemed dangerous and unpatriotic, first by then Attorney General A. Mitchell Palmer and the general public after a series of bombings and labor strikes in the country from 1919 to 1920 (Burnett, 2015).

The Bolshevik Revolution engulfing Russia in 1917 led to creation of the first communist state, later to become the Union of the Soviet Socialist Republics, a development that created deep anxiety in the United States, although thousands of miles from Europe and the fact that no other European country had fallen victim to communism despite the ongoing world war. American newspapers carried sensationalistic and often false reports about Bolshevism. The U.S. press described Bolshevik (communist) rule as one under which people are slaughtered, their property confiscated, and 500 heads guillotined per hour (Stone, 2004, p. 221). The nation seemed obsessed with communism and fear of the specter of an anti-capitalist workers' revolution taking place in America. Adding fire to the anxiety, the Socialist Party in the United States saw a growth in membership by one-third between 1918 and 1919 (Stone, 2004). The party itself broke apart due to struggle over direction and goals, with the more radical wing, the Communist Labor Party, advocating the overthrow of capitalism.

Following this incident, a series of other events occurred that heightened public hysteria. About 35,000 Seattle shipyard workers went on strike for higher wages and shorter working hours. As often was the case then and now, management refused the workers' demands, and even refused to negotiate. As a result, the Seattle Central Labor Council called for a general strike (Burnett, 2001). Sensing the potential effects of the strike, the public went into panic and rushed to stock up on food, medicines, and clothing; Seattle became paralyzed. Matters were made worse by the mayor proclaiming that the strike was the vanguard of an international conspiracy to start a communist revolution in the United States. Newspapers, including the *Cleveland Plain Dealer* and the *Chicago Tribune*, warned their readers that "the Bolshevik beast had now come into the open and it was only a middling step from Petrograd to Seattle" (Stone, 2004, p. 221).

Two months following the Seattle strike, there were persistent, though unsubstantiated, rumors of bombing attempts that had been thwarted. An apparent bombing plot against the mayor of Seattle was foiled, as he bragged about having put down the strike in the city; this was apparent payback (Burnett, 2001). Bombings or rumors of bombings were everywhere. As Stone (2004, p. 221) observes, "On April 28, 1919, a bomb arrived at the office of the Seattle mayor. No one was injured, but the following day a bomb exploded at the home of a former US senator in Atlanta, injuring two people. Two days later, the post office in New York discovered thirty-four bombs in the mail. They were addressed to the Postmaster General Burleson, Justice Oliver Wendell Holmes, Senator Lee Overman, Attorney General A. Mitchell Palmer, and John D. Rockefeller, among others. This triggered a firestorm of outrage, fear, and demands for intensified security measures" (Stone, 2004, p. 221). On May Day that same year, riots broke out in several American cities, including Boston, New York, and Cleveland, as police tried to harass and suppress May Day protesters, whom they described as radicals. Historical records show that in the Cleveland citizen-police confrontation, more than 100 May Day protesters were wounded by gunshots, two of whom died. On June 2, 1919, another multistate bomb plot was uncovered, leading to more fear of unseen anarchists and communists who could inflict destruction and death from afar. Retribution by the authorities was directed at any striking worker, since one cannot defend against an unknown enemy, the "known" enemy, which was those workers who chose to strike, became increasingly tempting targets for persecution (Burnett, 2001). That same day, there were simultaneous bomb explosions in eight U.S. cities, in which at least two people died. One of the exploded bombs destroyed part of the residence of then-Attorney General A. Mitchell Palmer, who immediately described the bombing as an attempt by anarchists to terrorize the country (Stone, 2004). Figure 6.1 shows Palmer's

FIGURE 6.1: Bombing at Washington, DC, home of Attorney-General Palmer

"THESE ATTACKS WILL ONLY INCREASE THE
ACTIVITIES OF OUR CRIME-DETECTING FORCES,"

Declares Attorney-General Palmer, whose Washington home, shown
above, was damaged by a bomb-explosion on June 2.

partially destroyed home following the bombing. Note his comments about the bombing at the bottom of the picture: "These attacks will only increase the activities of our crime-detecting forces."

Hysteria about a communist revolution, especially of workers, were to get worse, and immigrants would pay a heavy price for government overreaction. When Boston police went on strike on September, 9, 1919, rumors and accompanying panic developed that communists and anarchists were responsible, although there was no evidence of radicalization in the police force (Burnett, 2001). National newspapers again ran the usual sensationalistic stories about the dangers of communism and anarchism, concentrating on looting, vandalism, violence, and loss of property. There were reports of massive riots, reigns of terror, and federal troops firing machine guns on a mob (Independence Hall Association, 2015).

Barely weeks after the Boston police strike, 275,000 steel workers walked off their jobs, and shortly thereafter the number of striking workers increased to 365,000, resulting in the closure of three quarters of Pittsburgh's steel mills (Burnett, 2001). Newspapers tended to blame strikes and accompanying riots entirely on the workers without casting any blame on police overreaction and behavior, actions of management, or even those of politicians who used the various incidents to their advantage. Blaming communists and screaming that a Russian-style revolution was on its way to America was an easy way to win votes, garner public support, and even launch a platform from which to run for public office, including the presidency. This was exactly what the attorney general, Palmer, began doing in 1919. On August 1, 1919, Palmer created the General Intelligence Division of the Bureau of Investigation (FBI) to deal with "radicalism," and to lead it, he appointed the infamous J. Edgar Hoover. The mission of the new agency was to uncover Bolshevik conspiracies, and to find and imprison or deport conspirators (Independence Hall Association, 2015). Palmer's antiradical division compiled more than 200,000 records outlining details about "radical" organizations, individuals, and case histories throughout the country, and their work led to the imprisonment or deportation of thousands of supposed radicals and leftists, often humiliated without just cause and warrants (Burnett, 2001). Thus, one of the consequences of the Red Scare and Palmer's actions was erosion in civil liberties, a phenomenon that has all too often occurred at periods when the United States has found itself either at war, under some attack (real or imagined), or just undergoing hysteria and panic. One of the most bizarre, if not ridiculous, stories to come out of the Red Scare was that of a man who was arrested in Newark for looking like a radical. What does a radical look like?

As Burnett (2001, p. 1) recounts, "Even the most innocent statement against capitalism, the government, or the country could lead to arrest and incarceration. Moreover, arrestees were often denied counsel and contact with the outside world, beaten, and held in inhumane conditions. All told, thousands of innocent people were jailed or deported, and many more were arrested or questioned. On January 2, 1920 alone over 4,000 alleged radicals were arrested in thirty-three cities."

The Palmer Raids, as they were called, led to the arrest and deportation of 500 immigrants to Russia alone on a ship dubbed the "Soviet Ark" (Lemay & Barkan, 1999). Their alleged crime was suspicion of being radicals and anarchists; they were not allowed due process. Fortunately for civilization and American democracy, Palmer's ambition to be president of the United States by violating the civil and human rights of so many Americans and immigrants on suspicion of being radicals, anarchists, and communists was never realized. The country eventually woke up from its slumber, saw the light, and concluded that perhaps those fighting anarchism and Bolshevism were far more dangerous to the republic than the alleged radicals they were fighting.

In a major rebuke of Palmer and his vaunted "crime detecting units" in the Justice Department, a courageous Montana federal court judge, George M. Bourquin, granted a writ of habeas corpus to prevent the government from deporting an alien accused of being a "Red," noting that government officials had violated the constitutional rights of the alien when they seized him in a raid on a union meeting taking place at his home. Observed Judge Bourquin:

> There was no disorder save that of the raiders. [Acting without a warrant, these agents], mainly uniformed and armed, overawed, intimidated, and forcibly entered, broke, and destroyed property, searched persons, effects and papers ... cursed, insulted, beat, dispersed, and bayoneted union members. ... [They] perpetrated a reign of terror, violence and crime against citizen and alien alike, and whose only offense seems to have been peaceable insistence upon and exercise of a clear legal right ... Assuming petitioner is of the so-called "Reds," ... he and his kind are less of a danger to America than are those who indorse or use the methods that brought him to deportation. These latter are the mob and the spirit of violence and intolerance, ... the most alarming manifestation in America today ..." *(Stone, 2004, p. 225).*

REFERENCES

Bachelor, A. (2004). *U.S. immigration: A legislative history.* Available at http://www.prcdc. org/summaries/usimmighistory/usimmighistory.html. Retrieved December 15, 2015.

Black, E. (2003). *The horrifying American roots of Nazi eugenics.* History News Network. Available at http://hnn.us/article/1796. Retrieved March 18, 2016.

Black, E. (2012). *War against the weak: Eugenics and America's campaign to create a master race.* Washington, DC: Dialogue Press.

Bouche, T., & Rivard, L. (2014). *America's hidden history: The eugenics movement.* Available at http://www.nature.com/scitable/forums/genetics-generation/america-s-hidden-history-the-eugenics-movement-123919444. Retrieved March 18, 2014.

Bruinius, H. (2006). *Better for all the world.* New York, NY: Knopf.

Burnett, P. (2001). *The red scare.* Available at http://law2.umkc.edu/faculty/projects/ftrials/SaccoV/redscare.html. Accessed April 17, 2016.

Caswell, T. C. (2001). *Progressive era reform*. Available at http://regentsprep.org/regents/ushisgov/themes/reform/progressive.htm. Retrieved April 15, 2016.

Claude Moore Health Sciences Library (2004). *Buck v. Bell: The test case for Virginia's eugenical sterilization act*. Available at http://exhibits.hsl.virginia.edu/eugenics/3-buckvbell/. Retrieved March 24, 2016.

Cohen, A. (2016). *Imbeciles: The Supreme Court, American eugenics, and the sterilization of Carrie Buck*. New York, NY: Penguin Press.

Dorr, G. M. (2006). Defective or disabled?: Race, medicine, and eugenics in progressive era Virginia and Alabama. *Journal of the Gilded Age and Progressive Era*, 5(4): 359–392.

Galton, F. (1869). *Hereditary genius: An inquiry into its laws and consequences*. London, UK: Macmillan.

Grant, M. (1916/1919). *The passing of the great race*. New York, NY: Schribner's Sons.

Higham, J. (1955). *Strangers in the land: Patterns of American nativism, 1860–1925*. New Brunswick, NJ: Rutgers University Press.

Hitler, A. (1925/1999). *Mein Kampf* (translated by Ralph Manheim). New York, NY: Houghton Mifflin.

Independence Hall Association (2015). *The red scare*. Available at http://www.ushistory.org/us/47a.asp. Accessed April 16, 2016.

Jerome Law Library (1963). Eugenic sterilization in Indiana. *Indiana Law Journal*, 38(2), Article 4. Available at: http://www.repository.law.indiana.edu/ilj/vol38/iss2/4. Retrieved March 21, 2016.

Kaelber, L. (2012). *Eugenics: Compulsory sterilization in 50 American states*. Presentation about "eugenic sterilizations" in comparative perspective at the 2012 Social Science History Association. Available at http://www.uvm.edu/~lkaelber/eugenics/. Retrieved March 21, 2016.

Landman, J. H. (1932). *Human sterilization: The history of the sexual sterilization movement*. New York, NY: MacMillan.

Largent, M. A. (2008). *Breeding contempt: The history of coerced sterilization in the United States*. New Brunswick, NJ: Rutgers University Press.

Lemay, M., & Barkan, E. R. (1999). *U.S. immigration and naturalization laws and issues: A documentary history*. Westport, CT: Greenwood Press.

Lombardo, P. A. (2008). *Three generations, no imbeciles: Eugenics, the Supreme Court, and Buck v. Bell*. Baltimore, MD: Johns Hopkins University Press.

Lombardo, P. (2016). *Eugenic sterilization laws image archive on the American eugenics movement*. Available at http://www.eugenicsarchive.org/html/eugenics/essay8text.html. Retrieved March 24, 2016.

Norrgard, K. (2008). Human testing, the eugenics movement, and IRBs. *Nature Education* 1(1):170.

Roosevelt, T. (1913). T. Roosevelt letter to C. Davenport about "degenerates reproducing." Available at https://www.dnalc.org/view/11219-T-Roosevelt-letter-to-C-Davenport-about-degenerates-reproducing-.html. Retrieved March 22, 2016.

Stern, A. M. (2005). *Eugenic nation: Faults and frontiers of better breeding in modern America*. Berkeley: University of California Press.

Stern, A. M. (2011). From legislation to lived experience: Eugenic sterilization in California and Indiana, 1907–79. In *A century of eugenics in America*, pp. 95–116, edited by Paul A. Lombardo. Bloomington: Indiana University Press.

Stone, G. R. (2004). *Perilous times: Free speech in wartime*. New York, NY: W. W. Norton.

U.S. Department of Homeland Security (2006). Immigration by region and selected country of last residence, fiscal years 1820–2002. *2004 Yearbook of Immigration Statistics*, Table 2. Available at https://www.dhs.gov/publication/2004-yearbook-immigration-statistics. Retrieved March 8, 2016.

U.S. Supreme Court (1927). Buck v. Bell, 274 U.S. 200.

7 | Quantitative Restrictionism of the 1920s to 1965

Nativism and nativist movements have arisen at various times in American immigration history for both domestic and international reasons. Anti-immigration groups and their ideologies typically waned with time, or in some circumstances, as in the case of the Federalists, the leaders lost power and the causes they had espoused were reversed or simply fell into disfavor with the population. In the case of the Know Nothings, the movement literally imploded as divisions came out, and leaders could not decide which course of action to take. As has been noted elsewhere, the Know Nothings' preoccupation with slavery contributed to their downfall, and they never left a major legislative mark affecting immigration. The same cannot be said of the forces that came together to push immigration laws in the 1920s, because the acts that were passed as a result of the desire to keep some groups out due to ethnicity had a lasting effect on U.S. immigration for well over four decades.

Prior administration of immigration, with the exception of the 1882 Chinese Exclusion Act, had been aimed at controlling the quality of entrants. For example, excluding aliens described as "mentally retarded," "insane," having had one or more attacks of "insanity," afflicted with "psychopathic personality, sexual deviation, or a mental defect," aliens unable to care for themselves, coming for "polygamy," or aliens having committed "infamous crimes," and so forth. The acts passed in the early 1920s generally put an end to an immigration system that had been largely free and without numerical limits. Elimination of free migration and the placement of limits on number of people entering have both remained features of U.S. immigration to the present day.

Factors behind Immigration Restrictionism

Racism

In his 1916 book *The Passing of the Great Race*, Madison Grant divided and rank-ordered the European "races" into Nordic, Alpine, and Mediterranean, with the Nordics being superior. His book appeared within the context of already elevated racial anxieties about the immigration of people from southern and eastern Europe, including Poles, Italians, and Jews. It was believed by some (including Grant) that the United States had been "founded" by Nordics, a superior race, and that race mixing with perceived inferior groups would spell the end of White civilization in America. Accordingly, the migration into the country of "races" deemed inferior must be curtailed, if not stopped altogether, to protect and preserve Anglo-Saxons. Racial hatred was especially influenced by the Ku Klux Klan-inspired "100 percent Americanism" movement that began before World War I; it would influence political events in the 1920s. With the outbreak of war in 1914, and especially following America's entry into that Great European War, hatred was put aside to promote American nationalism and patriotism and enhance the war effort. In the war years themselves, there were scattered resentments against Americans of German ancestry. In some jurisdictions, the teaching of German in schools was banned, along with calls for controlling or curbing the printing of German newspapers. There were even calls for denaturalization of German Americans whose loyalty was questionable (Higham, 1988). Despite the anti-German sentiments in some circles, there was never a call for a German exclusion act, a fate that had been visited upon the Chinese. Following the war, racism, especially in the form of nativism, reemerged; it had never really died, but merely become dormant as unity in war temporarily concealed old hatreds. The racism of the 1900s and 1920s was not against minority groups as conceived today, but against groups and individuals from southern and eastern Europe, such as Greeks, Poles, Italians, Jews, and other Slavic persons, who were believed at the time to be inferior to those from western Europe, such as Scandinavians, Britons, and Germans (Daniels, 2002, p. 275). These groups (with ancestry in Old Europe) tended to be of more Protestant stock. Those to be targeted tended to be Catholic or Jewish. The 1920s essentially became a decade when everyone already in America (with ancestry in Old Europe) was trying to keep anyone else from entering if that person was perceived to be inferior in racial terms; it was a war of tribes, so to speak, in a period that has been described by some as the tribal twenties (Higham, 1988, 2004). Antipathy against individuals and groups based on national origin and a perception that such individuals or groups were inferior would continue and play a major role in passage of the Emergency Quota Act (1921) and the National Origins Quota Act (1924).

Economic Competition
In addition to pure racism, a second factor that contributed to immigration restrictionism was economic competition. Growth in the foreign-born population in the country had begun alarming labor unions from the late 1890s and concerns were heightened in the 1900s. After all, immigrants might compete for jobs; employers could use them as strike breakers; they might accept lower wages, an outcome that would have detrimental effect on the living standards of native-born people. The American Federation of Labor was highly complicit in the push to limit immigration out of fear that demobilization after World War I would lead to excess labor (an industrial reserve army) whose presence would destabilize labor markets in terms of job availability. Increasing immigration was also coming largely from southern and eastern Europe, an area of the world believed by labor to be especially wracked by poverty. If people from such poor areas entered America in large numbers, they might be willing and even eager to accept much lower wages, and if employers hired them in large numbers, the

overall result would be wage depression for most workers, and diminished power of the labor movement, especially the American Federation of Labor (AFL). So frightened was the labor union that in 1918 a special committee within the AFL held a secret meeting that came up with the idea of pushing Congress to suspend immigration for two years (Higham, 1988, p. 305). The two-year immigration suspension proposal would find its way into Congress in a modified form in 1920 when the House of Representatives (after reducing two years to 14 months) voted overwhelmingly (296–42) in favor of passage. Had it not been for the Senate's failure to go along with supporting the measure, there certainly would have been, for the first time in American history, a period when immigration was suspended through legislation.

Apart from fear that immigrants would have a decreasing effect on American wages, the AFL believed that new immigrants could not be easily assimilated, due to their origins, and therefore posed a threat to American national unity and homogeneity. Such an argument closely linked economic fears of immigration with racial concerns about newcomers' national origins and would contribute significantly to passage of restrictive legislation. We consider the first of two.

The Emergency Quota Act of 1921

Although short-lived, the significance of the Act of 1921 was in two areas: It was the first to place a numerical cap or ceiling on the number of people admitted into the United States each year. A numerical annual cap had never been placed before on admission of immigrants to the United States. Secondly, it was the first to introduce the notion of quotas into the administration of U.S. immigration policy. The first has remained a feature of U.S. immigration to the present day. The second was a rather controversial characteristic that was a cornerstone of U.S. immigration policy until 1965, though considered uncontroversial at the time of passage in 1921.

The emergency quota act of May 19, 1921, began as a temporary measure to control and curtail immigration until a more permanent solution for what was perceived as a problem (risk of old America potentially being replaced by new America) could be found. So popular was the bill in the House of Representatives that no records of voting were taken; it apparently passed by voice vote. The Senate voted by a margin of 78 in favor, one opposed, and 17 abstaining (Hutchinson, 1981, p. 180). It set an annual ceiling (numerical cap or limit) of 350,000 immigrants to be admitted in any fiscal year and established a formula of 3% of each nationality as recorded in the census of 1910. It was an effort to somewhat recreate the population of the United States as existed in 1910 on the basis of racial (ethnic) composition, with the clear aim of favoring countries in northwestern Europe (Old Europe) and reducing immigration from other countries, except those specifically excluded from quota restrictions within the legislation. Portions of the law are reproduced in the following section without editing so that readers can examine the original document without much interpretation. The title itself is self-explanatory; it was a law to limit or restrict the immigration of aliens into the United States. It probably should have been more appropriately labeled as an act to limit the immigration of undesirable aliens into the United States. Given that during the time of the earlier censuses the foreign-born from northern and western Europe already in the United States was higher than those from other regions of the world, the 3% quota formula gave a numerical advantage to potential entrants from that region. Therefore, immigration from northwestern Europe was really not limited as countries in those regions did not fill their quotas. The act of May 19, 1921, was set to expire in 1922, but was extended to June 1924, a feat that placed immigration restrictionism at the center of political campaigns for the general election later that year.

AN ACT TO LIMIT THE IMMIGRATION OF ALIENS INTO THE UNITED STATES

Be it enacted by the Senate and House of Representatives of the United States of America in Congress assembled ...

SEC. 2. (a) That the number of aliens of any nationality who may be admitted under the immigration laws to the United States in any fiscal year shall be limited to 3 per centum of the number of foreign born persons of such nationality resident in the United States as determined by the United States census of 1910. This provision shall not apply to the following, and they shall not be counted in reckoning any of the percentage limits provided in this Act: (1) Government officials, their families, attendants, and employees; (2) aliens in continuous transit through the United States; (3) aliens lawfully admitted to the United States who later go in transit from one part of the United States to another through foreign contiguous territory; (4) aliens visiting the United States as tourists or temporarily for business or pleasure; (5) aliens from countries immigration from which is regulated in accordance with treaties or agreements relating solely to immigration; (6) aliens from the so-called Asiatic barred zone, as described in section 3 of the Immigration Act (of 1917); (7) aliens who have resided continuously for at least one year immediately preceding the time of their admission to the United States in the Dominion of Canada, Newfoundland, the Republic of Cuba, the Republic of Mexico, countries of Central or South America, or adjacent islands; or (8) aliens under the age of eighteen who are children of citizens of the United States.

(b) For the purposes of this Act nationality shall be determined by country of birth, treating as separate countries the colonies or dependencies for which separate enumeration was made in the United States census of 1910.

(c) The Secretary of State, the secretary of Commerce, and the Secretary of Labor, jointly, shall, as soon as feasible after the enactment of this Act, prepare a statement showing the number of persons of the various nationalities resident in the United States as determined by the United States census of 1910, which statement shall be the population basis for the purposes of this Act.

Source: U.S. Congress (1921). Statutes at Large of the United States, 42 stat. 5; Public Law 67–5.

Shortly after passage of the Emergency Quota Act, debates began as to the bill's effectiveness, with many lawmakers and nativist groups suggesting it was not restrictive enough. One argument was that by 1910, there were already a sizable number of foreign-born people in the United States from countries in regions targeted for exclusion/restriction by the legislation. Accordingly, unless the census benchmark was altered, the percentage of immigrants from southern and eastern Europe would still, in due course, change the racial (ethnic) makeup of the American population in ways that disadvantaged Whites of Protestant European stock (Kposowa, 1998). The decade prior to 1910 had witnessed the end of the so-called Great Migration in which large numbers of entrants had come from southern and eastern Europe, and therefore setting the quotas to that year was a mistake, as it would not achieve what restrictionists wanted. The second area of contention was that the percentage value itself (3) was too high, and a smaller value (1 or 2) would be more effective in limiting immigration. The two issues (base year and percentage) would come to bear on what became known as the National Origins Quota Act of 1924.

The United States in the 1920s, especially 1924, appeared to be a country deeply divided, prosperous economically by modern standards, but resistant to social change, and hence ready to turn back history to an earlier period when White Protestants were dominant in population and culture. The divisions of the day tended to be between old stock Protestant America that lived mainly in rural areas and small towns, and immigrant stock, Catholic America, that lived in big cities (Daniels, 2002, p. 281). The great issues of the day over which these groups fought included immigration restriction, Prohibition, interpretation of sacred Scripture (whether the Bible was to be interpreted literally or allegorically), and the rise of the second Ku Klux Klan that was becoming increasingly involved in politics and debates on restricting immigration (Daniels, 2002, p. 281).

The conservatism that had gripped the country would become evident in positions on immigration incorporated into platforms of both Democratic and Republican parties at their 1924 conventions. For Democrats, discussion of immigration, both the Emergency Quota Act and the National Origins Quota Act, passed in May, just before the convention, was curiously missing from the party platform at the convention, held in New York City from June 24 to July 9, 1924. It may well have been that the large number of Klan members in the party, and at the convention, prevented incorporating immigration into the platform.

Indeed, efforts to condemn the Klan itself by name in the platform failed narrowly, with Klan members and supporters prevailing. The Democrats went on to pledge their support for Prohibition (an issue favored overwhelmingly by the Klan), accusing Republicans of trafficking in liquor permits and failing to enforce Prohibition. The Democratic Party further pledged to maintain its established position in favor of excluding what it called "Asiatic" immigration. Another strange omission, no doubt attributed to the large Klan presence in the Democratic Party at the time, was that no position was taken on lynching of African Americans; the issue was not discussed and not included in the platform. It is little wonder that in the ensuing presidential election that year, the Democrats (under the spell of the Klan) lost woefully.

The Republican National Convention, held in Cleveland from June 10 to July 12, 1924, had similar problems regarding the Klan. That party was divided as to whether to condemn the Klan in the platform. Participants chose to remain silent on the matter. On lynching, however, the Republicans appeared to express opposition to the practice by calling for passage of federal legislation. Leaving the matter to states was thought to be less effective, given the realities of racial politics prevailing in the various states, especially in the South. On immigration, the Republicans justified passage of the National Origins Quota Act ("the law recently passed") to declining living conditions created by World War I in Europe, which they believed would have led to mass migration (from Europe) to America. The law was couched in the platform as protecting Americans, citizens and noncitizens alike.

THE REPUBLICAN PARTY PLATFORM, JUNE 10, 1924

The Negro

We urge the congress to enact at the earliest possible date a federal anti-lynching law so that the full influence of the federal government may be wielded to exterminate this hideous crime. We believe that much of the misunderstanding which now exists can be eliminated by humane and sympathetic study of its causes. The president has recommended the creation of a commission for the investigation of social and economic conditions and the promotion of mutual understanding and confidence.

Immigration

The unprecedented living conditions in Europe following the world war created a condition by which we were threatened with mass immigration that would have seriously disturbed our economic life. The law recently enacted is designed to protect the inhabitants of our country, not only the American citizen, but also the alien already with us who is seeking to secure an economic foothold for himself and family from the competition that would come from unrestricted immigration. The administrative features of the law represent a great constructive advance, and eliminate the hardships suffered by immigrants under emergency statute. We favor the adoption of methods which will exercise a helpful influence among the foreign born population and provide for the education of the alien in our language, customs, ideals and standards of life. We favor the improvement of naturalization laws.

Source: Republican Party Platforms, 1924; June 10.

Platform politics (in terms of planks to include or exclude) showed that on immigration and other matters discussed previously, both parties were about to embark on a long road to conservatism, that is, setting the country on a backward-looking trajectory. No party had a progressive agenda. For Republicans, their choice of candidates was even more telling about the direction they wanted to lead. Calvin Coolidge, who had served as vice president under Warren Harding, became the 30th president on August 3, 1923, finishing Harding's term following his death at age 57 (History.com staff 2009). Coolidge was not only a eugenicist and believer in Nordic racial superiority, but an immigration restrictionist. Despite these extremist conservative credentials, he prevailed over more moderate Republican contenders and won reelection in 1924. He signed the infamous National Origins Quota Act of 1924 on May 26, before the election, and laid the groundwork for the Great Depression, beginning in 1929, barely a year following his departure from the White House.

The Klan's Influence on Immigration Restrictionism

The new Ku Klux Klan was quite influential politically in the mid-1900s through the 1920s. It had influence in some state legislatures, and many politicians were outright Klan members. In the area of immigration, it ran a campaign against what it described as "hyphenated Americans," suggesting that true Americans did not need to place a hyphen before America. Through its weekly publication, the *Imperial Night Hawk* (published at its Imperial Palace in Atlanta, Georgia), the Klan issued statements on its stance on immigration that very likely infuriated many immigrants but sounded like music in the ears of some politicians and immigration restrictionists. It called for the United States to place a moratorium on immigration and do what it called "stock taking'" of assets it already had, and decide which further actions were needed. The position of the Klan was laid out most clearly in a 1923 statement by the Grand Dragon of the Realm of South Carolina, in an August 29 issue of the *Imperial Night Hawk*, in which he stated that the Klan immigration commissioner should study immigration and provide the organization's advice to policy makers as they debated the national origin quota laws. His statement appears unedited here:

"I REGARD the regulation of immigration as one of the most perplexing and important questions confronting the American people today. And there are few questions that deserve the attention of this great organization, more than the immigration problem.

"The time has now come when the Knights of the Ku Klux Klan should take the leadership in this great fight, to prevent America from becoming the melting pot or dumping ground of the world for the millions of heterogeneous elements who are seeking admission to our shores.

"In my opinion, a law should be enacted restricting immigration to the United States for a period of at least ten years, while we take an inventory of human assets and liabilities within our borders, do a bit of house cleaning and set our domestic affairs in better order.

"The immigrants who come to this country form communities by themselves and congregate in the great cities. Paupers, diseased and criminals predominate among those who land upon American soil. They have a very low standard of morals, they are unable to speak our language and a great majority of them are unable to read and write their own language.

"We must insist that a law be enacted prohibiting the printing of any newspaper or magazine not printed in the English language, and to require all aliens within our borders to speak English within a limited period of time.

"Of the 805,000 admitted to the United States in 1921 more than half, 432,000 were Jews, Italians, Armenians, Greeks, Japanese, Chinese, and Finns, races which generation after generation maintain their own churches, customs, languages, schools, and social affiliations almost as intact as if they had remained in their native countries.

"The Japanese question is another great menace that confronts the American people today. And the Knights of the Ku Klux Klan can do no greater service than to take up the fight with those loyal citizens of California in their effort to prevent their State from becoming a little Japan.

"America has within her borders many of the so-called hyphenated Americans. They call themselves Hungarian-Americans, Polish-Americans, French-Americans, and German-Americans. Such a class of people do not deserve the respect of any decent, loyal, patriotic, red-blooded, pure and unadulterated American citizen. There is but one kind of American. One who would not for one moment tolerate any prefix to "America." Any alien who is not willing to measure up to the standard of true Americanism should be deported. We have no room for any individual … opposed to America.

Excerpt from: "Poorly Restricted Immigration is One of the Greatest Perils Confronting America," *Imperial Night Hawk*, vol. 1, no. 22, 1923. Copyright in the Public Domain.

"The Knights of the Ku Klux Klan should adopt a policy and program for combating the influence of individuals or organizations who are endeavoring to open the gates of our ports to the admission of aliens. Therefore, the Imperial Wizard should appoint an Imperial Immigration and Naturalization Commission to make a thorough study and outline a program."

The legislation passed in 1924 was relatively noncontroversial, and both parties appeared comfortable supporting it. Discussions in Congress never addressed issues of human rights, fairness, justice, or how future generations would judge how their representatives had behaved. Its key provisions included: (1) creation of a permanent quota system; (2) reducing worldwide ceiling of admissions from the 358,000 in the revised form of the Act of 1921 to 164,000; (3) calculating immigration from the 3% in 1921 to 2% of the nationality of foreign-born already in the United States; and (4) changing the census benchmark for calculating quotas from the 1910 census of population to the 1890 census, which had the effect of reducing the future total number of immigrants admitted to 154,000. The bill further stipulated that no person was to enter the United States without a visa, and consular officials abroad were to conduct interviews of prospective immigrants. This was intended to reduce the number of people coming to the country found to be inadmissible at ports of entry. Two copies of photographs were to be produced at interview, one of which was to be inserted into the issued visa; the other was to be discarded in a manner so prescribed by officials at the consulate. A fee of $9 was instituted for visa issuance. The term "immigrant" was defined. No quotas were established for countries in the Western Hemisphere, such as Canada, Mexico, nations in the Caribbean, and countries in Central or South America. It was felt by some that placing quotas on countries in that region would have negative effects on attempts by the United States to promote friendship and good (neighborly) relations. Nationals from countries in these regions were to fall under the label of "Non-Quota Immigrants" as in Section 4 (c). To keep away Asians, especially Japanese, the legislation introduced the statement that "no alien ineligible to citizenship shall be admitted to the United States ..."

The law was to be implemented in two phases. Phase 1 was scheduled to last until 1927, during which the base year of 1890 was to take effect, with quotas reduced from 3%, as had been set in 1921, to 2%. This phase allowed 300,000 entrants, with half coming from Europe (Daniels, 2002, p. 283). In Phase 2, quotas were to be based on findings from a scientific study of the origins of the American population as far back as the first census of 1790. Had such a study been carried out, the act of 1924 would have been even more restrictive given that in 1790 most of the White population had origins in Great Britain and surrounding isles. The study was impractical, but after 1927, a new quota did take effect, the calculation of which was to be based not just on the percentage of first-generation immigrants in the United States, but also on the ethnic background of the entire (White) population as recorded in the 1920 census. This did not make sense, given that calculations based on the entire population would still target foreigners as the native-born would not have had origins different from the United States; they were born in the USA! Relevant portions of the Act are shown here.

THE IMMIGRATION ACT OF 1924

An Act to Limit the Migration of Aliens into the United States, and for other Purposes

Be it enacted by the Senate and House of Representatives of the United States of America in Congress assembled, That this Act may be cited as the "Immigration Act of 1924"

IMMIGRATION VISAS

Sec. 2. (a) A consular officer upon the application of any immigrant (as defined in section 3) may (under the conditions hereinafter prescribed and subject to the limitations prescribed in this Act or regulations made thereunder as to the number of immigration visas which may be issued by such officer) issue to such immigrant an immigration visa which shall consist of one copy of the application provided for in section 7, visaed by such consular officer. Such visa shall specify (1) the nationality of the immigrant; (2) whether he is a quota immigrant (as defined in section 5) or a non-quota immigrant (as defined in section 4); (3) the date on which the validity of the immigration visa shall expire; and such additional information necessary to the proper enforcement of the immigration laws and the naturalization laws as may be by regulations prescribed. (b) The immigrant shall furnish two copies of his photograph to the consular officer. One copy shall be permanently attached by the consular officer to the immigration visa and the other copy shall be disposed of as may be by regulations prescribed. (c) The validity of an immigration visa shall expire at the end of such period, specified in the immigration visa, not exceeding four months, as shall be by regulations prescribed. In the case of a immigrant arriving in the United States by water, or arriving by water in foreign contiguous territory on a continuous voyage to the United States, if the vessel, before the expiration of the validity of his immigration visa, departed from the last port outside the United States and outside foreign contiguous territory at which the immigrant embarked, and if the immigrant proceeds on a continuous voyage to the United States, then, regardless of the time of his arrival in the United States, the validity of his immigration visa shall not be considered to have expired. (d) If an immigrant is required by any law, or regulations or orders made pursuant to law, to secure the visa of his passport by a consular officer before being permitted to enter the United States, such immigrant shall not be required to secure any other visa of his passport than the immigration visa issued under this Act, but a record of the number and date of his immigration visa shall be noted on his passport without charge therefor. This subdivision shall not apply to an immigrant who is relieved, under subdivision (b) of section 13, from obtaining an immigration visa. (e) The manifest or list of passengers required by the immigration laws shall contain a place for entering thereon the date, place of issuance, and number of the immigration visa of each immigrant. The immigrant shall surrender his immigration visa to the immigration officer at the port of inspection, who shall at the time of inspection indorse on the immigration visa the date, the port of entry, and the name of the vessel, if any, on which the immigrant arrived. The immigration visa shall be transmitted forthwith by the immigration officer in charge at the port of inspection to the Department of Labor under regulations prescribed by the Secretary of Labor. (f) No immigration visa shall be issued to an immigrant if it appears to the consular officer, from statements in the application, or in the papers submitted therewith, that the immigrant is inadmissible to the United States under the immigration laws, nor shall such immigration visa be issued if the application fails to comply with the provisions of this Act, nor shall such immigration visa be issued if the consular officer knows or has reason to believe that the immigrant is inadmissible to the United States under the immigration laws. (g) Nothing in this Act shall be construed to entitle an immigrant, to whom an immigration visa has been issued, to enter the United States, if, upon arrival in the United States, he is found to be inadmissible to the United States under the immigration laws. The substance of this subdivision shall be printed conspicuously upon every immigration visa. (h) A fee of $9 shall be charged for the issuance of each immigration visa, which shall be covered into the Treasury as miscellaneous receipts.

DEFINITION OF IMMIGRANT

SEC. 3. When used in this Act the term "immigrant" means an alien departing from any place outside the United States destined for the United States, except (1) a government official, his family, attendants, servants, and employees, (2) an alien visiting the United States temporarily as a tourist or temporarily for business or pleasure, (3) an alien in continuous transit through the United States, (4) an alien lawfully admitted to the United States who later goes in transit from one part of the United States to another through foreign contiguous territory, (5) a bona fide alien seaman serving as such on a vessel arriving at a port of the United States and seeking to enter temporarily the United States solely in the pursuit of his calling as a seaman, and (6) an alien entitled to enter the United States solely to carry on trade under and in pursuance of the provisions of a present existing treaty of commerce and navigation.

NON-QUOTA IMMIGRANTS

SEC. 4. When used in this Act the term "non-quota immigrant" means—(a) An immigrant who is the unmarried child under 18 years of age, or the wife, of a citizen of the United States who resides therein at the time of the filing of a petition under section 9; (b) An immigrant previously lawfully admitted to the United States, who is returning from a temporary visit abroad; (c) An immigrant who was born in the Dominion of Canada, Newfoundland, the Republic of Mexico, the Republic of Cuba, the Republic of Haiti, the Dominican Republic, the Canal Zone, or an independent country of Central or South America, and his wife, and his unmarried children under 18 years of age, if accompanying or following to join him; (d) An immigrant who continuously for at least two years immediately preceding the time of his application for admission to the United States has been, and who seeks to enter the United States solely for the purpose of, carrying on the vocation of minister of any religious denomination, or professor of a college, academy, seminary, or university; and his wife, and his unmarried children under 18 years of age, if accompanying or following to join him; or (e) An immigrant who is a bona fide student at least 15 years of age and who seeks to enter the United States solely for the purpose of study at an accredited school, college, academy, seminary, or university, particularly designated by him and approved by, the Secretary of labor, which shall have agreed to report to the Secretary of Labor the termination of attendance of each immigrant student, and if any such institution of learning fails to make such reports promptly the approval shall be withdrawn.

SEC. 11. (a) The annual quota of any nationality shall be 2 per centum of the number of foreign-born individuals of such nationality resident in continental United States as determined by the United States census of 1890, but the minimum quota of any nationality shall be 100. (b) The annual quota of any nationality for the fiscal year beginning July 1, 1927, and for each fiscal year thereafter, shall be a number which bears the same ratio to 150,000 as the number of inhabitants in continental United States in 1920 having that national origin (ascertained hereinafter provided in this section) bears to the number of inhabitants in continental United States in 1920, but the minimum quota of any nationality shall be 100.

SEC 12. 12 (a) For purposes of this Act nationality shall be determined by country of birth, treating as separate countries the colonies, dependencies, or self-governing dominions, for which separate enumeration was made in the United States census of 1890; except that (1) the nationality of a child under twenty-one years of age not born in the United States, shall be determined by the country of birth of such parent if such parent is entitled to an immigration visa, and the nationality of a child under twenty-one years of age not born in the United States, shall be determined by the country of birth of the father if the father is entitled to an immigrant visa; and (2) if a wife is of a different nationality from her alien husband and the entire number of immigration visas which may be issued to quota immigrants of her nationality for the calendar month has already been issued, her nationality may be determined by the country of birth of her husband if she is accompanying him and he is entitled to an immigrant visa, unless the total number of immigration visas which may be issued to quota immigrants of the nationality of the husband for the calendar month has already been issued. (b) The Secretary of State, the Secretary of Commerce, and the Secretary of Labor, jointly, shall, as soon as feasible after the enactment of this Act, prepare a statement showing the number of individuals of the various nationalities resident in continental United States as determined by the United States census of 1890, which statement shall be the population basis for the purposes of subdivision (a) of section 11.

EXCLUSION FROM UNITED STATES

SEC. 13. (a) No immigrant shall be admitted to the United States unless he (1) has an an unexpired immigration visa or was born subsequent to the issuance of the immigration visa of the accompanying parent, (2) is of the nationality specified in the visa in the immigration visa, (3) is a non-quota immigrant if specified in the visa in the immigration visa as such, and (4) is otherwise admissible under the immigration laws. (b) In such classes of cases and under such conditions as may be by regulations prescribed immigrants who have been legally admitted to the United States and who depart therefrom temporarily may be admitted to the United States without being required to obtain an immigration visa. (c) No alien ineligible to citizenship shall be admitted to the United States unless such alien (1) is admissible as a non-quota immigrant under the provisions of subdivision (b), (d), or (e) of section 4, or (2) is the wife, or the unmarried child under 18 years of age, of an immigrant admissible under such subdivision (d), and is accompanying or following to join him, or (3) is not an immigrant as defined in section 3. (d) The Secretary of Labor may admit to the United States any otherwise admissible immigrant not admissible under clause (2) or (3) of subdivision (a) of this section, if satisfied that such inadmissibility was not known to, and could not have been ascertained by the exercise of reasonable diligence by, such immigrant prior to the departure of the vessel from the last port outside the United States and outside foreign contiguous territory or, in the case of an immigrant coming from foreign contiguous territory, prior to the application of the immigrant for admission. (e) No quota immigrant shall be admitted under subdivision (d) if the entire number of immigration visas which may be issued to quota immigrants of the same nationality for the fiscal year already been issued. If such entire number of immigration visas has not been issued, then the Secretary of State, upon the admission of a quota immigrant under subdivision (d), shall reduce by one the number of immigration visas which may be issued to quota immigrants of the same nationality during the fiscal year in which such immigrant is admitted; but if the Secretary of State finds that it will not be practicable to make such reduction before the end of such fiscal year, then such immigrant shall not be admitted. (f) Nothing in this section shall authorize the remission or refunding of a fine, liability to which has accrued under section 16.

The Immigration Act of 1924 was signed into law by President Coolidge by the time the Democratic and Republican parties held their conventions in the run-up to the general election later that year. Perhaps their support for immigration restriction could not be reversed without major electoral consequences in 1924. In 1928, however, the quota acts had gone into effect, and so both parties had data enabling them to judge the merits of both the 1921 and 1924 laws. Yet at their conventions in 1928 the two parties were still strongly in favor of limiting immigration based on national origin, a practice that had been acknowledged even by many politicians as racist. They appeared to be falling over each other to demonstrate to the public which party was more restrictionist than the other. In their 1928 platform, Democrats called for restriction laws to be kept in full force; their only concern was that the law's provision that separated families was inhumane. Maybe it was inhumane, but what needed to be done about it, and what about the inhumanity of an entire piece of legislation based on exclusion of groups by race (national origin)? An overriding purpose of the law was to recreate the racial and ethnic composition of the U.S. population as had existed in 1890; it was a legislation aimed not at moving forward and embracing change, but going back to some glorious American past.

DEMOCRATIC PARTY PLATFORM 1928

Immigration

Laws which limit immigration must be preserved in full force and effect, but the provisions contained in these laws that separate husbands from wives and parents from infant children are inhuman and not essential to the purpose or the efficacy of such laws.

Source: Democratic Party Platforms, 1928; June 26.

For their part, Republicans went even further than Democrats in their support for the national origins law. As shown below, the party emphatically declared that it was necessary to restrict immigration, as without limitations, immigrants would contribute to unemployment and depression of American standard of living. Such claims that immigrants cause harm to native born Americans by bringing down wages, raising unemployment, and being a scourge on US living standards have survived throughout the ages to the present.

REPUBLICAN PARTY PLATFORM 1928

Immigration

The Republican Party believes that in the interest of both native and foreign-born wage-earners, it is necessary to restrict immigration. Unrestricted immigration would result in widespread unemployment and in the breakdown of the American standard of living. Where, however, the law works undue hardships by depriving the immigrant of the comfort and society of those bound by close family ties, such modification should be adopted as will afford relief. We commend Congress for correcting defects for humanitarian reasons and for providing an effective system of examining prospective immigrants in their home countries.

Source: Republican Party Platforms, 1928; June 12.

Impact of the Quota Acts on Immigration

Initial effects of the Act of 1924 on reducing immigration along lines envisaged by supporters of the bill are difficult to ascertain. As noted earlier, the law was enacted in phases, with the first lasting until 1927. Figure 7.1 shows a drop in immigration between 1921 and 1930 for those from southern and eastern Europe—the individuals targeted in the law. During the same period, immigration from Old Europe (western and northern) increased. If one were to focus only on the data, one would conclude that both laws were effective in at least curtailing immigration, but such a straightforward analysis is misleading as it does not take into account extraneous historical events that might have affected immigration. The Great Depression struck not long after implementation of the 1924 act, such that between 1932 and 1935 the United States experienced negative net immigration; more people were leaving the country on average than coming in (Kposowa, 1998, p. 20). Then from 1941 through 1950, immigration from southern and eastern Europe declined to their lowest levels since passage of both quota acts. Yet this period also experienced World War II, during which wartime exigencies would have slowed immigration with or without quotas. Nevertheless, immigration from northwest Europe increased sharply from 1920 through 1950, suggesting that overall it was far easier for people from those regions to move to America, and that quota restrictions did not hurt them at all. It appears from Figure 7.1 that the quota system did most of what it was intended to do, at least in the short run: slow immigration from eastern and southern Europe, and encourage immigration from northern and western Europe. This pattern held until 1950 when northern European immigration took a dive. Restrictionists in America had not studied or foreseen long-term historical trends, for example, that a point would come in history when Europeans from Old Europe would elect to stay in their own countries instead of moving to America. The postwar

FIGURE 7.1: Distribution of Immigration by Source Regions, United States 1821–1965

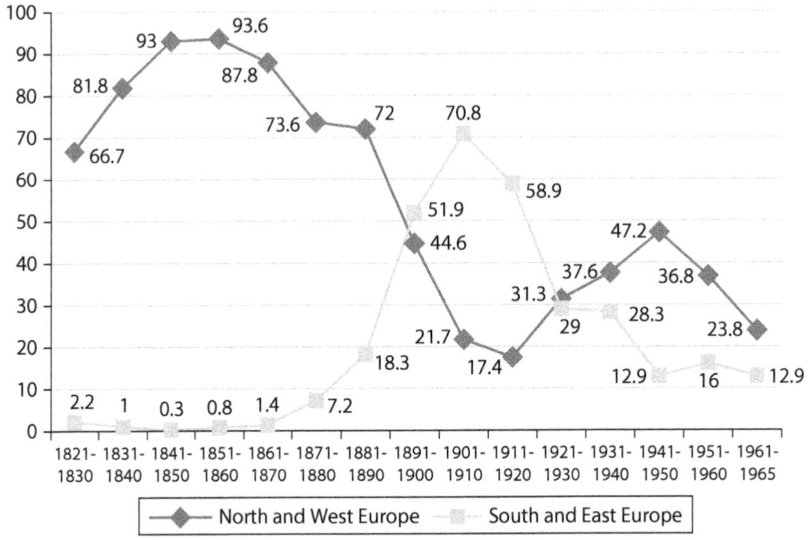

Source: US Census Bureau, "Distribution of Immigration by Source Regions, United States 1821-1965," *Historical Statistics of the United States Colonial Times to 1970.* Copyright in the Public Domain.

economic recovery in those nations meant that one could stay and live comfortably (perhaps more comfortably) economically in Europe than experience a lateral or downward move by migrating to the United States. Postwar problems created by Nazi invasions of other nations and persecution of people on the basis of race, religion, and even lifestyles meant that maintaining the quota system would be tested to its extreme and expose in a very embarrassing manner deep-seated American racism. What happened if persecuted groups had no place to go, wanted to enter the United States as refugees, but did not have quotas? Was the quota system so set in stone that it did not allow for any emergencies? Especially hard hit during World War II were Jews and Slavic individuals the quota acts had tried to exclude (such as Poles) and whose countries the Nazis had invaded and occupied.

Immigration, From Quota Acts to 1965

A persistent feature of U.S. immigration policies following World War II was preoccupation with subversives, national security, and a perception that individuals were entering who were potential threats to the peace and stability of the nation, especially communists. The atmosphere was eerily similar to what existed in 1798 before passage of the Alien and Sedition acts. Fears of the day led first to passage of the National Security Act of 1947 (amended in 1949), and then the Internal Security Act of 1950 (Subversive Activities Control Act), which demanded that communist front organizations register with the attorney general; members of such organizations were also barred from traveling abroad or getting defense-related jobs. Senator Joseph McCarthy of Wisconsin began his search for subversives and communists lurking in the State Department, and later elsewhere, in this period (1950s). Concerns over subversives and communists made it difficult to pass a comprehensive immigration statute that eliminated national origins. Some countries in northwestern Europe had unused quota slots, but many people elsewhere in the world desiring to immigrate could not do so due to relatively few quotas. Calls began to modify the immigration system from one based on ethnicity to one based on the country's labor market needs. Acknowledgment that the world had changed and the United States needed to reform its immigration policies eventually led to passage of the Immigration and Nationality Act (INA) of 1952, also known as the McCarran-Walter Act.

The 1952 legislation codified all existing U.S. immigration and naturalization laws and made revisions in some areas. It created a preference system to distribute visas within the quota allotments provided to each country (Harper, 1975). Four preference categories were created. The first category specified highly skilled immigrants with skills urgently needed in the United States and the spouses and children of such immigrants. This category was to receive up to 50% of quotas. The second preference consisted of parents of U.S. citizens over age 21, and the unmarried adult children of U.S. citizens. This group was to obtain up to 30% of quotas, plus any unused visas from preference one. The third preference consisted of spouses and unmarried adult children of permanent resident aliens. They were to get 20% of quotas, plus any unused visas from preferences one and two. Preference category four was made up of brothers, sisters, and married children of U.S. citizens and accompanying spouses and children. They were allotted 50% of visas not required for the first three preference categories. Non-preference applicants were those who were not entitled to any of the aforementioned preferences. They would get 50% of visas not required for the first three preferences, plus any not required for the fourth preference. Exempted from the preference system were spouses and unmarried minor children of U.S. citizens. They were not subject to numerical limitations and could come at any time (Harper, 1975). The Immigration and Nationality Act initiated labor certification as a requirement for admitting immigrants. The secretary of labor was to certify that admitting a person not related to a U.S. citizen did not adversely affect wages and working conditions for native workers (Kposowa, 1998).

The Immigration and Nationality Act is noted for its many provisions for excluding and deporting entire categories of people, such as subversives, communists, anarchists, homosexuals, and those with various health and moral problems. Most notable was that despite the passage of time (1952), the Act of 1952 maintained the national origin quota system favoring northwest Europe. It changed the census benchmark from 1920 to 1950 but did relatively nothing else. The continuing racial/ethnic discrimination inherent in the bill prompted President Harry S. Truman (1952) to veto it, but the veto was overridden by both chambers of Congress on June 27, 1952, leaving the law and the quota system intact until 1965.

Despite being overridden, the president's veto message is quite informative for scholars of immigration and its relationship to race/ethnicity at the time. The message is easily one of the best critiques and summary of U.S. immigration policy from 1798 to 1952. Truman seemed to understand the changing face of the world while members of Congress seemed stuck in the past. He reminded Congress that taking all its provisions together the bill was a step backward and not one forward. He added that he had long urged that racial or national barriers to immigration and naturalization be abolished:

"… But now this most desirable provision comes before me embedded in a mass of legislation which would perpetuate injustices of long standing against many other nations of the world, hamper the efforts we are making to rally the men of East and West alike to the cause of freedom, and intensify the repressive and inhumane aspects of our immigration procedures. The price is too high, and in good conscience I cannot agree to pay it …

"The bill would continue, practically without change, the national origins quota system, which was enacted, into law in 1924, and put into effect in 1929. This quota system—always based upon assumptions at variance with our American ideals—is long since out of date and more than ever unrealistic in the face of present world conditions …

"The greatest vice of the present quota system, however, is that it discriminates, deliberately and intentionally, against many of the peoples of the world. The purpose behind it was to cut down and virtually eliminate immigration to this country from Southern and Eastern Europe. A theory was invented to rationalize this objective. The theory was that in order to be readily assimilable, European immigrants should be admitted in proportion to the numbers of persons of their respective national stocks already here as shown by the census of 1920. Since Americans of English, Irish and German descent were most numerous, immigrants of those three nationalities got the lion's share—more than two-thirds—of the total quota. The remaining third was divided up among all the other nations given quotas …

"The desired effect was obtained. Immigration from the newer sources of Southern and Eastern Europe was reduced to a trickle. The quotas allotted to England and Ireland remained largely unused, as was intended. Total quota immigration fell to a half or a third—and sometimes even less—of the annual limit of 154,000. People from such countries as Greece, or Spain, or Latvia were virtually deprived of any opportunity to come here at all, simply because

Greeks or Spaniards or Latvians had not come here before 1920 in any substantial numbers ...

"The idea behind this discriminatory policy was, to put it baldly, that Americans with English or Irish names were better people and better citizens than Americans with Italian or Greek or Polish names. It was thought that people of West European origin made better citizens than Rumanians or Yugoslavs or Ukrainians or Hungarians or Baits or Austrians. Such a concept is utterly unworthy of our traditions and our ideals. It violates the great political doctrine of the Declaration of Independence that 'all men are created equal.' It denies the humanitarian creed inscribed beneath the Statue of Liberty proclaiming to all nations, 'Give me your tired, your poor, your huddled masses yearning to breathe free.'

"The basis of this quota system was false and unworthy in 1924. It is even worse now. At the present time, this quota system keeps out the very people we want to bring in. It is incredible to me that, in this year of 1952, we should again be enacting into law such a slur on the patriotism, the capacity, and the decency of a large part of our citizenry ...

"Today, we are 'protecting' ourselves, as we were in 1924, against being flooded by immigrants from Eastern Europe. This is fantastic. The countries of Eastern Europe have fallen under the communist yoke—they are silenced, fenced off by barbed wire and minefields—no one passes their borders but at the risk of his life. We do not need to be protected against immigrants from these countries—on the contrary we want to stretch out a helping hand, to save those who have managed to flee into Western Europe, to succor those who are brave enough to escape from barbarism, to welcome and restore them against the day when their countries will, as we hope, be free again.

"In no other realm of our national life are we so hampered and stultified by the dead hand of the past, as we are in this field of immigration. We do not limit our cities to their 1920 boundaries—we do not hold our corporations to their 1920 capitalizations—we welcome progress and change to meet changing conditions in every sphere of life, except in the field of immigration ...

"The only consequential change in the 1924 quota system which the bill would make is to extend a small quota to each of the countries of Asia. But most of the beneficial effects of this gesture are offset by other provisions of the bill. The countries of Asia are told in one breath that they shall have quotas for their nationals, and in the next, that the nationals of the other countries, if their ancestry is as much as 50 percent Asian, shall be charged to these quotas ...

"The bill would make it even more difficult to enter our country. Our resident aliens would be more easily separated from homes and families under grounds of deportation, both new and old, which would specifically be made retroactive. Admission to our citizenship would be made more difficult; expulsion from our citizenship would be made easier. Certain rights of native born, first generation Americans would be limited. All our citizens returning from abroad would be subjected to serious risk of unreasonable invasions of privacy. Seldom has a bill exhibited the distrust evidenced here for citizens and aliens alike—at a time when we need unity at home, and the confidence of our friends abroad.

"Some of the new grounds of deportation which the bill would provide are unnecessarily severe. Defects and mistakes in admission would serve to deport at any time because of the bill's elimination, retroactively as well as prospectively, of the present humane provision barring deportations on such grounds five years after entry. Narcotic drug addicts would be deportable at any time, whether or not the addiction was culpable, and whether or not cured. The threat of deportation would drive the addict into hiding beyond the reach of cure, and the danger to the country from drug addiction would be increased.

"These provisions are worse than the infamous Alien Act of 1798, passed in a time of national fear and distrust of foreigners, which gave the President power to deport any alien deemed 'dangerous to the peace and safety of the United States.' Alien residents were thoroughly frightened and citizens much disturbed by that threat to liberty.

"Such powers are inconsistent with our democratic ideals. Conferring powers like that upon the Attorney General is unfair to him as well as to our alien residents. Once fully informed of such vast discretionary powers vested in the Attorney General, Americans now would and should be just as alarmed as Americans were in 1798 over less drastic powers vested in the President.

"The bill would sharply restrict the present opportunity of citizens and alien residents to save family members from deportation. Under the procedures of present law, the Attorney General can exercise his discretion to suspend deportation in meritorious cases. In each such case, at the present time, the exercise of administrative discretion is subject to the scrutiny and approval of the Congress. Nevertheless, the bill would prevent this discretion from being used in many cases where it is now available, and would narrow the circle of those who can obtain relief from the letter of the law. This is most unfortunate, because the bill, in its other provisions, would impose harsher restrictions and greatly increase the number of cases deserving equitable relief."

With all its many flaws, the Immigration and Nationality Act of 1952 (INA) has remained the foundation of American immigration policy to the present day.

Subsequent acts were basically amendments, some major, as in 1965, but most others minor. The list of excludables has increased, but none present in 1952 has been eliminated. Communists, for instance, continue to be excluded, though one would be hard-pressed to find many in the 21st century, even in Russia or China. It is clear from Truman's veto message that had Congress paid attention to him, the National Origins Quota Act would have been repealed and U.S. immigration would have become progressive sooner. It is noteworthy today to ponder exit and reentry protocols at U.S. airports while reading his poignant prediction in 1952 that in the future, "All our citizens returning from abroad would be subjected to serious risk of unreasonable invasions of privacy." For aliens, the privacy invasions noted by President Truman may be even more serious.

REFERENCES

Daniels, R. (2002). *Coming to America: A history of immigration and ethnicity in American life*. New York, NY: Visual Education.

Democratic Party Platforms (1928). 1928 Democratic Party Platform, June 26, 1928. Online by Gerhard Peters and John T. Woolley, *The American Presidency Project*. http://www.presidency.ucsb.edu/ws/?pid=29594

Harper, E. J. (1975*). Immigration laws of the United States* (3rd ed.). New York, NY: Bobbs-Merrill.

Higham, J. (1988). *Strangers in the land: Patterns of American nativism, 1860–1925*. New Brunswick, NJ: Rutgers University Press.

History.com staff (2009). Calvin Coolidge. Available at http://www.history.com/topics/us-presidents/calvin-coolidge

Hutchinson, E. P. (1981). *Legislative history of American immigration policy, 1798–1965*. Philadelphia: University of Pennsylvania Press.

Knights of the Ku Klux Klan (1923). *Imperial Night Hawk*. Official weekly publication of the Knights of the Ku Klux Klan, Atlanta, GA: Imperial Palace, August 29, 1923, Vol. 1, No. 22. Available at http://www.authentichistory.com/1921-1929/4-resistance/2-KKK/nighhawk/index.html

Kposowa, A. J. (1998). *The impact of immigration on the United States economy*. Lanham, MD: University Press of America.

Republican Party Platforms (1924). Republican Party Platform of 1924, June 10, 1924. Online by Gerhard Peters and John T. Woolley, *The American Presidency Project*. http://www.presidency.ucsb.edu/ws/?pid=29636

Republican Party Platforms (1928). Republican Party Platform of 1928, June 12, 1928. Online by Gerhard Peters and John T. Woolley, *The American Presidency Project*. http://www.presidency.ucsb.edu/ws/?pid=29637

Truman, H. S. (1952). Veto of bill to revise the laws relating to immigration, naturalization, and nationality, June 25, 1952. Online by Gerhard Peters and John T. Woolley, *The American Presidency Project*. http://www.presidency.ucsb.edu/ws/?pid=14175

U.S. Census Bureau (2016). *Income, poverty and health insurance coverage in the United States*. Available at https://www.census.gov/content/dam/Census/library/publications/2016/demo/p60-256.pdf

U.S. Congress (1921). *An act to limit the immigration of aliens into the United States. Statutes at large of the United States, Public Law 67–5*.

U.S. Congress (1924). *An act to limit the migration of aliens into the United States, and for other purposes. Statutes at large of the United States*, 43 stat. 153, 1918–1925.

8

The New Immigration
1965 to the Present

The 1952 Immigration and Nationality Act (INA) passed over President Truman's veto was out of step with changing times. With all its flaws and heavy handedness pointed out by Truman, and with its excessive focus on punishing immigrants, excluding groups for political opinion, such as subversives and communists, it has remained the basis of present U.S. immigration law. It contains details of requirements for admission of foreign nationals into the United States (either on permanent or temporary basis), grounds for exclusion and removal of foreigners, document and entry-exit controls for U.S. citizens and foreigners, and eligibility rules for the naturalization of foreigners. Congress has amended the Immigration and Nationality Act numerous times since 1952, most notably by the Immigration Amendments of 1965, the Refugee Act of 1980, the Immigration Reform and Control Act (IRCA) of 1986, the Immigration Act of 1990, and the Illegal Immigration Reform and Immigrant Responsibility Act (IIRIRA) of 1996 (Congressional Research Service [CRS], 2014).

The most notable change to the INA (1952) took place in 1965, which followed extensive debate in both the House and Senate on various amendments, along with strong opposition to any attempts to remove national origins. Before going into relevant details of the 1965 act, it is informative in retrospect to once again see where the two main political parties stood. As we have seen, both were strongly in favor of the quota acts of the 1920s. The two parties strongly reaffirmed their support for those laws in 1928, and in 1952 none objected to maintaining the national origins provision in the Immigration and Nationality Act. Indeed, Truman's veto was overridden by a large majority in both chambers of Congress, with Democrats, including future Democratic President Lyndon Johnson, voting against Truman even though he (Truman) was a Democratic president. By 1960, it appeared that the two parties had changed, and Democrats were becoming critical of the racial aspects of the quota acts. This is evident in the position adopted in their platform at their 1960 convention, which began by recalling the party's first leader, Thomas Jefferson, and then moving on to positions that had become relatively "progressive" since 1924.

DEMOCRATIC PARTY PLATFORM 1960

In 1796, in America's first contested national election, our Party, under the leadership of Thomas Jefferson campaigned on the principles of "The Rights of Man."

Immigration

We shall adjust our immigration, nationality and refugee policies to eliminate discrimination and to enable members of scattered families abroad to be united with relatives already in our midst.

The national-origins quota system of limiting immigration contradicts the founding principles of this nation. It is inconsistent with our belief in the rights of man. This system was instituted after World War I as a policy of deliberate discrimination by a Republican Administration and Congress.

The revision of immigration and nationality laws we seek will implement our belief that enlightened immigration, naturalization and refugee policies and humane administration of them are important aspects of our foreign policy.

These laws will bring greater skills to our land, reunite families, permit the United States to meet its fair share of world programs of rescue and rehabilitation, and take advantage of immigration as an important factor in the growth of the American economy.

In this World Refugee Year it is our hope to achieve admission of our fair share of refugees. We will institute policies to alleviate suffering among the homeless wherever we are able to extend our aid.

We must remove the distinctions between native-born and naturalized citizens to assure full protection of our laws to all. There is no place in the United States for "second-class citizenship."

The protections provided by due process, right of appeal, and statutes of limitation, can be extended to non-citizens without hampering the security of our nation.

We commend the Democratic Congress for the initial steps that have recently been taken toward liberalizing changes in immigration law. However, this should not be a piecemeal project and we are confident that a Democratic President in cooperation with Democratic Congresses will again implant a humanitarian and liberal spirit in our nation's immigration and citizenship policies.

The Democrats for the first time called for elimination of the national origins system, which had already been passed in the Immigration and Nationality Act of 1952, which they had supported by helping Republicans override President Truman's veto in both chambers of Congress. In 1960, with the rise of young and dynamic new leadership in the party, especially Senator John F. Kennedy and his brothers, the inequalities in the 1952 legislation and others before were starting to bother the conscience of the party. In 1959, Kennedy had published the much-acclaimed book, *A Nation of Immigrants*, in which he had gone through the history of U.S. immigration, pointing out how various groups had come to the country and helped build it regardless of national origin, but how U.S. immigration policies were administered in a hypocritical and unequal manner. Some critics such as Daniels (2002, 2004) suggest that he was slow in moving immigration reform bills through Congress early in his administration, but they fail to realize other issues that may have severely slowed the president's agenda, including the Cuban Missile Crisis and continued opposition from some Southern senators to any effort to repeal national origins. Senator James O. Eastland of Mississippi, for example, chair of the powerful Senate Judiciary Committee, condemned drafts of the bill removing national origins as an assault on the immigration system by lobbyists who wanted to appease minority groups in the great urban areas (Hutchinson, 1981). The racially charged coded expression "urban areas" has long cast a shadow on American immigration history, an issue that was not absent from presidential primary campaigns leading to the 2016 general election in the United States. One often heard of the "inner city," "law and order," "lawlessness," and so on, as if there were a shooting war going on in the country when the real war was one waged by the rich and powerful against the less fortunate, not only in the metropolitan areas of the United States but also in the rural (red) areas. A newly sworn president pledged that some American "carnage" was going to stop immediately upon him taking over. The campaign of 2015–2016 was quite reminiscent of that leading to the 1924 election, though not in so much a dramatic fashion. Then as in 2016, immigration was a critical issue, though both parties appeared on the same page as far as turning back history and joining in passing perhaps the most restrictive immigration law ever passed in the history of the United States.

In his inaugural address in January 1961, Kennedy spoke of a torch being passed to a new generation of Americans:

> … Let the word go forth from this time and place, to friend and foe alike, that the torch has been passed to a new generation of Americans—born in this century, tempered by war, disciplined by a hard and bitter peace, proud of our ancient heritage—and unwilling to witness or permit the slow undoing of those human rights to which this nation has always been committed, and to which we are committed today at home and around the world *(Kennedy, 1961)*.

With his untimely death in 1963, however, and given the age and Southern origins of his successor, Lyndon Johnson, it appeared for all intents and purposes that the torch mentioned by the president had been taken back by the old generation. President Johnson, however, did carry through some of the policies of his predecessor, including the signing of the Act of 1965 on October 3 of that year at the Statue of Liberty.

For their part, the Republicans continued to uphold the national origins quota system. At their convention in 1960, the law was never challenged, but only procedural matters were brought up, such as changing the base year for calculating quotas from the 1920 census to that of 1960.

REPUBLICAN PARTY PLATFORM 1960

Immigration has historically been a great factor in the growth of the United States, not only in numbers but in the enrichment of ideas that immigrants have brought with them. This Republican Administration has given refuge to over 32,000 victims of Communist tyranny from Hungary, ended needless delay in processing applications for naturalization, and has urged other enlightened legislation to liberalize existing restrictions.

Immigration has been reduced to the point where it does not provide the stimulus to growth that it should, nor are we fulfilling our obligation as a haven for the oppressed. Republican conscience and Republican policy require that:

The annual number of immigrants we accept be at least doubled.

Obsolete immigration laws be amended by abandoning the outdated 1920 census data as a base and substituting the 1960 census.

The guidelines of our immigration policy be based upon judgment of the individual merit of each applicant for admission and citizenship.

In the 1964 presidential election, immigration was an issue again, and this time the party once under the spell of the Ku Klux Klan was taking an increasingly progressive position. It reiterated its stance in 1960 that the national origins quota system was inconsistent with American values, and that it needed to be eliminated.

DEMOCRATIC PARTY PLATFORM 1964

Immigration

In 1960, we proposed to—

Adjust our immigration, nationality and refugee policies to eliminate discrimination and to enable members of scattered families abroad to be united with relatives already in our midst.

The national-origins quota system of limiting immigration contradicts the founding principles of this nation. It is inconsistent with our belief in the rights of men.

The immigration law amendments proposed by the Administration, and now before Congress, by abolishing the national-origin quota system, will eliminate discrimination based upon race and place of birth and will facilitate the reunion of families.

In the run-up to the 1964 election, immigration did not appear in the platform of the Republican Party, and it is hard to judge the party's official position, though by nominating Barry Goldwater (an arch-conservative) it would have been extremely difficult for Republicans to adopt a more liberal and open view of immigration.

Some Provisions of the Act of 1965

The Act of 1965 was not new, but a series of amendments to the Immigration and Nationality Act of 1952. Indeed, its real title is *An Act to Amend the Immigration and Nationality Act and for Other Purposes*. Among the many purposes, it contained a very important statement that had never appeared in previous immigration statutes: "No person shall receive any preference or priority or be discriminated against in the issuance of an immigrant visa because of his race, sex, nationality, place of birth, or place of residence" (U.S. Congress, 1965). The nondiscrimination clause, which had appeared in civil rights legislation, was a turning point in U.S. immigration, as it minimized the tendency for visa officers at U.S. consulates abroad (especially in third world countries) to make arbitrary decisions that on face value might be based on racial or ethnic discrimination. The legislation also repealed the National Origins Quota System that had remained in effect from 1922. Nevertheless, it retained almost all of the exclusionary categories in the Act of 1952, including barring from entry individuals most likely to become public charges (LPC). It also added to the ever increasing list of persons or groups not welcome in the United States (deemed inadmissible), placing an increasingly heavy burden on those who might wish to immigrate but had otherwise been struck with unfortunate circumstances, such as having some disease, belonging previously to terrorist organizations (including Nelson Mandela's African National Congress), having a criminal history, seeking to work in the country without proper labor certification, seeking to enter without proper documentation, having previously entered without inspection, being ineligible for citizenship, and foreigners illegally present or previously removed (deported).

The Act of 1965 introduced a preference system that was heavy on family reunification and concerns about labor market needs, that is, preference for individuals having skills in short supply in the United States, provided the admission of such individuals did not displace U.S. citizen workers. Family reunification had been a feature of the Act of 1952, but it received even greater prominence in the 1965 amendments. The seven-point category system of visa allotment (preferences) included unmarried adult children of American citizens. This group was allocated 20% of visas. The second preference was spouses and unmarried adult children of permanent resident aliens ("green card" holders), assigned 20% of visas. The third category was composed of members of the professions along with scientists and artists deemed to have exceptional ability. Those from this category were to be assigned 10% of visas, but their immigration was subject to certification from the U.S. Department of Labor. There must be evidence that their immigration did not lead to adverse job or wage consequences on U.S. citizens. The fourth category was composed of married children of American citizens, allocated 10% of visas. The fifth preference category was made up of brothers and sisters of U.S. citizens above 21 years of age; their visa percentage was 24. Preference six was composed of skilled and unskilled workers in occupations for which there was a shortage of labor, including agriculture, and this group was assigned 10% of visas; their entrance or stay was to be subject to labor certification to ensure they did not displace qualified American workers. The final preference group was refugees from communist or communist-controlled nations, or countries in the Middle East; 6% of visas were allocated to them. Immediate family members, such as spouses, unmarried minor children, and parents of U.S. citizens were exempt from the preference system, meaning that an immigrant visa was immediately available to any family member who fit into this group. This meant that although the law placed a global numerical limit of 290,000, non-preference immigrants were not subject to this requirement. It was, therefore, no surprise when immigration began to rise sharply following passage of the legislation. Foreign-born individuals already in the country could easily bring family members from abroad. Addressing this point, Daniels (2004, p. 137) observed that "Legal immigration, which averaged a quarter of a million annually in the 1950s, expanded to nearly a third of a million in the 1960s, nearly 450,000 in the 1970s, more than 600,000 in the 1980s, and more than 970,000 in the 1990s. Increasingly this was immigration from Asia and Latin America."

The law placed a limit of 20,000 entrants per country in the Eastern Hemisphere in any fiscal year, but this too applied to only those coming under the preference system. Accordingly, the 20,000 per country cap has never been achieved. A diversity category would be later created in future immigration statutes to assist those from countries that had been disadvantaged by the abolishment of the national origin quotas. Some lawmakers had countries such as Ireland in mind, but this provision has since been used to bring in people from countries that had actually been disadvantaged by the maintenance of national origins in previous immigration laws. It has very likely helped individuals to come who do not have previous family connections in the United States given the legislation's focus on family reunification.

The 1965 law installed for the first time an annual cap of 120,000 on Western Hemisphere immigration, largely due to concerns over Mexican fertility and immigration. The law lifted the ban on Asian immigration by eliminating the "aliens ineligible for naturalization" language. The authors of the bill never foresaw the consequences of how immigration would change. Europeans were never going to come in large numbers as in previous decades; third world countries would send their people in larger numbers.

TABLE 8.1: Immigrants Admitted by Type of Admission, Selected Years, 1996 to 2005

Type and Class of Admission	1996	2000	2002	2004	2005
Total	915,560	841,002	1,059,356	957,883	1,122,373
New arrivals	421,403	407,279	384,289	373,962	384,071
Adjustments	494,157	433,723	675,067	583,921	738,302
Family-Sponsored Preferences	294,144	235,092	186,880	214,355	212,970
Unmarried sons/daughters of U.S. citizens and their children (first preference)	20,891	27,635	23,517	26,380	24,729
Spouses, unmarried sons/daughters of alien residents and their children (second preference)	182,824	124,540	84,785	93,609	100,139
Married sons/daughters of U.S. citizens (third preference)	25,450	22,804	21,041	28,695	22,953
Brothers or sisters of U.S. citizens (fourth preference)	64,979	60,113	57,537	65,671	65,149
Employment-Based Preferences	117,460	106,642	173,814	155,330	246,878
Priority workers	27,487	27,566	34,168	31,291	64,731
Professionals with advanced degrees or aliens of exceptional ability	18,458	20,255	44,316	32,534	42,597
Skilled workers, professionals, unskilled workers	62,744	49,589	88,002	85,969	129,070
Special immigrants	7,835	9,014	7,186	5,407	10,134
Employment creation (investors)	936	218	142	129	346
Immediate Relatives of U.S. Citizens	300,253	346,350	483,676	417,815	436,231
Spouses	169,673	196,405	293,219	252,193	259,144
Children	63,965	82,638	96,941	88,088	94,974
Parents	66,615	67,307	93,516	77,534	82,113
Refugees	118,447	56,091	115,601	61,013	112,676
Asylees	10,033	6,837	10,197	10,217	30,286
Diversity	58,244	50,920	42,820	50,084	46,234
Cancelation of Removal	5,806	12,144	23,642	32,702	20,785

The various preference categories created in 1965 and others crafted through subsequent amendments and global changes are shown in Table 8.1 for selected fiscal years, 1996 through 2005. As can be seen, family sponsored preferences (1, 2, 3, and 4) were prominent in bringing in large numbers of immigrants. In 1996, for example, there were 294,144 individuals who came through family preference. That number has remained high, but entrants from employment-based preferences have also been on the increase, going from 117,460 in 1996, to 246,878 in 2005. Note that immediate family members of U.S. citizens (spouses, children, and parents) are not part of the preference system; they can enter at any time regardless of visa allocations. These have generally dominated permanent immigration streams. For example, immediate relatives made up nearly 34% (300,253) of total class of admissions. If this number is combined with the family based preferences, in 1996 alone, the two categories accounted for 64.9% of all immigrants admitted that year.

The thrust of U.S. immigration policy in the direction of family reunification is further illustrated in Figure 8.1. As shown, family-based and family-sponsored immigrants far outnumber entrants from any other category or preference, including employment-based, in 2004 and 2014.

In 2013, 991,000 aliens became U.S. legal permanent residents, otherwise known as LPRs. Of this number, 65% entered on the basis of family ties (reunification). The pool of people potentially eligible to immigrate to the United States as legal permanent residents each year typically exceeds the worldwide ceiling set by the Immigration and Nationality Act. At the close of fiscal year 2014, most of the 4.4 million-approved petitions pending were for family members of U.S. citizens (CRS, 2014).

Immigration Trends Since 1965

One of the most tangible results of the 1965 amendments to the Immigration and Nationality Act was that it led to a dramatic shift in source countries. Since the 1970s, Europe has been replaced as a dominant sending region by counties in Latin America and Asia. As shown in Figure 8.2, the number of immigrants has also risen consistently since 1965. There were 296,697 entrants (for permanent residency) in 1965, but by 1980 there were 524,295 entrants. The unprecedented rise to 1,535,875 individuals obtaining permanent residency was due to both regular immigrants who had come with permanent visas issued abroad, and also those who had been in the United States illegally but were given the opportunity to adjust their status to permanent residency as a result of the Immigration Reform and Control Act of 1986 (IRCA). That legislation had as its goal curtailing illegal immigration, adjusting or regularizing the status of qualified illegal residents already in the United States, ensuring that labor demands in agriculture were met, and protecting citizens and legal immigrants against employment discrimination (Kposowa, 1998). The Immigration Reform and Control Act (IRCA) of 1986 enabled 2.1 million unauthorized people residing in the United States as of 1982 to become legal permanent residents. In addition, the number of refugees admitted increased from 718,000 in 1966–1980 to 1.6 million in 1981–1995, after enactment of the Refugee Act of 1980, which established permanent provisions for refugees and asylees to become legal permanent residents. These features contributed largely to the dramatic rise in 1990, shown in Figure 8.1, with regard to the number of people obtaining legal permanent residence.

FIGURE 8.1: Persons Obtaining Legal Permanent Resident Status, Selected Fiscal Years, 1950 to 2015

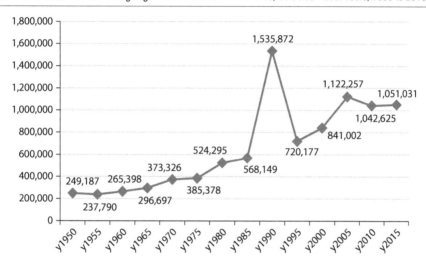

Source: U.S. Department of Homeland Security, "Persons Obtaininng Legal Permanent Resident Status, Selected Fiscal Years, 1950 to 2015," Department of Homeland Security, Office of Immigration Statistics, 2016. Copyright in the Public Domain.

Key provisions of IRCA included (1) employer requirements and sanctions under which it became a crime to hire undocumented workers; and (2) an anti-discrimination safeguard, which stipulated that employers may not discriminate against foreign-looking or foreign-sounding citizens or legal immigrants. Provision 3 created a workers' program that adjusted or legalized the status of immigrants who had lived continuously in the United States since 1982.

Provision 4 created the Special Agricultural Workers Legalization Program whereby the status of immigrants who had worked in agriculture through 1986 was adjusted. Provision 5 created a Replenishment Program, which granted further entry to additional immigrants for work in agriculture following 1990 if newly legalized immigrants under the previous provision had vacated the agricultural sector. It was anticipated by Congress that once previously undocumented workers became regularized, they would be free to take advantage of employment in other sectors of the labor market beyond agriculture, and that their departure would create labor shortages.

The sixth provision was a State Legalization Impact Assistance Grants Program (SLAG). Under it, the federal government was to pay states for additional costs incurred due to legalization of immigrants over a period of four years. Provision 7 instituted a Systematic Alien Verification for Entitlement Program by which determination could be made as to whether a noncitizen was eligible for public assistance programs financed by the federal government. The final provision was Increased Enforcement whereby more funds were provided to the then-Immigration and Naturalization Service (INS) and the U.S. Department of Labor to administer the new legislation (U.S. Congress, 1986).

The general verdict on the Immigration Reform and Control Act is that it was a failure. It failed to have any significant effect on reducing illegal immigration in the long run, and there are debates as to why the legislation failed. For example, although the legislation made it a crime to hire undocumented workers, companies generally ignored this provision, as enforcement was lax, and penalties were not severe. Economic expansion in the mid-1990s also created labor demands that could not be fulfilled by native-born workers. In that same decade, passage of the North American Free Trade Agreement (NAFTA) led to major economic dislocations in Mexico, which in turn encouraged more immigration.

The Act of 1990 raised levels of legal immigration; it tripled employment-related visas, and it created a diversity admissions visa category to assist countries such as the Republic of Ireland that had been negatively affected by the Act of 1965. The legislation raised the global annual ceiling of admissions from 270,000 to 700,000 for fiscal years 1992 through 1994, and to 675,000 thereafter. This number comprised 480,000 family-sponsored, 140,000 employment-based, and 55,000 "diversity" immigrants. The Act of 1990 allowed the entry of an unlimited number of visas for immediate relatives—children, parents, and spouses—of U.S. citizens, not counted under the numerical ceiling. As a result of these changes, by the close of the 1990s nearly 9 million immigrants had entered the United States (Department of Homeland Security, 2015; CRS, 2014).

There was a major immigration law passed amid the "tough on crime" rhetoric of both the William J. Clinton administration and the Republican-controlled House of Representatives in 1996 under the leadership of Newton L. Gingrich. This legislation has been faulted by some as one of the major drivers behind mass incarceration that now bedevils the United States and the omnipresent immigration raids in immigrant and minority neighborhoods, including the detention and deportation of immigrants, both documented and undocumented often for petty crimes, such as drug possession (Rabinovitz, 2014). The law was ostensibly passed to reform what was considered a broken immigration system that allegedly allowed an unknown—but presumably large—number of illegal entrants. It was passed to reduce illegal immigration and to apprehend those in the country without proper documentation. It was also intended to enhance border enforcement by introducing a pilot electronic employment eligibility verification system. This was in response to one of the perceived failures in the Immigration Reform and Control Act of 1986, which had included fines for punishing employers who hired undocumented foreigners but had not put into place adequate electronic monitoring. The law streamlined the removal process of individuals judged to have violated immigration laws, including entry without inspection, and allowed for a fence to be built on the U.S. border with Mexico at San Diego through "Operation Gatekeeper."

Officially known as the *Illegal Immigration Reform and Immigrant Responsibility Act* (enacted September 30, 1996), it barred legal immigrants entering the United States after 1996 from most federal means-tested programs (food stamps, Medicaid) for five years. It raised the income and legal standards for U.S. residents who sponsor immigrants; it made the affidavit of support provided by U.S. residents to would-be new entrants enforceable. It barred illegal immigrants from participating in most federal, state, and local public assistance. Some thought that one way to discourage illegal entry was to cut down on social ("welfare") benefits, which was believed to "attract" movement of individuals to the United States. It was widely believed by some policy makers in the House of representatives, especially on the Republican side, that illegal immigration was causing harm to the United States in terms of the effect on U.S. (native-born) people in higher taxes, unemployment, and reduced social services. The law was in response to these concerns.

The Illegal Immigration Reform and Immigrant Responsibility Act of 1996 further required the attorney general, within two years of enactment (September 30, 1998), to develop an automated entry and exit control system that would collect records of immigrant arrivals and departures, and allow the attorney general through online searches to match such arrivals and departures, thereby identifying nonimmigrant aliens who remain in the United States beyond their visa periods (i.e., visa overstayers). The legislation further required the attorney general to annually report to Congress on the number of visa overstayers and their countries of origin (CRS, 2015).

Today, the number of foreign-born residents in the United States is at its highest level in U.S. history, reaching 41.3 million in 2013. In 2013 the foreign-born comprised 13.1% of the U.S. population; these high levels have not been seen since 1910 when the percentage of foreign-born residents in the country reached 14.8% (U.S. Congressional Research Service [CRS], 2014).

Naturalization rates have also been increasing, especially since the attacks of September 2001 on New York and Washington, DC, and subsequent greater scrutiny of individuals entering the United States not only on valid nonimmigrant visas, but also even permanent resident visas ("green cards"). Indeed, holding a resident visa is no guarantee against deportation or barring an individual who has left the country from returning. Figure 8.2 shows new naturalizations by states in 2014.

The prospect of being denied entry even with a valid visa took on international significance in January 2017 following President Donald J. Trump's Executive Order 13769 of January 27, 2017. The order temporarily (for 90 days) barred entry to individuals from selected countries (Iraq, Iran, Yemen, Sudan, Somalia, Libya, Syria), and refugees (for 120 days) to allegedly do more "vetting." Caught up in the maze of confusion that followed immediate implementation of the order were U.S. permanent residents who had traveled abroad from the selected countries, and the holders of valid visas who had obtained permission to travel to the United States, including students. Although the courts placed a temporary hold on final implementation of the order, the reprieve was temporary, as the Trump administration wrote what was described as a watered-down version of the first. Like its earlier counterpart, it was struck down by the courts, but the administration appealed the lower court decisions, and the Supreme Court allowed portions of the second version of the president's executive order to be in effect, promising hearings on constitutional merits in October 2017. It is unclear what would happen, and whether the president himself would still be in office much longer. Investigations of his campaign's alleged collusion with Russia in the 2016 presidential election were ongoing as of fall 2017, along with possible financial irregularities by senior members of his campaign and the president himself.

Presidents and congresses have frequently left their marks on U.S. immigration policies. The Clinton administration left its blueprints on the Act of 1996; the following Bush administration (2001–2009) left its marks via the USA Patriot Act; and regardless of the final adjudication and disposition of Executive Order 13769, the Trump administration will leave an indelible mark, for better or for worse, on U.S. immigration for years to come. In July 2017, President Trump signaled that he favors reducing legal immigration, though in the run-up to the 2016 election his focus had been on illegal immigration.

Administration of U.S. immigration laws has historically often appeared to be based on an attitude of suspicion of—and hostility—toward foreigners, especially if coming from non-desirable countries. The laundry list of excludable categories is an enduring testament to this, along with the unwelcoming looks and cold treatment given to entrants by U.S. customs and immigration officials at ports of entry, especially airports.

FIGURE 8.2: U.S. Citizens Naturalized in 2014 by State

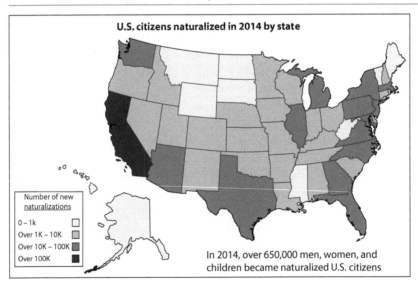

Immigration and the Changing Face of America

The population composition of the United States has changed—and continues to change. At the passage of the 1965 Amendments to the Immigration and Nationality Act, more than 84% of the U.S. population comprised non-Hispanic whites; in 2016 that number was much smaller. At the same time, as shown in Figure 8.3, the share of other groups has increased with Asians and those of Hispanic origin showing elevated percentage distributions (U.S. Census Bureau, 2012). Data from the American Community Survey show that immigrants with origins in Latin America and the Caribbean comprised 53.1% of all foreign-born persons in the United States in 2010. When these groups are disaggregated further, Mexican-origin immigrants made up 29.3 of the 53%, while Central America, South America, and Caribbean nations comprised 7.6%, 6.8%, and 9.3%, respectively. Immigrants with ancestry in Asia made up 28.2% of all foreign-born individuals.

In 2014, the share of non-Hispanic Whites in the population was at an all-time low, at 62%. This represents a 26% decline in the non-Hispanic White population since passage of the 1965 amendments to the Immigration and Nationality Act. Current projections provide evidence to suggest that by 2065, the percentage of non-Hispanic Whites in the U.S. population will be only 46%, with the American population becoming very demographically diverse, and increasingly "brownish" in terms of racial/ethnic composition. This will be a far cry from makeup of the population based on immigrant streams to the country from 1901 to 1960, as illustrated in Figure 8.3.

FIGURE 8.3: Top Sending Countries Comprising at Least Half of Legal Permanent Residents, 1901–2010

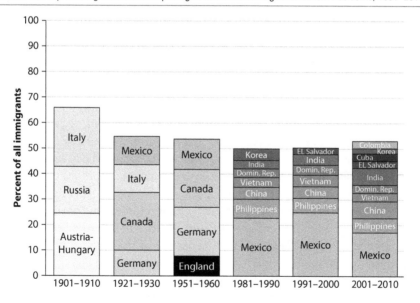

Source: Congressional Research Service, "Top Sending Countries Comprising at Least Half Legal Permanent Residents, 1901-2010," Congressional Research Service (2014), R42988. Copyright in the Public Domain.

FIGURE 8.4: Foreign-Born Residents by Region of Origin, 1960–2010

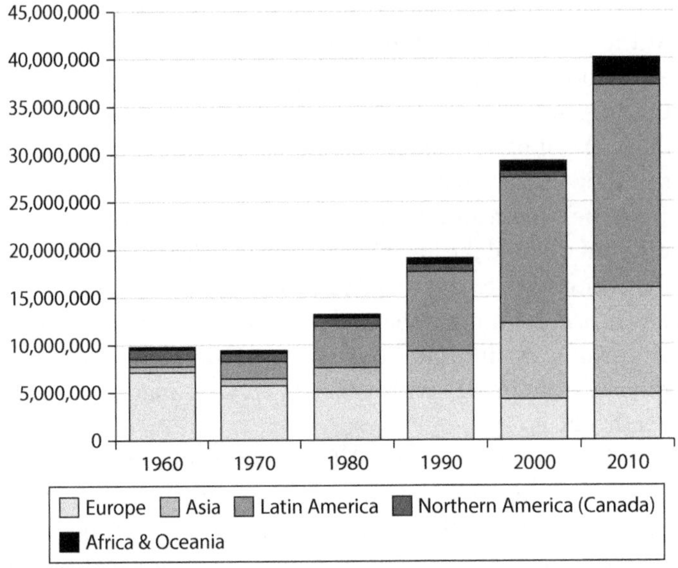

Source: US Census Bureau, "Foreign Born Residents by Region of Origin, 1960- 2010," *Decennial Censuses, 1960 to 2000; American Community Survey 2010.* Copyright in the Public Domain.

If we use the decennial census alone, the long-term consequences of the 1965 amendments are even much clearer. Europe has increasingly become a less significant source of immigration (except England periodically), while Latin America and Asia have taken over as dominant sources; Africa and Oceania are catching up, though slowly. These trends are reflected in the data shown in Figure 8.4.

As various changes in immigration policy have been since 1960, the focus on family reunification and the exceptional difficulties inherent in the process of securing U.S. visas abroad for legal entry, undocumented immigration has also increased. Instead of making changes to allow easier entry for people who wish to come, the focus has been on enforcement, expulsion, or removal, and what some would even characterize as "militarization," especially of the U.S.– Mexico border, to prevent individuals from coming outside the usual categories cited previously. As a result, there is now a sizable group of foreigners in the country without proper documentation. Some came with valid visas and stayed beyond the time assigned at a port of entry. Others crossed land borders without inspection. Figure 8.5 shows the estimated number of unauthorized aliens in the United States from 2000 to 2013. The data show that from 10 million to 11 million undocumented foreign nationals have been in the United States since 2004. The notion of building walls and stepping up removals may pose real ethical dilemmas and prove a challenge to the new Trump administration.

Change in racial/ethnic composition entails some changes in culture, religion, and even language. The specter of different languages written on the fronts of stores and restaurants in places such as Westminster, California, may not quite

FIGURE 8.5: Estimated Number of Unauthorized Aliens in the United States, 2000 to 2013

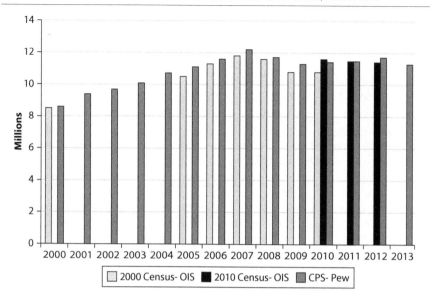

Source: Congressional Research Service, "Estimated Number of Unauthorized Aliens in the United States, 2000 to 2013," Congressional Research Service (2014), R42988. Copyright in the Public Domain.

Notes: OIS stands for Office of Immigration Statistics at the Department of Homeland Security; CPS is the Current Population Survey.

look like the melting pot that was once expected in America, for that melting pot envisaged only European immigrants believed to easily assimilate. It is easy to forget that even Whites who came to the United States following independence did not necessarily all speak English. Germans came with German and spoke it. Poles spoke Polish, the French spoke French, Spaniards spoke Spanish, and the Portuguese spoke Portuguese. Yet over time, these groups learned to speak English, and their unique backgrounds added to what became America.

Although some Americans view the changing racial/ethnic composition, largely brought about by immigration, as positive and use the concept "diversity," there is another side that views the change in a negative light. Some, especially older Whites, may be seeing something very different from the country they once knew or grew up in, and embracing this transformation is not easy. Hence, cries such as "we want our country back" or "make America great again" are nothing more than coded racial slogans masquerading as patriotic calls to move the country back to earlier times when it was less heterogeneous in terms of skin tone. To a large extent, these were the same sentiments prevailing in the 1920s that ultimately led to passage of the quota laws. If the 1920s were the Tribal Twenties, the current period (2015 to 2021) may well be another "tribal" period in immigrant acceptance and treatment.

REFERENCES

Congressional Research Service (2014). *U.S. immigration policy: Chart book of key trends.* CRS Report for Congress, R42988.

Congressional Research Service (2015). *Border security: Immigration inspections at ports of entry.* CRS Report for Congress, R43356.

Daniels, R. (2004). *Guarding the golden door.* New York, NY: Hill and Wang.

Daniels, R. (2002). *Coming to America.* New York, NY: Visual Education.

Democratic Party Platforms (1960). 1960 Democratic Party Platform, July 11, 1960. Online by Gerhard Peters and John T. Woolley, *The American Presidency Project.* http://www.presidency.ucsb.edu/ws/?pid=29602

Kennedy, J. F. (1959). *A nation of immigrants.* New York, NY: Anti-defamation League of B'nai B'rith.

Kennedy, J. F. (1961). Inaugural Address, January 20, 1961. Online by Gerhard Peters and John T. Woolley, *The American Presidency Project.* http://www.presidency.ucsb.edu/ws/?pid=8032

Kposowa, A. J. (1998). *The impact of immigration on the United States economy.* Lanham, MD: University Press of America.

Republican Party Platforms (1960). Republican Party Platform of 1960, July 25, 1960. Online by Gerhard Peters and John T. Woolley, *The American Presidency Project.* http://www.presidency.ucsb.edu/ws/?pid=25839

Democratic Party Platforms (1964). 1964 Democratic Party Platform, August 24, 1964. Online by Gerhard Peters and John T. Woolley, *The American Presidency Project.* http://www.presidency.ucsb.edu/ws/?pid=29603

Rabinovitz, J. (2011). *Ending the laws that fuel mass detention and deportation.* Available at https://www.aclu.org/blog/ending-laws-fuel-mass-detention-and-deportation. Accessed February 12, 2017.

Republican Party Platforms (1964). Republican Party Platform of 1964, July 13, 1964. Online by Gerhard Peters and John T. Woolley, *The American Presidency Project.* http://www.presidency.ucsb.edu/ws/?pid=25840

U.S. Bureau of the Census (2012). *The foreign-born population in the United States 2010: American Community Survey Reports.* Washington, DC: Department of Commerce.

U.S. Congress (1965). *An act to amend the immigration and nationality act and for other purposes.* Public Law 89–236. Available at http://www.gpo.gov/fdsys/pkg/STATUTE-79/pdf/STATUTE-79-Pg911.pdf.

U.S. Congress (1986). *Immigration reform and control act of 1986.* Public Law 99–603, S.1200, November 6. Washington, DC: Government Printing Office.

U.S. Department of Homeland Security, Office of Immigration Statistics (2005). *2005 yearbook of immigration statistics.* Available at http://uscis.gov/graphics/shared/statistics/yearbook/index.htm.

U.S. Department of Homeland Security (2015). *Persons obtaining lawful permanent resident status, 1994, 2004 and 2014.* Available at https://www.dhs.gov/immigration-statistics/visualization.

U.S. Department of Homeland Security (2015). *U.S. citizens naturalized in 2014 by state.* Available at https://www.dhs.gov/immigration-statistics/visualization.

9 Changing Immigrant Characteristics

I
n the 1980s and early 1990s, one frequently heard the expression "the New Immigration" even in academic circles (peer-reviewed journal articles and books). Chiswick's "Is the New Immigration Less Skilled?" (1986), Altonji and Card's "The Effects of Immigration on the Labor Market Outcomes of Less-Skilled Natives" (1991), and numerous other articles devoted an inordinate amount of coverage to the new immigration and its alleged effect on U.S. natives. Peter Brimelow (1995), himself an immigrant, though of White British stock, in his book *Alien Nation: Common Sense About America's Immigration Disaster* blamed the Kennedy administration and the 1965 amendments to the Immigration and Nationality Act as some disaster that had befallen the country in allowing thousands of non-White immigrants to enter the nation. He echoed earlier claims of nativists that the United States had been founded by Nordics, and should remain so, that immigration laws of the previous 30 years should be repealed, that the U.S. southern border should be sealed, and that undocumented immigrants should be arrested and deported. The new immigration designation was in reference to entrants to the United States following the 1965 amendments to the Immigration and Nationality Act.

It was alleged from the 1980s through early 1990s that the "floodgates" had been opened, and that new immigrants were not as skilled as their counterparts of earlier times, and would most likely have negative effects on native-born Americans and on the U.S. economy as a whole. In short, the newcomers were bringing down the United States. The debates and controversies over the consequences of immigration, in light of increasing numbers entering from developing nations, were so intense and at times so acrimonious that Congress asked the U.S. Commission on Immigration Reform to review and evaluate implementation of U.S. immigration policy, and the effect of U.S. immigration (National Research Council, 1997, p. 17). In 1995, the commission asked the National Academy of Sciences to convene a panel of experts across various disciplines in the social sciences to examine the consequences of U.S. immigration on society, focusing on three main areas: (1) demographic consequences, (2) economic consequences, and (3) fiscal consequences.

The panel's findings were published in a book aptly titled *The New Americans: Economic, Demographic, and Fiscal Effects of Immigration* (National Research Council, 1997). Since the effects of the post-1965 legislation would have been felt at least five years after the law went into effect, the base year for many statistical analyses and reporting was 1970. The report, covering 434 pages, examined issues of immigration history, characteristics of immigrants immediately before and after 1965, marriage patterns between immigrant cohorts, source countries of the new immigrants, characteristics of new entrants relative to the native-born, gender disparities in immigration, and the projection of what was called the face of the U.S. population from 1950 to 2050 in terms of racial composition. One estimate, for example, was that while non-Hispanic Whites made up 87% of the population in 1950, following passage of the 1965 legislation, they had already dropped to 83% of the population in 1970, and this trend would remain through 2010, when Whites (non-Hispanic) would comprise 67% of the population. It was projected that by 2050, non-Hispanic Whites would make up only 51% of the population (National Research Council, 1997, p. 121). By comparison, Hispanics, who represented only 3% of the American population in 1950, would emerge as the largest visible minority group in 2010 (15% of the population), projected at 20% in 2030, and by 2050 are expected to have a 26% share of the U.S. population. Although population projections in demography are made with uncertainty, the panel's analyses have been relatively accurate at the national level as of 2010, and there is every indication its estimates would come very close for 2050.

Of an estimated population of 311,116,000, there were 40,107,000 foreign-born residents in the United States in 2013 (U.S. Census Bureau, 2013). The share of the foreign-born was nearly 13%. Figure 9.1 shows trends in source countries for the foreign-born population by cohorts of entry. As may be seen, immigration has risen in every cohort and from each region of the world since 1970, though some regions have increased the foreign-born pool at a higher rate than others. For instance, prior to 1970, Europeans comprised 24.1% of the foreign-born in that cohort. In that same period, Latin Americans made up only 5.6% of immigrants. In every cohort since 1970, Latin Americans have seen their share of the foreign-born rise, to 9.3% (1970–1979), 17.8% (1980–1989), 29% (1990–1999), and 38.3% between 2000 and 2013. Immigrants from Asia have made remarkable strides as well. Their share of the foreign-born population was a mere 3.6% before 1970, but between 1970 and 1979, they accounted for 10% of that cohort, representing a phenomenal growth of nearly 178%. Of the 11,763,000 arriving from Asia since 1970, 43.4% entered in the 2000 to 2013 period.

As shown in Figure 9.2, about 62% of the foreign-born population came to live in the United States in 1990 or later, and this includes 35% that entered the country in 2000 or later (U.S. Bureau of the Census, 2010).

Seventy-eight percent of the foreign-born population from Africa entered the United States in 1990 or later, a figure that includes nearly 52% that entered in 2000 or later. By comparison, more than 50% of the foreign-born population from Europe and northern America (Canada) entered prior to 1990 (U.S. Bureau of the Census, 2010).

Geographic Distribution of the Foreign-Born

Immigrants (foreign-born) are not evenly distributed in the United States, though every state in the Union does have immigrants. In 2010, more than one in four

FIGURE 9.1: Year of Entry of the Foreign-Born Population by Sex and World Region of Birth: 2013

Sex and Year of Entry	Total		Asia		Europe		World Region of Birth — Latin America — Total Latin America		Mexico		Other Latin America[1]		Other areas[2]	
	Number	Percent	Number	Percent	Number	Percent	Number	Percent	Number	Percent	Number	Percent	Number	Percent
Both sexes	40,106	100.0	11,763	100.0	4,442	100.0	21,047	100.0	11,497	100.0	9,549	100.0	2,856	100.0
Entered 2000 or later[3]	15,876	39.6	5,110	43.4	1,210	27.2	8,070	38.3	4,226	36.8	3,843	40.2	1,487	52.1
Entered 1990–1999	10,739	26.8	2,901	24.7	1,130	25.4	6,108	29.0	3,619	31.5	2,489	26.1	599	21.0
Entered 1980–1989	6,775	16.9	2,146	18.2	553	12.5	3,738	17.8	2,005	17.4	1,733	18.1	339	11.9
Entered 1970–1979	3,792	9.5	1,182	10.0	479	10.8	1,962	9.3	1,096	9.5	866	9.1	171	6.0
Entered before 1970	2,924	7.3	424	3.6	1,070	24.1	1,169	5.6	551	4.8	618	6.5	260	9.1
Male	19,538	100.0	5,404	100.0	2,089	100.0	10,582	100.0	6,036	100.0	4,546	100.0	1,463	100.0
Entered 2000 or later[3]	7,848	40.2	2,357	43.6	573	27.4	4,152	39.2	2,258	37.4	1,894	41.7	767	52.4
Entered 1990–1999	5,279	27.0	1,351	25.0	577	27.6	3,064	29.0	1,871	31.0	1,192	26.2	287	19.6
Entered 1980–1989	3,327	17.0	1,001	18.5	242	11.6	1,900	18.0	1,057	17.5	843	18.5	184	12.6
Entered 1970–1979	1,821	9.3	519	9.6	231	11.0	969	9.2	587	9.7	382	8.4	102	7.0
Entered before 1970	1,263	6.5	176	3.3	466	22.3	498	4.7	263	4.4	234	5.2	123	8.4
Female	20,569	100.0	6,359	100.0	2,352	100.0	10,465	100.0	5,461	100.0	5,004	100.0	1,393	100.0
Entered 2000 or later[3]	8,028	39.0	2,752	43.3	637	27.1	3,918	37.4	1,968	36.0	1,949	39.0	721	51.7
Entered 1990–1999	5,460	26.5	1,551	24.4	552	23.5	3,045	29.1	1,748	32.0	1,297	25.9	312	22.4
Entered 1980–1989	3,448	16.8	1,145	18.0	311	13.2	1,838	17.6	948	17.4	890	17.8	155	11.1
Entered 1970–1979	1,971	9.6	662	10.4	248	10.5	993	9.5	509	9.3	484	9.7	68	4.9
Entered before 1970	1,661	8.1	249	3.9	604	25.7	672	6.4	288	5.3	384	7.7	137	9.9

[1]Those born in 'other Latin America' are from all sub-regions of Latin America (Central America, South America, and the Caribbean), excluding Mexico.

[2]Those born in 'other areas' are from Africa, Oceania, Northern America, and Born at Sea.

[3]The category '2000 or later' includes 2000–2013.

Note: Numbers in thousands. Universe is the foreign-born civilian noninstitutionalized population of the United States, plus Armed Forces members who live in housing units—off post or on post—with at least one other civilian adult.

Source: US Census Bureau, "Year of Entry of the Foreign-Born Population by Sex and World Region of Birth: 2013." *Current Population Survey, Annual Social and Economic Supplement.* Copyright in the Public Domain.

FIGURE 9.2: Period of Entry of the Foreign-Born, 2010

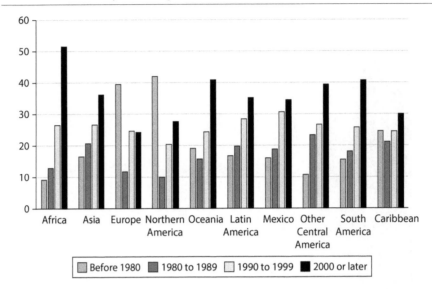

Source: US Census Bureau, "Period of Entry of the Foreign-Born, 2010," www.census.gov/acs/www/, pp. 10. Copyright in the Public Domain. Data entered into Excel by author.

FIGURE 9.3: Percent Foreign Born Population by State, U.S. 2010

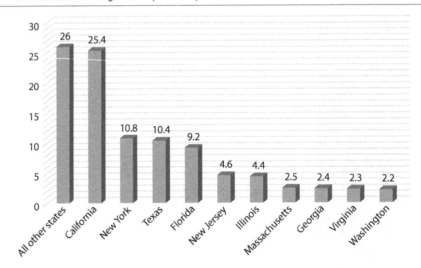

Source: US Census Bureau, "Percent Foreign Born Population by State, U.S. 2010," https://www.census.gov/prod/2012pubs/acs-19.pdf. Copyright in the Public Domain. Data entered in Excel by author.

foreign-born persons lived in the state of California. Other high immigrant destination states were New York, Florida, and Texas.

The pattern shown in Figure 9.3 on immigrant destinations has not changed since the 1970s. In 1974, 21 percent of legal immigrants entering the United States reported to the then Immigration and Naturalization Service (INS) that California was their intended destination, with New York ranking a very close second at 20%. In 1984, California began to pull away from New York, with 26% of immigrants selecting the Golden State as their intended place of residence, while New York had fallen to 20%. In 1994, California was the preferred destination for 26% of immigrants and 18% reported New York as their state of intended residence (U.S. Immigration and Naturalization Service, 1975, 1985, 1996).

Rates of Naturalization

Naturalization is usually the end of the path to citizenship for an immigrant or foreign-born person. Becoming a citizen confers on an immigrant benefits not open to noncitizens, primarily voting and some federal jobs, especially sensitive ones only open to citizens, such as working for the U.S. Census Bureau; some defense department positions; and some positions at think tanks that undertake contracts with the Department of Defense, such as RAND Corporation. There is also the added benefit of applying for, and obtaining, an American passport, which enables one to travel to countries with visa reciprocity agreements with the United States and bypassing the hassles of applying for a visa. Of course, in times of crisis, and in countries hostile to the United States, it is possible for an American passport to be a liability, and benefits may be proportionate to the degree of cordial relations between the United States and the country to which one travels.

Rates of naturalization have varied historically by region of origin, and even within regions, countries vary. In 2010, 43.7% of the foreign-born were naturalized U.S. citizens. Immigrants from Europe had the highest rate of naturalization (61.8%), followed by those from Asia (57.7%).

FIGURE 9.4A: Percent Naturalized by World Regions, 2010

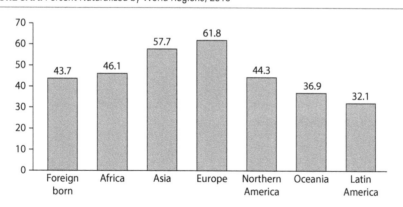

Source: US Census Bureau , "Percent Naturalized by World Regions, 2010," www.census.gov/acs/www/. Copyright in the Public Domain.

The lower naturalization for immigrants from Latin America (42.1%) masks significant variation when it is broken down by subregions or countries. For instance, within the Latin region, Caribbean immigrants have the highest naturalization rate (54.1%), followed by South American countries (44.4%). Immigrants from Mexico have the lowest naturalization rate (22.9%). Other Central American nationals experienced a naturalization rate of 39.6% by 2010.

Naturalization varies by time of arrival, and duration of residence in the United States. The type of visa used by a person at time of initial entry may also affect how soon an individual may get naturalized. In general, individuals arriving in the United States on immigrant visas obtained abroad may become naturalized sooner than those arriving as students on temporary (nonimmigrant) visas.

Data from the 2010 American Community Survey show that in 2010, 79.9% of the foreign-born who entered the United States prior to 1980 were naturalized. Of those coming between 1980 and 1989, 63.1% had been naturalized. Nearly 43% of those entering between 1990 and 1999 were naturalized, but only 13.7% of immigrants who entered after 2000 were naturalized. Important factors that may account for the differentials include the residency requirement, and the often long-drawn process of getting naturalized, including paper work, adjustment of status for those arriving on nonimmigrant visas, and the financial costs involved. It also makes a big difference as to whether someone came under family reunification or under one of the other preference categories cited in the previous chapter.

Human Capital and Other Social Characteristics

Educational Attainment

Of the total U.S. population, 14.4% had less than a high school education in 2010; 28.5% had a high school education or equivalency. Nearly 29% had some college or associate's degree, and 28.2% had a bachelor's degree or higher.

Among the native-born, 11% had less than a high school education, 29.7% were high school graduates, and 30.9% had some college or associate's degree, while 28.4% had a bachelor's degree or higher. Disparities in educational attainment of the population 25 years and older by nativity status are shown in Table 9.1. At the highest level of educational attainment, near parity has been achieved by immigrants and the native-born. There is only 1.4% difference between the two groups.

TABLE 9.1: Educational Attainment, Native and Foreign-Born, 25 years and Older, United States 2010

Education	Total	Native-Born	Foreign-Born
Less than high school graduate	14.4%	11.0%	31.7%
High school or equivalency	28.5%	29.7%	22.5%
Some college or associate's degree	28.9%	30.9%	18.8%
Bachelor's degree or higher	28.2%	28.4%	27.0%

Source: US Census Bureau, "Educational Attainment, Native and Foreign Born, 25 Years and Older, United States 2010," https://www.census.gov/data/tables/2013/demo/foreign-born/cps-2013.html. Copyright in the Public Domain.

Educational attainment of immigrants varies significantly by region of birth. As shown in Figure 9.4, the highest educational attainment of the foreign-born was among immigrants from Asia, 48.5% of whom had a bachelor's degree or higher. They were followed by those from northern America (Canada), 42.5% of whom were in that educational category. The African immigrant group had 40.3% with a bachelor's degree or higher. European immigrants were at 36.4%, while those from Latin America were at 11.2%.

FIGURE 9.4B: Educational Attainment of the Foreign Born, 25 years and Older by Region of Birth, 2010

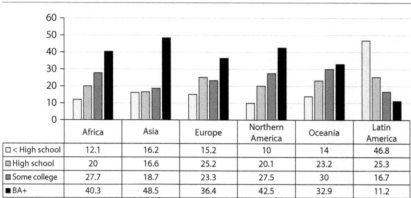

	Africa	Asia	Europe	Northern America	Oceania	Latin America
□ < High school	12.1	16.2	15.2	10	14	46.8
▨ High school	20	16.6	25.2	20.1	23.2	25.3
▦ Some college	27.7	18.7	23.3	27.5	30	16.7
■ BA+	40.3	48.5	36.4	42.5	32.9	11.2

□ < High school   ▨ High school   ▦ Some college   ■ BA+

Source: US Census Bureau, "Educational Attainment of the Foreign Born, 25 years and Older by Region of Birth, 2010," www.census.gov/acs/www/. Copyright in the Public Domain.

Substantial variations were observed in the lowest educational strata and by region of birth. The total foreign-born average for those with less than a high school education was 31.7%, but when broken down by regions, it was observed that those from Canada (northern America) had the lowest percentage (10%), followed by African immigrants (12.1%), immigrants from Oceania (14%), Europeans (15.2%), and those from Asia (16.2%). Among Latin American immigrants, 46.8% had less than a high school education, but this number differs by subregion. For instance, while South Americans had 17.3% with less than a high school education, comparable figures for Caribbean and Mexican immigrants were 26.7% and 60.1%, respectively.

Educational attainment of the foreign-born is shown in greater detail in Table 9.2, based on the 2013 Current Population Survey. The percentage with less than a high school education for all immigrants is 27.9, which is below the 31.7% recorded in the 2010 American Community Survey.

Labor Force Participation

In 2010, the labor force participation rate of immigrants was higher than that of the native-born population. For example, among immigrants 16 years and older, 68% were in the labor force. The comparable labor force participation rate of the native-born was 64%. Sex differences in labor force participation were especially pronounced, with 79% of immigrant males more likely to be actively in the labor

TABLE 9.2: Educational Attainment of the Foreign-Born Population 25 Years and Over by Region of Birth, 2013

Sex and Educational Attainment[1]	World Region of Birth													
	Total		Asia		Europe		Latin America						Other Areas[3]	
							Total Latin America		Mexico		Other Latin America[2]			
	Number	Percent	Number	Percent	Number	Percent	Number	Percent	Number	Percent	Number	Percent	Number	Percent
Both sexes	34,462	100.0	10,046	100.0	3,931	100.0	18,117	100.0	9,797	100.0	8,320	100.0	2,368	100.0
Less than 9th grade	5,949	17.3	631	6.3	197	5.0	4,987	27.5	3,489	35.6	1,498	18.0	134	5.7
9th to 12th grade (no diploma)	3,653	10.6	510	5.1	154	3.9	2,880	15.9	2,003	20.4	878	10.5	108	4.6
High school graduate	8,799	25.5	2,018	20.1	1,082	27.5	5,179	28.6	2,653	27.1	2,527	30.4	520	22.0
Some college or associate's degree	5,673	16.5	1,605	16.0	847	21.5	2,700	14.9	1,052	10.7	1,648	19.8	521	22.0
Bachelor's degree	6,219	18.0	2,977	29.6	966	24.6	1,665	9.2	455	4.6	1,210	14.5	611	25.8
Master's degree	2,850	8.3	1,518	15.1	481	12.2	531	2.9	108	1.1	423	5.1	320	13.5
Professional degree	533	1.5	299	3.0	60	1.5	102	0.6	20	0.2	82	1.0	72	3.0
Doctorate degree	787	2.3	489	4.9	145	3.7	72	0.4	19	0.2	54	0.6	81	3.4
Less than high school diploma	9,602	27.9	1,141	11.4	351	8.9	7,868	43.4	5,492	56.1	2,376	28.6	242	10.2
High school graduate or more	24,860	72.1	8,905	88.6	3,580	91.1	10,250	56.6	4,305	43.9	5,944	71.4	2,125	89.8
Less than bachelor's degree	24,074	69.9	4,764	47.4	2,279	58.0	15,747	86.9	9,197	93.9	6,551	78.7	1,283	54.2
Bachelor's degree or more	10,388	30.1	5,282	52.6	1,651	42.0	2,370	13.1	601	6.1	1,769	21.3	1,084	45.8
Less than master's degree	30,293	87.9	7,741	77.1	3,245	82.6	17,412	96.1	9,651	98.5	7,761	93.3	1,895	80.0
Master's degree or more	4,169	12.1	2,305	22.9	686	17.4	705	3.9	146	1.5	559	6.7	473	20.0

[1]Educational attainment is measured as highest level of school completed or degree received.

[2]Those born in 'other Latin America' are from all sub-regions of Latin America (Central America, South America, and the Caribbean), excluding Mexico.

[3]Those born in 'other areas' are from Africa, Oceania, Northern America, and Born at Sea.

Note: Numbers in thousands. Universe is the foreign-born civilian noninstitutionalized population of the United States, plus Armed Forces members who live in housing units—off post or on post—with at least one other civilian adult.

Source: US Census Bureau, "Educational Attainment of the Foreign Born Population 25 years and over by Region of Birth, 2013." Current Population Survey, Annual Social and Economic Supplement. Copyright in the Public Domain.

force than native-born males at 68%. Sixty percent of native-born females were more likely to have participated in the labor force than foreign born females at 57% (U.S. Census Bureau, 2010).

Labor force participation rates, including employment figures, can be derived from the decennial census, the American Community Survey, the Current Population Survey (CPS), and especially from the Annual Economic Supplement (AES) of the CPS. Table 9.3 shows the employment status of the foreign-born (immigrant) population in the United States, in 2013, from the Annual Economic Supplement of the CPS. As can be seen, 76% of the foreign-born were employed full time in 2013. Distinctions between full time and part time are based on hours worked per week. Typically, individuals working 35 hours a week or more are employed full time, while those who report working less than 35 hours a week are employed part time. Nearly 8% of the foreign-born were unemployed. A major flaw in the U.S. official definition of unemployment is the fact that no provision is made for long-term unemployment. For a person to be considered unemployed, he or she has to be actively looking for work, and available to work in the week of the survey. The downside to such a definition is that those who have become discouraged due to not finding a job after seeking work are missing from the classification of the "unemployed." Such a narrow definition may severely underestimate unemployment among visible minorities and immigrants due to issues such as labor market discrimination, and a lack of access to networks (such as exclusive social and country clubs) that many of the more disadvantaged are excluded (Davison & Kposowa, 2012). After all, in America, as in many other societies, access to jobs is not merely a question of merit, but who you know (or who knows you). Thus for many, including native-born and foreign-born, but especially visible minorities, expressions such as "equal opportunity," "you can be anything you want to be," or even an "American dream" are nothing more than empty slogans, if not cruel jokes. They ignore real hurdles that people who are not well connected, or who face daily realities of prejudice, have to contend with.

Income

Recent research shows a strong correlation between skin tone and income for new immigrants. Grubbs (2016), for example used the New Immigrant Survey and reported that as skin color darkens for immigrants, income decreases. Similar observations were made by Bideshi and Kposowa (2012) in their comparison of White African and Black African immigrants to the United States, using data from the 2000 decennial census and the American Community Survey.

There is evidence to suggest disparities in income between immigrants and native-born (Table 9.4). In 2010 the median household income of immigrant households was $46,224 while that of native-born households was $50,541. The differential in income was larger for family households, where the median income was $62,358 for families with a native householder, but $49,785 for families with an immigrant householder (U.S. Census Bureau, 2010).

TABLE 9.3: Employment Status of the Foreign-Born Civilian Population 16 Years and Over by Sex and Region of Birth, 2013

Sex and Employment Status[1]	World Region of Birth													
	Total		Asia		Europe		Latin America						Other Areas[3]	
							Total Latin America		Mexico		Other Latin America[2]			
	Number	Percent	Number	Percent	Number	Percent	Number	Percent	Number	Percent	Number	Percent	Number	Percent
Both sexes	25,290	100.0	7,169	100.0	2,422	100.0	13,834	100.0	7,480	100.0	6,354	100.0	1,865	100.0
Employed	23,359	92.4	6,757	94.3	2,273	93.8	12,623	91.2	6,809	91.0	5,814	91.5	1,706	91.5
Full-time[4]	19,221	76.0	5,614	78.3	1,827	75.4	10,381	75.0	5,555	74.3	4,826	75.9	1,399	75.0
Part-time[4]	4,138	16.4	1,143	15.9	445	18.4	2,242	16.2	1,255	16.8	988	15.5	307	16.5
Unemployed	1,931	7.6	412	5.7	150	6.2	1,211	8.8	670	9.0	541	8.5	159	8.5
Male	14,597	100.0	3,849	100.0	1,338	100.0	8,359	100.0	4,889	100.0	3,469	100.0	1,052	100.0
Employed	13,562	92.9	3,634	94.4	1,268	94.8	7,693	92.0	4,518	92.4	3,175	91.5	967	91.9
Full-time[4]	11,966	82.0	3,204	83.2	1,126	84.2	6,779	81.1	3,987	81.5	2,792	80.5	857	81.5
Part-time[4]	1,596	10.9	431	11.2	142	10.6	914	10.9	531	10.9	383	11.0	109	10.4
Unemployed	1,035	7.1	215	5.6	70	5.2	665	8.0	371	7.6	294	8.5	85	8.1
Female	10,693	100.0	3,320	100.0	1,085	100.0	5,475	100.0	2,590	100.0	2,885	100.0	813	100.0
Employed	9,797	91.6	3,123	94.1	1,005	92.6	4,930	90.0	2,291	88.5	2,639	91.5	740	91.0
Full-time[4]	7,255	67.8	2,411	72.6	701	64.6	3,601	65.8	1,568	60.5	2,034	70.5	542	66.6
Part-time[4]	2,542	23.8	712	21.5	303	28.0	1,329	24.3	724	27.9	605	21.0	198	24.4
Unemployed	896	8.4	197	5.9	80	7.4	545	10.0	299	11.5	246	8.5	73	9.0

[1] Employment status is based on week of the survey

[2] Other Latin America includes Central America, South America, and the Caribbean (excluding Mexico)

[3] Other areas include Africa, Oceania, Northern America, and born at sea

[4] Full time means working 35 hours or more per week; part-time means working less than 35 hours

Source: US Census Bureau, "Employment Status of the Foreign Born Civilian Population 16 Years and Over by Sex and Region of Birth, 2013," https://www.census.gov/prod/2012pubs/acs-19.pdf. Copyright in the Public Domain.

TABLE 9.4: Median Household Income by Type, Natives, and Immigrants, 2010

	Total	Native	Immigrant
All households	$50,046	$50,541	$46,224
Family households	$60,609	$62,358	$49,785
Non-Family households	$30,440	$30,585	$28,287

Source: US Census Bureau, "Median Household Income by Type, Natives and Immigrants, 2010," www.census.gov/acs/www/. Copyright in the Public Domain.

When immigrants are disaggregated by world region of birth, there are major differences in median household income. For all households, immigrants from Oceania (which includes Australia and New Zealand) had the highest income ($71,441), followed by those from northern America (Canada) at $64,095. Latin American-origin immigrant households have the lowest ($38,234). Figure 9.5 shows median household income by household type and world region of birth. As shown in the figure, the median income for households with an immigrant householder born in Oceania was $71,441. This exceeded the median income of the native-born household population, and that of households with householders born in all other regions of birth. At the same time, among family households, the median income of families with an immigrant family householder from northern America (Canada) was the highest, at $83,369.

There are variations in income within regions, notably Latin America. The median income for households with a foreign-born householder born in Latin America was $38,238, but when concentrating on specific countries or subregions,

FIGURE 9.5: Median Household Income of the Foreign-Born by Household Type 2010

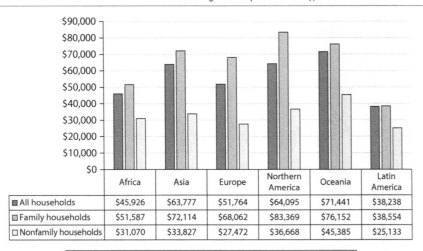

	Africa	Asia	Europe	Northern America	Oceania	Latin America
■ All households	$45,926	$63,777	$51,764	$64,095	$71,441	$38,238
▨ Family households	$51,587	$72,114	$68,062	$83,369	$76,152	$38,554
☐ Nonfamily households	$31,070	$33,827	$27,472	$36,668	$45,385	$25,133

■ All households   ▨ Family households   ☐ Nonfamily households

Source: U.S. US Census Bureau, "Median Household Income of the Foreign-Born by Household Type 2010," American Community Survey 2010. Copyright in the Public Domain.

TABLE 9.5: Total Earnings of Full-Time, Year-Round, Foreign-Born Workers 25 Years and Over with Earnings by Educational Attainment and Region of Birth, United States 2012

Educational Attainment[1] and Total Earnings[2]	Total		Asia		Europe		World Region of Birth — Latin America — Total Latin America		Latin America — Mexico		Latin America — Other Latin America[3]		Other Areas[4]	
	Number	Percent	Number	Percent	Number	Percent	Number	Percent	Number	Percent	Number	Percent	Number	Percent
Total	16,287	100.0	4,964	100.0	1,650	100.0	8,497	100.0	4,463	100.0	4,034	100.0	1,176	100.0
$1 to $24,999 or loss	4,628	28.4	760	15.3	216	13.1	3,421	40.3	2,028	45.4	1,393	34.5	231	19.7
$25,000 to $49,999	5,821	35.7	1,497	30.2	517	31.3	3,427	40.3	1,806	40.5	1,622	40.2	380	32.3
$50,000 to $74,999	2,648	16.3	1,058	21.3	378	22.9	978	11.5	398	8.9	580	14.4	234	19.9
$75,000 to $99,999	1,353	8.3	660	13.3	212	12.8	364	4.3	119	2.7	245	6.1	118	10.1
$100,000 and over	1,836	11.3	990	19.9	327	19.8	307	3.6	112	2.5	194	4.8	212	18.0
Median earnings ($)	36,871	X	52,437	X	52,152	X	28,475	X	26,284	X	31,548	X	47,124	X
Up to 12th grade (no diploma)	3,624	100.0	292	100.0	58	100.0	3,206	100.0	2,262	100.0	944	100.0	68	100.0
$1 to $24,999 or loss	2,061	56.9	156	53.4	13	21.5	1,843	57.5	1,281	56.6	562	59.6	49	72.1
$25,000 to $49,999	1,316	36.3	112	38.4	30	51.6	1,157	36.1	840	37.1	317	33.6	17	24.4
$50,000 to $74,999	178	4.9	13	4.6	11	18.2	152	4.8	104	4.6	49	5.2	2	3.2
$75,000 to $99,999	44	1.2	5	1.8	4	6.1	35	1.1	22	1.0	13	1.4		
$100,000 and over	25	0.7	5	0.7	2	2.6	18	0.6	15	0.7	2	0.3	2	0.4
Median earnings ($)	22,545	X	23,772	X	41,501	X	22,411	X	22,809	X	21,741	X	20,422	X
High school graduate	3,942	100.0	847	100.0	377	100.0	2,498	100.0	1,320	100.0	1,177	100.0	221	100.0
$1 to $24,999 or loss	1,466	37.2	290	34.3	94	24.9	989	39.6	517	39.1	472	40.1	93	42.3
$25,000 to $49,999	1,818	46.1	401	47.4	171	45.3	1,148	46.0	596	45.1	552	46.9	98	44.5
$50,000 to $74,999	456	11.6	113	13.3	69	18.4	254	10.2	140	10.6	114	9.7	20	8.9
$75,000 to $99,999	120	3.0	25	3.0	19	5.1	69	2.7	42	3.2	27	2.3	7	3.3
$100,000 and over	82	2.1	18	2.1	24	6.3	38	1.5	26	2.0	13	1.1	2	0.9
Median earnings ($)	30,036	X	30,718	X	37,254	X	28,130	X	28,385	X	27,737	X	27,670	X

(Continued)

TABLE 9.5: (Continued)

Educational Attainment[1] and Total Earnings[2]	Total Number	Total Percent	Asia Number	Asia Percent	Europe Number	Europe Percent	World Region of Birth — Latin America: Total Latin America Number	Total Latin America Percent	Mexico Number	Mexico Percent	Other Latin America[3] Number	Other Latin America[3] Percent	Other Areas[4] Number	Other Areas[4] Percent
Some college or associate's degree	2,693	100.0	720	100.0	339	100.0	1,379	100.0	515	100.0	864	100.0	256	100.0
$1 to $24,999 or loss	610	22.6	115	16.0	59	17.3	397	28.8	148	28.8	249	28.8	39	15.0
$25,000 to $49,999	1,191	44.2	345	47.9	119	35.2	619	44.9	241	46.9	378	43.7	108	42.1
$50,000 to $74,999	593	22.0	183	25.5	95	28.1	255	18.5	88	17.0	167	19.3	60	23.4
$75,000 to $99,999	189	7.0	47	6.5	38	11.2	73	5.3	25	4.9	47	5.4	31	12.2
$100,000 and over	111	4.1	29	4.0	28	8.2	36	2.6	12	2.3	24	2.7	18	7.2
Median earnings ($)	38,391	X	41,289	X	47,105	X	35,601	X	35,629	X	35,583	X	43,702	X
Bachelor's degree	3,450	100.0	1,640	100.0	483	100.0	979	100.0	273	100.0	706	100.0	348	100.0
$1 to $24,999 or loss	376	10.9	147	9.0	31	6.3	155	15.8	63	23.1	92	13.0	43	12.3
$25,000 to $49,999	1,107	32.1	446	27.2	152	31.4	398	40.7	111	40.7	287	40.7	111	32.0
$50,000 to $74,999	843	24.4	436	26.6	114	23.6	216	22.1	43	15.7	173	24.6	77	22.1
$75,000 to $99,999	536	15.5	290	17.7	88	18.2	110	11.3	22	8.0	89	12.6	48	13.9
$100,000 and over	588	17.1	321	19.6	99	20.5	99	10.1	34	12.6	65	9.2	69	19.7
Median earnings ($)	55,322	X	60,911	X	60,559	X	44,937	X	40,769	X	46,751	X	51,988	X
Advanced degree	2,578	100.0	1,465	100.0	394	100.0	435	100.0	93	100.0	342	100.0	284	100.0
$1 to $24,999 or loss	116	4.5	51	3.5	21	5.3	36	8.4	19	20.2	18	5.2	8	2.7
$25,000 to $49,999	389	15.1	193	13.2	45	11.5	104	24.0	17	18.6	87	25.5	46	16.3
$50,000 to $74,999	578	22.4	312	21.3	89	22.6	101	23.2	24	25.9	77	22.5	75	26.6
$75,000 to $99,999	464	18.0	292	19.9	63	16.1	77	17.8	8	8.9	69	20.2	31	11.1
$100,000 and over	1,030	40.0	616	42.0	175	44.5	115	26.6	24	26.4	91	26.6	123	43.3
Median earnings ($)	82,355	X	88,399	X	87,818	X	70,340	X	56,357	X	71,557	X	81,659	X

[1]Educational attainment is measured as highest level of school completed or degree obtained.

[2]Earnings are the sum of wages, salaries per calendar year.

[3]Other Latin American countries are from South American, Central America, and the Caribbean (excluding Mexico).

[4]Other areas include Africa, Oceania, Canada, and those born at sea.

Source: US Census Bureau, "Total Earnings of Full-Time, Year Round, Foreign-Born Workers 25 Years and Over with Earnings by Educational Attainment and Region of Birth, United States 2012," https://www.census.gov/prod/2012pubs/acs-19.pdf. Copyright in the Public Domain.

immigrant households with a householder born in Mexico had the lowest median household income, at $35,254, compared with householders born in South America who had the highest median household income in the sub-region ($49,741).

Earnings vary by educational attainment among the foreign-born. Without considering educational attainment, 11.3% of immigrants made $100,000 or more in 2012. By world region of birth, 19.9% of Asian immigrants were in this income category, followed by immigrants from Europe (19.8%), and other areas (Africa, Canada, Oceania, and those born at sea) at 18%. Among 2,578 immigrants with advanced degrees, 40% had median incomes in the $100,000 or more bracket in 2012. European immigrants had an edge in this group, with 44.5% in the $100,000 or more median income.

Occupation

Immigrants are more likely than the native-born to work jobs having to do with service, construction, and production. More than half of the civilian-employed immigrant population 16 years and older work in either management, business, science and the arts (29%), or service occupations (25%). When compared with the native-born population, more than one third work in management, business, science and the arts (37%), with about 25% working in sales and office-based occupations. Data from the 2010 American Community Survey (U.S. Census Bureau, 2010) show that management, business, science and the arts make up the largest share of civilian immigrant population from Canada (59%), Asia (47%), Europe (45%), Oceania (41%), and Africa (38%). The immigrant population from Latin America were the least likely to work in management, business, science and arts occupations (14%). As shown in Figure 9.6, they were the most likely, however, compared with immigrants from all other regions of the world, to work in service occupations (U.S. Census Bureau, 2010, p. 18).

FIGURE 9.6: Occupation of the Immigrant Population by Wold Region of Birth, 2010

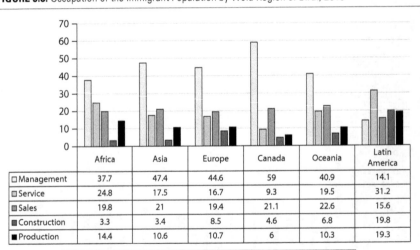

	Africa	Asia	Europe	Canada	Oceania	Latin America
☐ Management	37.7	47.4	44.6	59	40.9	14.1
☐ Service	24.8	17.5	16.7	9.3	19.5	31.2
▣ Sales	19.8	21	19.4	21.1	22.6	15.6
■ Construction	3.3	3.4	8.5	4.6	6.8	19.8
■ Production	14.4	10.6	10.7	6	10.3	19.3

☐ Management ☐ Service ▣ Sales ■ Construction ■ Production

Source: US Census Bureau, "Occupation of the Immigrant Population by Wold Region of Birth, 2010," www.census. gov/acs/www/. Copyright in the Public Domain.Figure by author from data entered in Excel.

When Latin America is broken down into further components, Mexican immigrants are the least likely to work in management, business, science and the arts (8.6%), and they are over represented in construction (25.2%).

Household Size

Immigrant households are typically much larger than that of native-born households. They also tend to have more children under 18, and more likely to spread over longer generations. The average household size of immigrants is 3.4 persons, while that of native-born is 2.5 persons. Duration of U.S. residence leads to reductions in household size due to assimilation and other factors, such as the high cost of having and raising children in the United States. Another reason for the difference between native-born and foreign-born is that a higher proportion of immigrant family households tends to have children under 18 years old. A lower percentage of native-born households includes children under 18 years old.

TABLE 9.6: Total and Family Household Size, by Nativity Status, 2010

	Total	Native-Born	Immigrants
Average household size	2.6	2.5	3.4
Average family household size	3.3	3.2	4.0

Source: US Census Bureau, "Total and Family Household Size, by Nativity Status, 2010," www.census.gov/acs/ www/. Copyright in the Public Domain.

Total and family household sizes vary by world region of birth. They are highest for immigrants from Latin America (3.9), and lowest for those from Canada (2.3). Within Latin America, Mexican immigrant households are the largest (4.4) and Caribbean households are the lowest (3.1). Percent of immigrant households with children under 18 years is highest among Mexican immigrants (77.1), followed by immigrants from other Central American nations (71.7).

Poverty Rate

The poverty rate of immigrants is higher than that of the native-born. As shown in Table 9.7, nearly 19% of immigrants live below the poverty level. This compares with nearly 15% of the native-born. At every age group, the poverty rate of immigrants exceeds that of native-born Americans. The difference is especially startling for children under 18 years. In this group, while the poverty rate among the native-born is 21.2%, among immigrants it is nearly 31%. Regardless of nativity status, the high percentage of children living in poverty in the United States is a very sad commentary on national priorities and policy. After all, the true symbol of a nation's greatness lies not in arms of war, number of missiles loaded and ready to be fired, number of militarized police forces and armored personnel carriers, not on how shiny the uniforms of police forces or the latest models of cruisers they drive, or number of citizens behind bars, but how it treats its most vulnerable. It seems from Table 9.7 that the nation has failed its children, regardless of nativity status.

TABLE 9.7: Poverty Rate of Native and Immigrants by Age, 2010

	Total	Native-Born	Immigrants
All ages	15.3%	14.8%	18.8%
Under 18	21.6%	21.2%	30.9%
18 to 64	14.2%	13.4%	18.2%
65 and older	9.0%	8.1%	15.8%

Source: US Census Bureau, "Poverty Rate of Native and Immigrants by Age, 2010," www.census.gov/acs/www/. Copyright in the Public Domain.

Health Insurance

To many outside the United States, the country often appears as a place where unregulated capitalism and privatization have gone too far. This is especially true when it comes to health care, and the notion that it exists in America as a profit-making enterprise, no different from any other industry or business. Why, it might be asked, does a nation that claims to be exceptional and the best not provide medical care for all its population, but relies on profit-making corporations to decide who lives and who dies? The ability to obtain medical care has remained a persistent source of controversy for ages, with many vested interests fighting to prevent universal coverage, or making health care a right for all citizens. There are physician groups, such as the American Medical Association, and insurance companies, each wanting to maintain the status quo for their own benefits.

The American Medical Association historically discouraged the notion of universal health care out of fear that ability to make high incomes by providers would be eroded, but often argued under the disguise of diminished quality of care (Quadagno, 2004, 2006; Derickson, 2005), an argument reminiscent of its opposition to barring foreign physicians from practicing in the United States. More physicians might lead to excess supply, which in turn could heighten competition, leading to a fall in compensation.

Insurance companies opposed universal (and single-payer system) out of concern that their profit margins would decline, and indeed, if the state took over administering health care, some insurance companies might literally go out of business. Health care thus remains in the United States a largely profitable industry with many lucrative stakeholders.

Until the Patient Protection and Affordable Care Act (ACA), insurance companies often and routinely refused to cover people described as having "preexisting conditions," a rather strange, if not cruel, policy. People typically do not go out to purchase diseases, but are either born with predispositions, inherit them, or acquire diseases as they get old, especially with increasing life expectancy, reduced organ functioning, and more chronic conditions that are not curable, but at best manageable. The idea that they should not be treated because their conditions are preexisting never answered the moral question as to what should happen to such individuals. Successive U.S. administrations largely ignored the plight of the "preexisting" people. Likewise, prescription drug prices continued to rise uncontrolled, and lawmakers would make dubious, if not nonsensical, claims that patients should be prevented from purchasing drugs from Canada because they were unsafe—even though Canadians who used those drugs were not dying in thousands or hundreds by the wayside, and the same corporations manufactured the same drugs. Of course, the restrictions on drug importation from Canada were designed to artificially keep the cost of prescription medications high in the United States, an outcome that benefitted the pharmaceutical industry. At every step of the way, capitalist quest for profit prevailed, along with campaign contributions from pharmaceutical industries to politicians, and special interests that made huge profits from the dysfunctional status quo.

The much-praised Patient Protection and Affordable Care Act (ACA) or Obamacare (as derided by its opponents), while helping to insure millions of Americans, was not as revolutionary as one would have thought because it only succeeded in bringing more customers to the private insurance industry. It failed to make provision for single-payer universal coverage. Some had hoped a public option provision would lay a foundation for the eventual movement of the United States away from a profit-driven private insurance orientation in health care to a more humane system that never again allowed insurance company abuse of citizens (Baucus, 2008; Cohn, 2010). The public option was never allowed into the ACA for many reasons. One was the refusal of Republican legislators in the Senate to associate themselves with anything having to do with President Barack Obama, whose presidency they seemed determined to turn into some blemish on American history; the president was, after all, the first non-White person to ever hold that office, and this was just too much for some to stomach. Prejudice against the president and his skin color (and by extension to his racial background) was often hidden under his alleged "liberal" tendencies, though many policies he espoused or failed to champion often left many progressives disappointed, confused, and frustrated. Given that the ACA's eventual passage required a two-thirds majority in the Senate (60 senators), and Democrats did not have a foolproof number, they needed all in their party to vote for the public option, along with securing the vote of an independent senator from Connecticut, Joseph Lieberman.

Unfortunately, and perhaps oddly, Lieberman opposed the public option idea, and with that opposition, Democrats lacked the 60 votes needed (Brasfield, 2011). It is on one of those unexpected and thin threads of history in liberal democracies that the entire future of a nation sometimes depends. Had Lieberman joined Democrats and voted yes, the future of health care in the United States would have most likely taken a major step toward a universal single-payer coverage. Insurance companies would have very likely been compelled for the first time in American history to put people first, and not money. As things turned out, and as late as September 2017, the future of even the modest and still private insurance friendly ACA remains in doubt. Republicans have continued their rhetorical opposition to what they call Obamacare, with the House of Representatives voting numerous times to repeal the ACA. Republicans' near total control of government following the 2016 presidential election makes the future even more uncertain, especially with the election of President Donald Trump, whose chief message during the 2015–2016 campaign was to repeal the legislation. In the first six months of the Trump administration, the Republican majority in the House of Representatives passed a bill to repeal and replace the ACA, to the consternation of many Americans who would have lost health care. Instead of wisely letting the House bill die, Senate Majority Leader Mitch McConnell created a group of all-male senators to write the Senate version (of "Repeal and Replace") in secret. No public hearings were held; no committees were created to debate the provisions of the Republican Senate bill, and McConnell continued to display his total contempt for regular order in the Senate. Although in the end, Republican efforts to repeal and replace what they call Obamacare failed in a rather spectacular fashion, there is no guarantee the ACA will survive. Should Republicans continue to gain seats in the House, given the gerrymandering of districts, or increase their representation in the Senate, they might continue efforts to repeal the legislation. A silver lining is that in the eventual bill signed by President Obama in March 2010, there is nothing that bars individual states in the Union from moving to single-payer insurance coverage or "public options." States such as California may well be positioned to move in that direction given the political landscape and economic recovery from the Great Recession. Indeed, some have argued that the seeds of a public option in health insurance markets were planted in California in 2001 when progressives in the state supported it as a way to gradually move to universal single-payer health coverage (Halpin & Harbage, 2010, p. 1118).

Given the background and the continuing role of private companies in health care markets, it is time to examine health care coverage among immigrants, as it is plausible that a hidden resistance by some to universal single-payer coverage may well stem from fear that immigrants, especially the undocumented, might participate in a program funded by U.S. taxpayers. Table 9.8 presents health insurance coverage for the native and foreign-born populations in 2010. It appears from the data that immigrants were less likely (65.7%) than native-born Americans (87.3%) to have health insurance; immigrants were slightly less likely to be covered by private insurance (75.3%) than the native-born (78.2%).

TABLE 9.8: Percent of Population With Health Insurance by Nativity, 2010

	Total	Native-Born	Immigrants
All insurance	84.5%	87.3%	65.7%
Private insurance	77.9%	78.2%	75.3%

Source: US Census Bureau, "Percent of Population with Health Insurance by Nativity, 2010," www.census.gov/acs/www/. Copyright in the Public Domain.

Coverage varies by region of the world of origin of immigrants, with coverage highest among those from Canada (91.8%) and lowest among those from Latin America (50.7%). Within the Latin American region, the lowest coverage is among immigrants from Mexico (42.2%) and highest among those from the Caribbean (71.2%). Immigrants from the Caribbean, however, are least likely to be covered by private health insurers (63.4%) among all immigrant groups.

REFERENCES

Altonji, J. G., & Card, D. (1991). *The effects of immigration on the labor market outcomes of less-skilled natives.* Chicago, IL: National Bureau of Economic Research. Available at http://www.nber.org/chapters/c11773

Baucus, M. (2008). *Call to action: Health reform 2009.* Washington, DC: Senate Finance Committee.

Bideshi, D., & Kposowa, A. J. (2012). African immigrants and capital conversion in the U.S. labor market: Comparisons by race and national origin. *The Western Journal of Black Studies, 36*(3), 181–200.

Brasfield, J. (2011). The politics of ideas: Where did the public option come from and where is it going? *Journal of Health Politics, Policy and Law, 36*(3), 455–459.

Brimelow, P. (1995). *Alien nation: Common sense about America's immigration disaster.* New York, NY: Random House.

Chiswick. B. R. (1986). Is the new immigration less skilled than the old? *Journal of Labor Economics, 4*(2), 168–192.

Cohn, J. (2010). How they did it: The inside account of health care reform's triumph. *New Republic*, June 10, 14–25.

Derickson, A. (2005). *Health security for all: Dreams of universal health care in America.* Baltimore, MD: Johns Hopkins University Press.

Grubbs, S. (2016). *The income color line: The significance of race for new immigrants in the United States* (Master's thesis). Department of Sociology, University of Oklahoma.

Halpin, H. A., & Harbage, P. (2010). The origins and demise of the public option. *Health Affairs, 29*(6), 1117–1124.

National Research Council (1997). *The new Americans: Economic, demographic, and fiscal effects of immigration.* Washington, DC: National Academy Press.

Quadagno, J. (2004). Why the United States has no national health insurance: Stakeholder mobilization against the welfare state, 1945–1996. *Journal of Health and Social Behavior,* 45 (extra Issue), 25–44.

Quadagno, J. (2006). *One nation, uninsured: Why the U.S. has no national health insurance.* New York, NY: Oxford University Press.

U.S. Census Bureau (2013). Year of entry of the foreign-born population by sex and world region of birth, 2013. *Current population survey, annual social and economic supplement.* Washington, DC: Department of Commerce. Table 3.17. Available at https://www.census.gov/data/tables/2013/demo/foreign-born/cps-2013.html

U.S. Census Bureau (2010). *The foreign-born population of the United States, 2010.* American Community Survey. Available at www.census.gov/acs/www/

U.S. Census Bureau (2013). *Current population survey, annual social and economic supplement.* Washington, DC: Department of Commerce.

U.S. Immigration and Naturalization Service (1975). *Statistical yearbook of the Immigration and Naturalization Service, 1974.* Washington, DC: Department of Justice.

U.S. Immigration and Naturalization Service (1985). *Statistical yearbook of the Immigration and Naturalization Service, 1984.* Washington, DC: Department of Justice.

U.S. Immigration and Naturalization Service (1996). *Statistical yearbook of the Immigration and Naturalization Service, 1994.* Washington, DC: Department of Justice.

10

Effects of Immigration and the Politics of Immigration Reform

Perhaps no topic arouses more passion in political and social discourse than the consequences of immigration on the United States. Typically, United States is understood as native-born citizens, and what uncontrolled immigration might be doing to them. Debates over the consequences of immigration on the host society, in this case, the United States, have a long tradition (Kposowa, 1998). A quick reminder of public concerns about perceived negative effects of immigration is the old and persistent "likely to become a public charge" clause in U.S. immigration policy, which forbids granting of visas to would-be foreigners who most likely would presumably become dependent on American taxpayers upon their arrival.

The claim that immigrants cause harm to the nation is not new but has a long tradition. Immigration restrictionists argued in the early 19th century that foreigners comprised a high percentage of criminals, that they placed excessive demands on charitable institutions, and that they damaged American quality of life (Taylor, 1971; Kposowa, 1998). Typically, concerns about negative immigration effects on the nation tend to rise in periods of domestic disturbances, especially economic crises, such as a surge in unemployment or during a recession or depression when immigrants might be blamed for allegedly taking jobs away from natives, or accepting lower pay than natives. In times of prosperity, anti-immigration feelings might be low, although the numbers being admitted might alarm some people, especially if the newcomers are coming from cultures that are perceived to be very different from European American culture or what is typically clothed as "American values." In short, it is often facile to blame immigrants or use them as scapegoats, especially for problems not of their making.

A 2016 Pew Research Center survey of 5,006 U.S. adults found that a sizable percentage of Whites living in the United States had very negative views on immigration, and believed that immigrants took away jobs. To the question: "A growing number of immigrants working in the United States is hurting American workers", 65% of rural Whites agreed; 52% of suburban Whites agreed, and 48% of urban Whites agreed (Pew Research Center, 2016). The survey analysts concluded that "Most rural white residents (65%) say American workers are being hurt by the growing number of immigrants working in the U.S., compared with about half of urban (48%) and suburban (52%) white residents. Among whites, both rural men and women (65% for both groups) are more likely than urban

181

men (46%) and women (49%) or their suburban counterparts (55% and 49%, respectively) to say immigration has a negative impact on workers."

This chapter presents and discusses various areas in which there is controversy over the effects of immigration. The central question undergirding discussions over the effects of immigration is relatively simple: Do immigrants constitute a burden or liability on American taxpayers? It is within this simple, but fundamental question that others arise, such as perceived differential use of public social and health services; effects of immigration on housing costs, including home prices and rents; earnings depression and rising unemployment; population diversity; cost of goods and services (prices); crime (so-called "street" or violent crimes); interracial/ethnic marriages; and segregation in the nation's urban environment. There are also real fears and concerns over whether new immigrants, now coming largely from countries not in Europe, will assimilate and accept Euro-American values previously brought by earlier immigrants from Europe. Will the nation, for example, continue to have residents who accept and speak English or will there be language bifurcation? Will the new immigrants adhere to traditional Euro-American cultural norms, or will they bring their own cultural habits and try to impose them on others once they have achieved some level of numerical majority in states in which they settle?

Addressing the above and related questions is often risky in social science academic circles in the event that the researcher investigating them is perceived as being "anti-immigration" or anti some group of immigrants. Research questions, instead, tend to be couched in safer terms, with a focus on issues perceived to be more politically or socially acceptable, a potentially disastrous development even in higher education. Should students be exposed to controversial ideas that generate rigorous debate? Or should they be presented with sanitized materials so that they are not made uncomfortable? Following such a path could undermine not only academic freedom, but constitutional provisions of free speech itself. If a researcher were to argue, for example, that having bilingual education is poor for democracy, or having store and street signs in Spanish or Mandarin instead of English does not promote national integration, and might be harmful to assimilation, would his or her work lead to protests from immigrant groups or the politically correct group?

Ironically, ignoring these issues (out of fear of offending someone) has left the door wide open for an immigrant backlash, propelled to the surface at times through the writings and speeches of non-academics such as Lamm & Imhoff (1985), Brimelow (1995), the Center for Immigration Studies (2017), and so on. Commenting on the paucity of sociological interest in the anti-immigrant reaction among non-Hispanic Whites—a fear of cultural change and a deep-seated worry that European Americans will be displaced from their dominant position in American society—Massey (1995, p. 632) remarked that "While social scientists have analyzed the state of the trees, the public has worried about the future of the forest, and no amount of empirical research has quieted these anxieties."

From the early establishment of the United States, most immigrants came from northwest Europe and quickly assimilated, in part because they transmitted western European culture to the continent. Later in history, as waves and waves of newcomers entered from southern and Eastern Europe, and despite the discrimination they faced, they eventually assimilated into the broader European American culture that had emerged. They discarded their ethnic origins, and as second and third generations came of age, original ethnic boundaries were increasingly forgotten. This is the model that nativists and immigration restrictionists had hoped or expected.

But as some researchers have warned, it might be a mistake to view the process of European assimilation as a model by which Asians, Latin Americans, Middle Easterners, and sub-Saharan Africans would be incorporated into American society. There are fears of ethnic fragmentation and insistence by some new immigrants on maintaining their ethnic and cultural practices (Jasso & Rosenzweig, 1990) and even looking down on traditional (European American) cultural practices as inferior. It is gratifying to recall, however, that fears over ethnic division may be displaced by recalling that historically as Poles, Italians, and Jews entered the United States in the late 1890s and early 1920s, similar anxieties and worries (of ethnic fragmentation) were expressed about their assimilation. Worries by immigration restrictionists and nativist groups should be assuaged by the fact that immigrants of today, though not from Europe, are displaying the same signs of assimilation as those of the past with European ancestry.

There is ample evidence that as duration of residence in the United States increases, income and occupational status rise (Kposowa, 1998, 2002), and patterns of fertility, language, and residence come to resemble those of natives (Lee, 1966; Massey, 1981; Jasso & Rosenzweig, 1990). Furthermore, as socioeconomic status increases, interracial and interethnic marriages may increase with each generation, resulting in population diversity of such a nature that old ethnicities may no longer be discernible in many cases. This appears to be the case in the United States over the past two decades, as interracial marriages, once illegal in most states, have become popular and commonplace (Livingstone & Brown, 2017; Pew Research Center, 2017).

Immigration and Emigration

No discussion of the effects of immigration can be complete without acknowledging the reality that not everyone who comes to the United States stays or even intends to remain permanently, though as mentioned previously, the presumption of stay is at the heart of U.S. immigration policy and visa issuance. A substantial percentage of immigrants do leave the United States, and estimates suggest that between 35% and 45% of immigrants emigrate, either returning to their home country or moving on to third countries (Warren & Peck, 1980; Jasso & Rosenzweig, 1990, p. 124; Smith & Edmonston, 1997, p. 40). Immigrants most likely to return are those from Europe and Asia. A high proportion of even illegal entrants stay temporarily, living in the United States for several years, but eventually returning to their home countries. Given that data on emigration are either nonexistent (especially before the September 2001 attacks on the United States) or highly unreliable, estimates of immigrants, especially undocumented ones, must be interpreted with caution. If the primary focus is only on those who have entered, but without knowing how many have left, there is a risk of severely dramatizing and overestimating the perceived effects of immigration, thereby making it more difficult to come up with legalization programs.

Immigration, Housing Rents, and Home Prices

Relatively little is known about the effects of immigrants on housing markets of cities where immigrants opt to settle. There is scattered evidence from the economic literature that locally, immigration affects U.S. cities; immigration pushes up demand for housing, rents increase, and in time general housing prices also increase (Saiz, 2007, p. 363). The causal mechanism by which immigrants contribute to rental and home prices is that they bring about population increase, along with demand for housing in the midst, often leading to housing shortages. Property owners and real estate markets (including owners of property available for rent) may raise prices to fill demands, and this yields benefits overall. The relationship between immigration and rising rental costs is not necessarily universal for the whole country, since there is variation in dispersal or concentration of old and new immigrants. New immigrants tend to settle in metropolitan areas where there is already a sizable group of previous immigrants. Therefore, their contribution to housing and rental increases is partly a function of their tendency to move to urban centers (or gateway cities) and elevate concentration of the stock of immigrants already in those cities (Saiz, 2003).

Another pathway of how immigrants cause rising rental and housing prices is that some native-born living in cities that witness rapid increases in immigration might decide to leave or escape the rising number of immigrants (Filer, 1992; Borjas, 1994). The end result is that in at least the short run, home values and rental values might increase as the overall population size expands. Native-born residents, especially minorities and the poor, may be unable to afford higher prices, and some may end up leaving the area where they may have lived for decades or, in some cases, generations.

The situation between immigration and rise in rents and home values may be compared to that between home mortgage interest and rising home and mortgage values. Homeowners are allowed under the U.S. tax code to reduce their taxable income by writing off interest paid to financial institutions on their home mortgage, along with property taxes. It is plausible that this practice (at least until the Great Recession of 2008) encouraged some to upgrade houses, purchase even bigger houses, or buy houses (often at variable interest rates) that they could not afford in the expectation that mortgage interest deductions would help them at tax time. The rush to buy houses (though unaffordable based on income) contributed to rising home values in some U.S. metropolitan areas. Accordingly, at the start of the recession, some homeowners realized that the value of their homes was much lower than the debt they held on those same homes. The end result was a collapse in housing markets as foreclosures increased. It is plausible that as new immigrants come in, especially in states and urban areas that are traditionally high immigrant-reception regions, real estate brokers, financial markets, and others with money may speculate on a future increase in home values. In the process, highly artificial demands are created; city governments embark upon revitalization campaigns; downtowns must be rebuilt in anticipation of some highly educated "yuppies" moving in and drinking coffee or bottled water at Starbucks; and a heretofore unknown "Route 38" sign appears to remind those unfamiliar with the past that the street was once a historic site. Few bother to ask where these yuppies will get jobs and how they would pay for the increasing home and rental costs.

Effect of Immigration on Public Social and Health Services

The perception that immigrants participate disproportionately in taxpayer entitlement programs such as Medicare, Medicaid, "welfare," and others has figured considerably in anti-immigration debates of the past 30 years. The belief that immigrants use social services and, indeed, come to the United States to take advantage of existing programs, is again a reflection of changes in source countries of immigrants following the Act of 1965 that eliminated the quota system and opened the door to entrants from countries previously unable to send emigrants. Passage of the Save our State Initiative (Proposition 187) in California in 1994, and the *Personal Responsibility and Work Opportunity Reconciliation Act of 1996* (P.L. 104–193), a welfare reform plan supported by both Republicans and Democrats, and signed into law on August 22 by President Bill Clinton, a Democrat, was in response to the view that there were too many people dependent on the government who presumably did not want to work. Chief on the minds of the president and lawmakers were immigrants and minorities, especially African Americans.

Campaigning to portray himself as a middle-of-the-road president, Clinton often used the slogan "Ending welfare as we know it." Even before passage of this federal act, various states, especially those with high immigrant populations, had been complaining about the high cost of "welfare." As the assistant secretary for planning and evaluation at the federal Department of Health and Human Services observed in 1996, "Even before Congress passed welfare reform legislation acceptable to President Clinton, states were acting to try new approaches. With encouragement, support, and cooperation from the Clinton Administration, 43 states have moved forward with 78 welfare reform experiments." The Clinton administration required teen mothers to stay in school, mandated that federal employees pay their child support, and cracked down on people who owed child support and crossed state lines. It was claimed by Health and Human Services that due to these efforts and President Clinton's desire to strengthen the American economy, child support collections increased by nearly 50%, to $11.8 billion, in fiscal year 1996, and there were 1.9 million fewer people on welfare in 1996 than before Clinton took office (U.S. Department of Health and Human Services, 1996).

The new law was to ostensibly allow states flexibility to reform their welfare systems and to build on demonstrations initiated under the Clinton administration. No one knows for certain the number of casualties left in the wake of Clinton's welfare reform act. Among other provisions, the legislation barred undocumented immigrants from receiving any form of public assistance, except emergency Medicaid. Legal immigrants who arrived in the United States after August 22, 1996, are not eligible for federally funded Temporary Assistance for Needy Families (TANF), Medicaid, or State Children's Health Insurance Program benefits during their first five years in the United States.

Immigrant adults are not eligible for food stamps (Supplemental Nutrition Assistance Program), irrespective of the date of entry into the United States, until they naturalize or prove that they, their spouse, or their parents were employed in the United States for a combined total of at least 10 years. Following a flurry of criticism for the meanness of the legislation, especially for children, food stamps for children, disabled individuals, and older adults were later restored, but working-age immigrants are not eligible.

The general conclusion over whether the various reforms were successful depends on the state of the economy. Since a major goal was to limit reception of welfare benefits (to no more than five years for an adult for the duration of life), and to prevent people from receiving cash benefits unless they were engaged in work or work-related activity, research findings show that welfare reception was already dropping before the law went into effect (Schoeni & Blank, 2000), thereby making it difficult to draw a causal effect. Relatedly, the legislation went into effect when the U.S. economy was booming, making it easier for individuals to find jobs. There is also ample research evidence that for most recipients of "welfare," dependency is a short-term phenomenon (Kposowa, 1995a; Harris, 1996). For instance, single mothers may need assistance following a marital breakdown, when undergoing some major economic crisis, or having a non-marital birth (Duncan, 1984; Blank, 1989). It is unclear how the law has worked during periods of economic recession. Immigrants, undocumented or not, were clearly in the bullseye of the Personal Responsibility and Work Opportunity Reconciliation Act of 1996. The bulk of the empirical evidence on immigration and welfare or public assistance dependency is that immigrants arriving in the United States are much less likely to depend on welfare benefits (Simon, 1984; Ku & Bruen, 2013). After analyzing five decades of census data, Kposowa (1995, 1998) reported that immigrants were less likely to use public social services (welfare). Interestingly, although the focus of much of the anti-immigration rhetoric and nativist feelings has been directed at post-1965 entrants, Kposowa (1995, 1998) reported that immigrants (from White countries) arriving before 1965 were much more likely to depend on welfare than their native-born counterparts; post-1965 immigrants, however, were less likely to depend on welfare.

There are three other programs often believed by some to be used disproportionately by immigrants. The three are not strictly speaking public assistance but trust funds that offer a mix of mainly health coverage and social services to the elderly and/or to the more vulnerable members of society. Some disparagingly at times refer to them as "entitlement programs." First, each program is described, and then evidence is provided as to whether immigrants use them, their extent of usage, and if they use the programs more than the native-born. The first to examine is the health program referred to as Medicare.

Medicare is the federal health insurance program for people who are 65 or older, certain younger people with disabilities, and people with permanent kidney failure that require dialysis (U.S. Centers for Medicare & Medicaid Services, 2017). The bill creating the program (H.R. 6675) was signed into law by President Lyndon B. Johnson on July 30, 1965, in Independence, Missouri. At the ceremony, the first person to receive a Medicare card was former President Harry S. Truman (U.S. Centers for Medicare & Medicaid Services, 2017).

The program has many parts, depending on the type of care that an enrollee wishes to have. There is, for example, Medicare Part A, which is a type of hospital insurance that covers inpatient hospital stays, care in a skilled-nursing facility, hospice care, and some home health care. Part B is a medical insurance component that covers certain physician services, outpatient care, medical supplies, and preventive services.

Part C is a lot of different plans, referred to as Medicare Advantage Plans. Under this category are entities such as Health Maintenance Organizations, Preferred Provider Organizations, Private Fee-for-Service Plans, Special Needs Plans, and Medicare Medical Savings Account Plans. An individual enrolled in a Medicare Advantage Plan is typically covered for most Medicare services that are not paid for under the original legislation. Most Medicare Advantage Plans carry prescription drug coverage (U.S. Centers for Medicare & Medicaid Services, 2017).

Finally, Part D adds prescription drug coverage to Original Medicare, some Medicare Cost Plans, some Medicare Private-Fee-for-Service Plans, and Medicare Medical Savings Account Plans. Typically, the plans are provided by private insurance companies and others approved by Medicare (U.S. Centers for Medicare & Medicaid Services, 2017). Not all services under Medicare are free; premiums and co-pays apply, and there are limits on the availability and supply of prescription drugs.

The second program is **Medicaid**. As with Medicare, Medicaid is a public insurance program that provides health coverage to Americans under 65 years such as eligible low-income adults, children, pregnant women, elderly adults, and people with disabilities. Medicaid is administered by states, according to federal requirements. The program is funded jointly by states and the federal government, and it was signed into law by President Lyndon B. Johnson the same day that he signed the bill creating Medicare (U.S. Centers for Medicare & Medicaid Services, 2017). Medicare is funded by federal payroll taxes. Medicaid is also funded by federal payroll taxes, general tax revenues, and beneficiary premiums, but unlike Medicare, Medicaid is a cost-sharing program in which the federal government pays states for a specified percentage of program expenditures (Federal Medical Assistance Percentage or FMAP). FMAP varies by state based on criteria such as per capita income. The usually small percentage not covered by the federal government is paid by the state (U.S. Centers for Medicare & Medicaid, 2017). Each state operates its own program, and benefits may, therefore, vary depending on one's state of residence.

What is the effect of immigration on Medicare? The preponderance of the research evidence shows that immigrants, especially those who are not U.S.

citizens, provide heavy subsidies for the Medicare trust fund. Contrary to much popular belief and also that of nativists, immigration restrictionists, and others who hold much animosity toward immigrants, especially those from third world countries, immigrants, particularly noncitizens, contribute far more to the health insurance trust fund (Medicare) than they use. Indeed, without immigration, the long-term viability of the program itself would be in danger. A 2013 study (Zallman et al., 2013, p. 1156) using data from the 2010 Current Population Surveys and the 2009 Medical Expenditure Panel Surveys reported that in 2009 alone, immigrants contributed $13 billion more to the Medicare (health insurance) trust fund than it paid out on their behalf, and most of the surplus came from *noncitizens*. The study authors further found that from 2002 to 2009 the cumulative surplus contributions originating from immigrants amounted to $115.2 billion. In other words, from 2002 to 2009, immigrants contributed $115.2 billion more to the Medicare trust fund than they took out. On a yearly basis, in 2009 immigrants made 14.7% of Medicare contributions, but they accounted for only 7.9% of its expenditures, resulting to a surplus of $13.8 billion (Zallman et al., 2013, p. 1153). What about the wonderful native-born? U.S. native-born in contrast with the foreign-born generated a deficit $30.9 billion. While immigrants contribute far more to a system that they underutilize, the native-born who use it far more often derive considerably more benefits than what they put into the system. The native-born consume far more than what they contribute to the system. In this view, immigrants (as much derided as they are) provide subsidies to the native-born.

How to explain the differential usage of Medicare by the native-born and immigrants? First, Medicare is administrated through payroll taxes of workers. To be on a payroll in the United States means for the most part that one has to have a valid Social Security number as required by federal law; employers are obligated to obtain the number from would-be employees. For immigrants who are in the United States legally, this is not a problem; they can easily obtain Social Security numbers if they do not have them already. Immigrants whose status is legal have money taken out of their pay for each pay period. Immigrants who are not in the country legally use Social Security numbers as well, but these are often connected to invented or fictitious names; in some cases, undocumented individuals use numbers that belong to other people (Gross, 2007).

Another reason why immigration generates a surplus for Medicare is the high labor-force participation rates of immigrants due to a higher percentage of the group in the working-age population (typically 16 to 64 years). Accordingly, immigrants who are noncitizens tend to be younger, and since in the United States a five-year residency requirement is needed to become a citizen, noncitizens may work for years, contributing to Medicare before they become citizens, if ever. As noncitizens, they may not be qualified to partake of the system's health benefits, and being younger, they may not require health care as readily as U.S.-born citizens who, on average, are older than immigrants, especially noncitizen immigrants. Medicare is a health insurance trust fund that is typically not available to younger persons under 65 years of age (with exceptions, such as disability).

As stated earlier in this chapter, an unknown number of immigrants return to their home countries after years of residence in the United States. People who qualify for Medicare after 65 but return to retire in their countries of birth are unlikely to have access to or utilize a program they might have funded with years of working in the United States and contributing to it through payroll deductions. There are people who may return to home countries because of the much higher cost of health care in the United States, even with Medicare. Some services, including prescription costs, hospital visits and stays, and medical office visits, tend to be cheaper in other countries (even in third world nations) than in the United States. There may also be greater social support provided by extended family members or children that might outweigh any benefits received in the United States under the Medicare program.

What is the effect of immigration on Medicaid? In an analysis of the March 2012 Current Population Survey data, Ku and Bruen (2013, p. 2) observed that when health insurance in general was investigated, 27.9% of native-born, low-income elderly (those falling below 200% of the poverty line) were uninsured, while 31.3% of naturalized citizens in the same category were uninsured. Health insurance coverage was even much lower for low-income elderly, native-born Americans (27.9%). The same analysis showed that while 25.6% of native-born, low-income adults were on Medicaid, 29% of naturalized citizens were utilizing the program, but only 19.7% of noncitizens were covered. Two-thirds of low-income citizen children receive health insurance through Medicaid, and 48.9% of noncitizens do so; low-income noncitizen immigrants were the least likely to receive Medicaid (Ku & Bruen, 2013, p. 2).

Similar findings of a lower Medicaid enrollment by immigrants and immigrant children have been reported in other studies (Simon, 1984; Wang & Holahan, 2003; Ku et al., 2003). Ku et al. (2003, p. 5) concluded, following analysis of data from the Current Population Surveys that between 1996 and 2001, noncitizens were less likely than the native-born to be enrolled in Medicaid, and the proportion receiving benefits had decreased since 1996. The authors concluded that noncitizens were much more likely than native citizens to be uninsured. One reason given for the lower rate of utilization by noncitizens is that they are less likely to have employer coverage for insurance, owing to the types of jobs they occupy. Among studies that find noncitizens less likely to be enrolled in Medicaid (or other public assistance programs in general), the big outlier is one done by the Center for Immigration Studies in Washington, DC, which suggests noncitizens enrolled in Medicaid at a higher rate than native citizens even after welfare reform (Krikorian et al., 2003). The center's findings on this and many other immigration-related topics should be read with caution as the center has a declared goal of reducing immigration to the United States, which it believes to be too high, while claiming to be "pro-immigrant" (Center for Migration Studies, 2017). Although it describes itself as a nonpartisan research center, what it parades as objective scientific research often fails to stand up to closer scrutiny. Mark Krikorian, the center's chief executive officer, is believed to be responsible for a concept called immigration "enforcement by attrition" (Dickson, 2017). In the 2012 U.S. presidential election, the American public was introduced to this rather cynical, if not immoral, idea by Republican candidate Mitt Romney when he described it as "self-deportation."

Attrition can be used in many instances, including war, to deprive the enemy or some undesired group of valuable and needed resources so that in the end, the enemy or other side gives up and decides to withdraw or give in. Used as an immigration policy, attrition would in essence prevent any meaningful immigration reform; it would make it extremely difficult, if not impossible, for undocumented immigrants to work or receive any benefits or protection. Such persons can be continuously monitored and harassed through police powers, using such tactics as requiring them to carry papers at all times; failure would result in arrest if stopped by police personnel. The ultimate objective is to make life for the potential undocumented immigrant so unbearable that he or she decides to return to the country of origin, and hence, the words "attrition" or "self-deport." The cynicism lies in the fact that although it is the government in the destination country that created circumstances that forced the undocumented person to vacate the country, the general public will never know and the government will never publicly accept responsibility for the "deportation" or risk being blamed for it. After all, the government or its agents never physically ordered the alien to depart; he or she did so "voluntarily."

Effect of Immigration on Prices

That immigration leads to lower prices for the native-born seems easy to understand, but it has been quite difficult to measure the effects of immigration on prices quantitatively. One of the main difficulties is that the analyst would first have to identify the amount consumers spend on particular goods, and then partial out the cost share of immigrant labor in the production of the goods. The National Research Council's Panel on the Demographic and Fiscal Impacts of Immigration study of the issue ran into this problem (Smith & Edmonston, 1997, p. 231), and came to the conclusion that "to correctly infer the amount of immigrant labor involved in producing a dollar's worth of consumer spending requires detailed knowledge about the production process along every step of the way." After an exhaustive quantitative analysis, however, the panel observed that immigration leads to a lowering of prices for the native-born, and the benefits are spread rather uniformly across most types of native-born consumers. Panel members added that "Benefits from lower prices are higher for households with very high levels of wealth and education" (Smith & Edmonston, 1997, p. 235). That immigrants do more to lower prices for the wealthier members of society is relatively easy to understand. Immigrants are overrepresented in building construction, in agriculture and gardening, in the garment industry, in child care, in caring for the elderly in nursing homes, in domestic (house) cleaning work, in major hotels cleaning rooms or opening and closing doors, in cooking, and in chauffeuring. Natives who are most likely to need these services or be able to pay for them are not the poor, but wealthier or middle-class individuals. A lower-middle-class individual who purchases a car is unlikely to hire a driver to be taking him or her around, and the car bought or leased is much less likely to be a Cadillac or Lincoln stretch limousine. Millionaires and billionaires, however, are in a much better position to afford expensive housing, stay in 5-star-rated hotels, have nannies living with them and caring for their children, and enjoying the many finer things of life that rely on cheap immigrant labor. For all the immigrant bashing, could average native-born Americans truly imagine a week, a month, or a year without any undocumented immigrants in the United States?

Effect of Immigration on Crime

In the United States, immigration restrictionists and politicians have long debated and claimed that immigration is a cause of high crime rates. The perception or fear that immigrants contribute to crime is a recurrent theme in American history. In the middle of the 19th century, nativist organizations, including the American Party and its affiliate the Know Nothings, often offered crime as justification for restricting immigration (Taylor, 1971, p. 239). In 1859, for example, 55% of those arrested in New York City were Irish immigrants, and 22% were born in other foreign countries (Jones, 1992, p. 1140; Smith & Edmonston, 1997, p. 386). Yet, most of the alleged crimes were minor infractions, including such "high" offenses as drinking in public or engaging in "disorderly" conduct (Kposowa et al., 2010, p. 160).

An accumulating body of social science research findings show that contrary to popular belief, and also claims of the classical Chicago School of Sociology, large immigrant populations might be associated with lower rather than higher rates of criminal violence; increases in immigration are associated with lower violent and property crimes (Lee et al., 2001; Stowell et al., 2009, p. 889; Ousey & Kubrin, 2009; Kposowa et al., 2010). It is also noticeable that crime rates (violent and property) have been on a downward slope in the United States over the past decade, during which immigration rates have been on an upward trajectory. If immigration per se were a cause of crime, it would seem that the past decade would have been one of the most violent periods in American history. Of course, the nation saw sustained episodes of violence in the same period, but a considerable proportion of the violence was not coming from immigrants, but from police abusing citizens, especially young African American men and women, either through direct shooting deaths or other vicious types of behavior.

Despite the consistently negative research findings on immigration and crime, politicians have continued to parrot and promote "tough on crime" rhetoric and policies, which combined with misguided policies and laws of the past (including mandatory minimum sentences and a crime bill) have led to the creation of a massive prison industrial complex through which the rich get richer and the poor and less fortunate get prison (Reiman & Leighton, 2013). In building such a complex, while beneficial to groups such as peddlers of private prisons and individuals whose careers depend on the maintenance of harsh punishment for even the most mundane of human failings, it should be noted that higher incarceration rates are not without societal costs in both human misery and public taxation. As observed by Yates (2017), "Since 1980, the U.S. prison population has exploded from 500,000 to more than 2.2 million, resulting in the highest incarceration rate in the world and costing more than $80 billion a year. The federal prison population has grown 700 percent, with the Federal Bureau of Prisons budget now accounting for more than 25 percent of the entire Justice Department budget." A nation that wastes so much of its human capital ultimately pays a heavy price, not just in the unnecessary money spent in the process, but also in terms of losing out on contributions those now in prison would have made to the development of the country had enough resources been spent on, for instance, public education, job creation, and building and modernizing infrastructure (bridges, railways, roads, communication, airports, and so on). Every dollar now spent on imprisoning some low-level nonviolent drug offender is a dollar that the country does not have to build a new school, replace a bridge built before the World War I, modernize a train track that now only accommodates locomotives traveling at barely 50 miles per hour, build a new hospital in a rural area, or even provide better health care. How did the nation become so punitive, angry, and divided and in the process lose its priorities: its people and their potential?

Effect of Immigration on Native Earnings

Does immigration have negative effects on the wages (earnings) of the native-born population? Responding to this question is one of the underlying concerns in public and even academic debates on immigration. The evidence from economic and sociological research findings is that overall the effect of immigration on the earnings of native-born workers is small. The Panel on the Demographic and Economic Impacts of Immigration (Smith & Edmonston, 1997, p. 220) concluded that immigration might reduce earnings of competing native-born workers by 1 to 2%. Panel members argued that the effect of immigration is so small and negligible because the U.S. economy is extremely large and complex, running at $7.6 trillion a year. The Panel (Smith & Edmonston, 1997, p. 220) stated that "it is simply not plausible that immigration, even across a decade, by increasing the supply of workers by 4 percent could seriously impact such an economy." Although in most studies, immigration is not found to reduce native earnings considerably, there are studies that show earnings of African Americans are reduced as a result of immigration if the immigrants reside in the same metropolitan area as African Americans (Kposowa, 1998). One explanation given is that the two groups may compete for the same jobs, and employers could take advantage of excess labor supply to bring down wages. Kposowa (1998) warned that analysts run the risk of minimizing the effect of immigration on native earnings if they focus on the country as a whole; in local labor markets, it is possible for immigration to have greater negative effects. Smith and Edmonston (1997, p. 221) acknowledge this possibility by cautioning that in a specific labor market such as Los Angeles, the effects of immigration may be larger simply because there is a higher percentage of foreign-born people in the city than in other areas. Some studies also show that one group whose wages are negatively affected by immigration is previous immigrants, an indication that newer immigrants into a metropolitan area might be in competition with earlier immigrants from the same country.

Effect of Immigration on Unemployment

Research findings on the effect of immigration on unemployment are similar to those regarding earnings. In general (when the country as a whole is considered), immigration does not appear to have a major negative influence on native-born employment. At the same time, displacement cannot be ruled out within specific occupations or industries or specific localities, primarily those metropolitan areas with large concentrations of immigrants. Some studies have found displacement effects in some industries, meaning that native-born workers vacate as immigrants penetrate the industry. For example, in Waldinger's (1996) study of the garment and hotel industries in New York City, the proportion of native-born workers declined as the proportion of immigrant workers increased. Kposowa (1995b) also reported that while immigration had no significant effect on unemployment for the native-born as a whole, African American/Black native-born were displaced by immigrants in urban areas with large immigrant populations. He found that unemployment increased among African Americans as more immigrants entered the area.

In view of the evidence that, in general, immigration has only a negligible effect on both native-born earnings and native-born unemployment, an inevitable question to address is why there remain anxieties over increasing immigration. For earnings or wages, one possibility is that despite all the talk of economic recovery following the recession, and even years prior to that recession, the U.S. economy has been precarious for many workers. Real median household income in the country since 1967 has shown stagnation, along with vast income inequality. Americans work harder and harder but cannot seem to make it or achieve a widely held slogan of the "American dream." The real median household income in the United States was $47,335 in 1967, and by 2015 it stood at $56,516 (U.S. Census Bureau, 2017a). Income varies significantly by race. The median income for non-Hispanic White individuals was $62,950 in 2015. Corresponding figures were $36,898 for African American/Black individuals, $45,148 for Hispanic people (of any race), and $77,166 for Asian people (U.S. Census Bureau, 2017a). With such wide variation, it is difficult not to seek explanations. High levels of immigration could easily be cast as one of those.

The Great Recession cost job loss for millions of middle-class Americans; some never got back the jobs back, or the homes they lost. While unemployment fell from 10% in 2009 at the height of the recession to 5% in 2015 (U.S. Census Bureau, 2017b), median household income, *adjusted for inflation*, has fallen in the United States. In 1999, median household income was $57,843, adjusted for inflation; in 2014, it was $53,657. The middle class that built the country appears to be collapsing as income inequality grows. Although unemployment has declined, many languish in very low-paying jobs with minimum wages that are not living wages; many struggle to make ends meet by having more than one job. Housing and general costs of living have increased in many localities despite the fact that income and earnings have remained stagnant.

Responding to economic uncertainties and difficulties, some in the United States have turned to right-wing politics and nationalism, with not so hidden anti-immigrant flavor. Immigration may well have played some role in recent dramatic political outcomes. Despite all the clamor about Donald Trump being insensitive to—or even insulting of—women, Blacks, Hispanics, the disabled, immigrants, and Muslims, he won the 2016 presidential election on a misleadingly simplistic, but clearly reactionary, slogan of "Make America great again." Not so hidden beneath this slogan were calls to increase racist fears and anxieties and an appeal to populism or nationalism. If people embrace it, they are acknowledging a willingness to return to the past in both social and economic terms, and that history had never fully embraced equality for all. Despite all the allegations of sexism against Trump, in a CNN exit poll of 24,558 respondents, he won White women by 52%, while his opponent, a white woman, had only 43% (CNN, 2016). Clinton did win a greater percentage of all women regardless of race or ethnicity by 54%, while Trump carried 41% of women, but her margin of victory over Trump was due largely to the much higher percentage of African American/ Black women (94%) who voted for her versus only 4% that voted for Trump. Had other minority groups (Latinos, Asians, Native Americans, Middle Easterners, etc.) voted for Clinton in percentages as large as that of African Americans, the outcome of the 2016 presidential election would have been much different.

Trump carried previously assumed to be reliable and "safe" Democratic-leaning states of Michigan, Pennsylvania, and Wisconsin. His election has reignited deep racial, ethnic, gender, and class divisions that have always been apparent to even the most casual visitor to America, but denied by even pro-gressives, and their existence buried in the grave of "political correctness." With Trump's triumph over Clinton, immigration restrictionists have achieved some victory, even if it is brief, and even if the cost of building a wall on the U.S. south-ern border is so prohibitive that they deviate from their plan. With his victory in the previously Democratic-leaning states of Michigan, Pennsylvania, and Wisconsin, his economic populist message appears to have been taken seriously by some voters, no matter how few they may have been. The three states are part of the so-called rust belt, places that once had heavy manufacturing industries, such as automobile plants that offered well-paying union jobs that made for a comfortable living with decent middle-class wages; there was solace in the hope that one could work, retire at some age, and still maintain acceptable material, quality of life; and there was job security. Loss of these jobs in the great economic transformation of the United States from reliance on heavy manufacturing to service occupations, roughly from the early 1970s to the middle 1980s (Wilson, 1987), has led to a new economic system characterized by low-paying jobs, often with few benefits, or high-education-intensive occupations (Wilson, 1996) with excessive competition. Politicians have often reacted to the economic fallout by asking for retraining, but how do you tell a 60-year-old worker nearing retirement to go back and retrain for a new job that offers income several times lower than what he or she used to make? What about lost health care, or reduced pension benefits, thanks to the recession? In the midst of so much economic anxiety, Trump's message of making America great again was translated by some as bringing back high-paying industrial jobs that had been lost, including coal-mining jobs, and immigrants figured highly as scapegoats to blame for presum-ably taking away nonexistent jobs.

A critical issue rarely brought to the attention of the American public is the role of automation in job loss, and the ills of capitalism itself. Simply put, many jobs are lost not because of immigrants or other humans taking them away, but because machines are replacing human beings. Left uncontrolled and unregulated, capitalism generates greed, and instead of profits "trickling down" to the lower classes they are accumulated ever more by the wealthy and owners of industry and stockholders, so that the rich get ever richer, and the poor get poorer. Ever since the neoliberal policies preached by people such as former UK Prime Minister Margaret Thatcher and former U.S. President Ronald Reagan (Harvey, 2005), privatization has been viewed as the solution for almost every aspect of state operation, and music in the ears of capitalist elites. If capitalists could find a way to harness the air citizens breathe, they would very likely sell each person an oxygen mask and perhaps charge a dollar for each breath taken in. If fast food restaurant chains could find a way to let robots prepare hamburgers and sell them in the drive-through, they would probably replace cashiers. Many banks have reduced the number of human tellers in the age of the ATM. Maybe in time drones will replace delivery people in big chain stores. One only has to place an order online for a product, and a machine will deliver it to the door. In such a brave new world, no one will blame immigrants anymore, but only some blind faith in technology, capitalism, and human greed. Maybe in the not too distant future, professors might find themselves replaced by podcasts, webinars, and teleconferenced lectures. The increase in the adjunct professoriate across many college campuses present ominous warnings of things to come.

Barriers to Comprehensive Immigration Reform

The expression comprehensive immigration reform has often been used in the past on how to solve the issue of undocumented immigration. Although definitions are hard to come by, it means creating some mechanism for those in the country illegally to come into the open, acknowledge that they entered without inspection or overstayed visas, regularize their status, and be placed on a path through which they will become citizens. The idea seems simple enough but is unlikely to be heeded by Washington politicians any time soon.

For decades, Republican politicians at all levels (federal, state, and local) have rallied around alleged damaging consequences of undocumented immigration. At the 1992 Republican National Convention, presidential candidate Patrick Buchanan spoke of a culture war going on in the country when he commented in a rather frightening voice at the time: "There is a religious war going on in this country, a cultural war as critical to the kind of nation we shall be as the Cold War itself, for this war is for the soul of America" (Buchanan, 1992, cited in Fiorina et al., 2005, p. 1). Buchanan's culture war speech, delivered to thousands at the convention and to millions of television viewers, was taken by some as reference to his belief that immigrants (both documented and undocumented) were changing the face of America, and also modifying traditional American values. Whether a cultural war truly exists may be emblematic of one of the factors very likely preventing comprehensive immigration reform: the belief that a considerable number of immigrants now in the country are from cultures far different from the traditional Euro-American one and that welcoming these immigrants would somehow radically change America in racial, ethic, and cultural values. Thus, one obstacle to immigration reform most likely has to do with the skin configurations of the newcomers, though many may not accept this, at least publicly. Assume for a moment whether there would be pushbacks to comprehensive immigration reform if most undocumented immigrants were known to be from Britain, France, Ireland, or Germany!

Against heated criticism, President Barack Obama in 2012 undertook executive actions, generally described as *Deferred Action for Childhood Arrivals* (DACA), to shield children who had been brought to the United States illegally by parents and to provide work permits. DACA would not have been necessary, and the number of such individuals, now estimated to be about 800,000 young adults, could have been protected and their status legalized had the Republican-controlled House of Representatives supported Obama's push for comprehensive immigration reform in 2010. The "Dreamers," as the individuals are sometimes called, could have been placed on a path to citizenship; after all, most know no other country, having lived in the United States for nearly all their lives. The Tea Party reactionary tactics against the president and his policies, expressed in taunts and demonstrations of "We want our country back," and Democratic loses in the 2010 midterm elections ensured that comprehensive immigration reform was dead. Republicans were certainly not going to bring it up for a vote in the House. And although an immigration bill had passed in a lame-duck Democratic Senate, there were no prospects for reconciliation so long as Republicans controlled the House—and in time, even the Senate—and viewed the bill as some "amnesty" legislation. The president was left with no choice but executive actions if the Dreamers were to be given any chance of having some peace of mind.

Some might argue that President Obama should have undertaken immigration reform as a priority when his administration came to power in 2009 while Democrats controlled both chambers of Congress. Opponents, however, fail to acknowledge the terrible circumstances and choices facing the new president when he took over the White House. The country was in a deep recession, with thousands of jobs lost every month; there was a housing market crisis, and an overall deep uncertainty about the global economy itself. Under these circumstances, the new president prioritized saving the economy and carrying out health care reform, both of which were accomplished largely without Republican support. As noted earlier, during this period (before the midterm elections) a comprehensive immigration reform bill passed in the Senate, but it was not taken up by the House because in the midterms the Tea Party wave, which pushed the position that the bill passed in the Senate was "amnesty" legislation, turned the House over to Republicans. It may not be fair to blame President Obama for failure by Republicans to support immigration reform, and for continuously trying to derail his administration's agenda. After all, who would have imagined that Senate Majority leader Mitch McConnell would set a dangerous precedent in the nation's history by refusing to hold hearings on a Supreme Court nominee for purely political reasons—reserve the seat until a Republican president is elected! On September 25, 2017 McConnell was still leading another effort to repeal and replace the ACA with no Democratic support or consultation despite past failures.

To the consternation of many, but fully keeping in line with the extreme partisanship now prevailing in the government, where the aim is to "please the base" and the president's supporters, President Trump announced in early September 2017 that he had rescinded President Obama's executive order creating DACA, and was giving Congress six months to act. It is uncertain whether a dysfunctional Republican-controlled Congress with a long history of anti-immigration rhetoric and ideology would pass meaningful legislation to protect the Dreamers.

The second major obstacle to comprehensive immigration reform, and one also rarely talked about openly, has to do with electoral politics. Undocumented immigrants are already within the United States and many, including the Dreamers, have resided in the country for decades. While here, they have access to information; they watch television, read newspapers, read stories online, most likely follow politics, attend schools and universities, and so forth. They are, therefore, very familiar with U.S. politics. They know which party tends to demonize them and which one appears to be more open and welcoming. For decades, the Republican Party in particular has pushed itself into a corner by having candidates who repeatedly rail against illegal immigration. If, for example, the call is not for "self-deportation," other derogatory language is used.

At a campaign rally at Mount Pleasant, South Carolina, on December 7, 2015, for example, a Republican candidate read a statement as follows: "Donald J. Trump is calling for a total and complete shutdown of Muslims entering the United States until our country's representatives can figure out what the hell is going on." Trump added that based on polls he had read, there was a great deal of hatred of Americans by large segments of the Muslim population, and other polls had suggested that 25% of Muslims surveyed within the United States had agreed with a statement that violence against Americans within U.S. borders was justified as part of the global jihad. Such language and sentiments would be unlikely to come from a candidate more receptive of immigration.

The Republican Party finds itself in a dilemma: With such a long history of immigrant bashing, would a sudden policy change in favor of immigration seem credible? More perplexing and probably worrisome is the following question: If the presently undocumented were provided a pathway to citizenship and they registered to vote, for which party would they vote in large numbers? It is plausible that some Republican operatives and politicians have some genuine fear about the voting preferences of undocumented immigrants should their status be regularized. Cries of voter fraud, purging of voter rolls to allegedly prevent dead people from voting, and requirements in some states that identification documents be presented at voting stations are often aimed at intimidating targeted groups believed to be less likely to vote for Republican candidates. Thus, uncertainty about how immigrants might vote in elections will very likely remain a major barrier to comprehensive immigration reform.

REFERENCES

Blank, R. M. (1989). Analyzing the length of welfare spells. *Journal of Public Economics* 39, 245–273.

Borjas, G. (1994). The economic benefits of immigration. *Journal of Economic Perspectives*, 9, 3–22.

Brimelow, P. (1995). *Alien nation: Common sense about America's immigration disaster.* New York, NY: Random House.

Buchanan, P. (1992). Speech to the Republican National Convention. In Fiorina, M. P., Abrahams, S. J., & Pope, J. C. (edited) *Culture war: The myth of a polarized America* (2005). New York, NY: Pearson Longman.

Centers for Medicare & Medicaid Services (2017). *Medicaid.* Available at https://www.medicaid.gov/about-us/program-history/index.html. Accessed June 30, 2017.

Center for Immigration Studies (2017). *Low-immigration, pro-immigrant.* Available at https://cis.org/. Accessed July 4, 2017.

CNN (2016). *Election 2016 exit polls, November 2016.* Available at http://www.cnn.com/election/results/exit-polls. Accessed July 1, 2017.

Dickson, C. (2017). Inside the Center for Immigration Studies, the immigration false-fact think tank. *The Daily Beast.* Available at http://www.thedailybeast.com/inside-the-center-for-immigration-studies-the-immigration-false-fact-think-tank. Accessed July 4, 2017.

Duncan, G. J. (1984). *Years of poverty, years of plenty.* Ann Arbor, MI: Institute for Social Research.

Filer, R. K. (1992). Immigrant arrivals and the migratory patterns of native workers. In G. J. Borjas, & R. B. Freeman (eds.) *Immigration and the workforce.* Chicago, IL: University of Chicago Press.

Gross, S. C. (2007). Letter to the honorable Richard J. Durbin. Washington, DC: Social Security Administration Office of the Chief Actuary, June 5.

Harris, K. M. (1996). Life after welfare: Women, work, and repeat dependency. *American Sociological Review*, 61, 407–426.

Harvey, D. (2005). *A brief history of neoliberalism.* Oxford, UK: Oxford University Press.

Jasso, G., & Rosenzweig, M. (1990). *The new chosen people: Immigrants in the United States.* New York, NY: Russell Sage.

Jones, M. A. (1992). *American immigration* (2nd ed.) Chicago, IL: University of Chicago Press.

Kposowa, A. J. (1995a). Immigration and economic dependence in the U.S.: Approaches to presenting logistic regression results. *Applied Behavioral Science Review*, 3, 65–83.

Kposowa, A. J. (1995b). The impact of immigration on unemployment and earnings among racial minorities in the United States. *Ethnic and Racial Studies*, *18*(3), 605–628.

Kposowa, A. J. (1998). *The impact of immigration on the United States economy.* Lanham, MD: University Press of America.

Kposowa, A. J., Adams, M.A., & Tsunokai, G. T. (2010). Citizenship and arrest patterns in the United States: Evidence from the arrestee drug abuse monitoring program. *Crime, Law and Social Change*, 53, 159–181.

Krikorian, M., Camarota, S. A., Rector, R., & Besharov, D. (2003). *An examination of trends in immigrant welfare use since welfare reform.* Panel transcript available at http://cis.org/search?search_api_fulltext=Back+where+we+started. Accessed July 4, 2017.

Ku, L., Farmstead, S., Broaddus, M. (2003). *Noncitizens' use of public benefits has declined since 1996: Recent report paints misleading picture of eligibility restrictions on immigrant families.* Center on Budget and Policy Priorities, April.

Ku, L., & Bruen, B. (2013). Poor immigrants' use of public benefits at a lower rate than poor native-born citizens. *CATO Institute Economic Development Bulletin*, No. 17, March 4, 1–8.

Lamm, R., & Imhoff, G. (1985). *The immigration time bomb: The fragmenting of America.* New York, NY: Dutton.

Lee, E. S. (1966). A theory of migration. *Demography*, 3, 47–59.

Lee, M. T., Martinez, R., & Rosenfeld, J. (2001). Does immigration increase homicide? Negative evidence from three border cities. *The Sociological Quarterly*, 42, 559–580.

Livingston, G., & Brown, A. (2017). *Intermarriage in the U.S. 50 years after Loving v. Virginia.* Washington, DC: Pew Research Center. Available at http://www.pewsocialtrends.org/. Accessed June 19, 2017.

Massey, D. S. (1981). Dimensions of the new immigration to the United States and the prospects for assimilation. *Annual Review of Sociology*, 7, 57–85.

Ousey, G. C., & Kubrin, C. E. (2009). Exploring the connection between immigration and violent crime rates in U.S. cities, 1980 to 2000. *Social Problems*, 56, 447–473.

Peri, G. (2012). The effect of immigration on productivity: Evidence from U.S. states. *Review of Economics and Statistics*, 94, 348–358.

Pew Research Center (2016). *Behind Trump's win in rural white America: Women joined men in backing him.* Available at http://www.pewresearch.org/fact-tank/2016/11/17/behind-trumps-win-in-rural-white-america-women-joined-men-in-backing-him/. Accessed June 18, 2017.

Pew Research Center (2017). *Intermarriage in the U.S. 50 years after Loving v. Virginia.* Washington, DC: Pew Research Center. Available at http://www.pewsocialtrends.org/. Accessed June 19, 2017.

Reiman, J., & Leighton, P. (2013). *The rich get richer and the poor get prison: Ideology, class, and criminal justice* (11th ed.). New York, NY: Routledge.

Saiz, A. (2003). Room in the kitchen for the melting pot: Immigration and rental prices. *Review of Economics and Statistics*, 85, 502–521.

Saiz, A. (2007). Immigration and housing rents in American cities. *Journal of Urban Economics*, 61, 345–371.

Schoeni, R. F., & Blank, R. M. (2000). *What has welfare reform accomplished? Impacts on welfare participation, employment, income, poverty, and family structure.* National Bureau of Economic Research (Working Paper 7627). Available at http://www.nber.org/papers/w7627. Accessed July 1, 2017.

Smith, J. P., & Edmonston, B. (1997). *The new Americans: Economic, demographic, and fiscal effects of immigration.* Washington, DC: National Academy Press.

Simon, J. (1984). Immigrants, taxes, and welfare in the United States. *Population and Development Review*, 10, 55–69.

Stowell, J. I., Messner, S. F., McGeever, K. F., & Raffalovich, L. E. (2009). Immigration and recent violent crime drop in the United States: A pooled, cross-sectional time series analysis of metropolitan areas. *Criminology*, 47, 889–928.

Taylor, P. (1971). *The distant magnet.* London, UK: Eyre and Spottiswoode

Trump, D. J. (2015). *Trump calls for Muslim ban.* Available at https://www.youtube.com/watch?v=LRxozK6Bpvk

U.S. Centers for Medicare & Medicaid Services (2017). *What is Medicare?* Available at https://www.medicare.gov/sign-up-change-plans/decide-how-to-get-medicare/whats-medicare/what-is-medicare.html. Accessed July 1, 2017.

U.S. Census Bureau (2017a). *Current population survey, annual social and economic supplements.* Available at https://www.census.gov/data/tables/time-series/demo/income-poverty/historical-income-households.html. Accessed July 4, 2017.

U.S. Census Bureau (2017b). *The American Community Survey 2015*. Available at https://factfinder.census.gov/faces/tableservices/jsf/pages/productview.xhtml?pid=ACS_15_5YR_DP03&src=pt

U.S. Department of Health and Human Services (1996). *The personal responsibility and work opportunity reconciliation act of 1996*. Washington, DC: Office of the Assistant Secretary for Planning and Evaluation. Available at https://aspe.hhs.gov/report/personal-responsibility-and-work-opportunity-reconciliation-act-1996. Accessed July 1, 2017.

Waldinger, R. (1996). *Still the promised city?* Cambridge, MA: Harvard University Press.

Wang, M., & Holahan, J. (2003). *The decline in Medicaid use by noncitizens since welfare reform*. Urban Institute Health Policy Online. Available at http://www.urban.org/sites/default/files/publication/59661/900621-The-Decline-in-Medicaid-Use-by-Noncitizens-since-Welfare-Reform.PDF. Accessed June 30, 2017.

Warren, R., & Peck, J. M. (1980). Foreign-born emigration from the United States: 1960 to 1970. *Demography*, 17, 71–84.

Wilson, W. J. (1987). *The truly disadvantaged: The inner city, the underclass, and public policy*. Chicago, IL: University of Chicago Press.

Wilson, W. J. (1996). *When work disappears: The world of the new urban poor*. New York, NY: Random House.

Yates, S. Q. (2017). Making America scared again won't make us safer. *Washington Post*. Available at https://www.washingtonpost.com/opinions/making-america-scared-again-wont-make-us-safer/2017/06/23/f53d238e-578a-11e7-ba90-f5875b7d1876_story.html. Accessed June 24, 2017.

Zallman, L., Woolhandler, S., Himmelstein, D., Bor, D., & McCormck, D. (2013). Immigrants contributed an estimated $115.2 billion more to the Medicare Trust Fund than they took out in 2002–09. *Health Affairs*, 32(6), 1153–1160.

Author Index

Subject Index

CPSIA information can be obtained
at www.ICGtesting.com
Printed in the USA
BVHW012130010222
627858BV00009B/283